Praise for *The Living Beach*

"Brilliant storytelling ... What makes *The Living Beach* such a fine book is Cameron's enthusiasm and exuberance."
— *The Globe and Mail*

"I haven't been so charmed or learned so much from a book of nature writing in years."
— *Vancouver Sun*

"Once in an extremely blue moon, a writer finds a subject that perfectly suits his talents, passions, life and even the place he calls home. As this book eloquently proves, Cameron and the living beach were made for each other."
— *Halifax Sunday Herald*

"For those who delight in words, *The Living Beach* is a gold mine."
— *Toronto Star*

"... an easily understood, authoritative style that admirers of American author John McPhee (*The Control of Nature etc*) will find instantly attractive."
— *Georgia Straight*

"... gracefully written, elegant ... this book about our beaches works, metaphorically, as a look at the larger human experience."
— UBC *Alumni Chronicle*

"If you love the sea, or think you might if only you could get near one, you are going to love this book."
— *Ottawa Citizen*

The
Living

Beach

LIFE, DEATH AND POLITICS WHERE THE LAND MEETS THE SEA

SILVER DONALD CAMERON

Red Deer Press

Published in Canada by Red Deer Press, 195 Allstate Parkway, Markham, Ontario L3R 4T8
Published in the United States by Red Deer Press, 311 Washington Street, Brighton, Massachusetts 02135

10 9 8 7 6 5 4 3 2 1

Red Deer Press acknowledges with thanks the Canada Council for the Arts, and the Ontario Arts Council for their support of our publishing program. We acknowledge the financial support of the Government of Canada through the Canada Book Fund (CBF) for our publishing activities.

Canada Council for the Arts **Conseil des Arts du Canada**

ONTARIO ARTS COUNCIL CONSEIL DES ARTS DE L'ONTARIO
50 YEARS OF ONTARIO GOVERNMENT SUPPORT OF THE ARTS
50 ANS DE SOUTIEN DU GOUVERNEMENT DE L'ONTARIO AUX ARTS

Library and Archives Canada Cataloguing in Publication
ISBN 9780889955097
Cataloguing data available from Library and Archives Canada

Publisher Cataloging-in-Publication Data (U.S.)
ISBN 9780889955097
Data available on file

First published by Macmillan Canada in 1998
Cover design by Kerry Designs
Text design by Daniel Choi

Printed in Canada by Friesens Corporation

MIX
Paper from responsible sources
FSC® C016245
www.fsc.org

When I have seen the hungry ocean gain
Advantage on the kingdom of the shore,
And the firm soil win of the watery main,
Increasing store with loss, and loss with store;
When I have seen such interchange of state.
Or state itself confounded to decay;
Ruin hath taught me thus to ruminate—
That Time will come, and take my love away.

—William Shakespeare, "Sonnet LXIV"

For Charlie and Noel
and in memory of Lulu

Time did come and take my love away.

Contents

Acknowledgments   11

Foreword to the Second Edition   13

1. Gaia's Fingernail   19
   A Boy's Beach   28

2. The Sea and The Waves   32
   Oceanographer   50

3. The Sand and The Shore   58
   Le Concours National des Chateaux du Sable   75

4. Rising Sea and Rolling Islands   79
   Spanish Horses   99

5. The Animate Beach   104
   She Sells Sea Shells   140

6. The Human Beach   148
   The Demon Lover   179

7. The Armored Beach   184
   The Spicy Shores of Araby   216

8. The Politics of The Beach   221
   The Celtic Mass for the Sea   253

9. The Living Beach   258

Further Reading   272

Index   274

Acknowledgments

"The Living Beach" has now been the title of an article in *Canadian Geographic*, a two-hour documentary series for CBC Radio's *Ideas*, a television documentary broadcast by Vision TV and ATV, a video produced by Needham Gate Productions, and a half-hour CBC Nova Scotia show for *Land and Sea*. Along the way, it has benefited from the advice and insights of more people than I can possibly thank. Dozens of people consented to be interviewed, and most of them are quoted in the text. I am grateful to all of them. Beyond that, I am vividly conscious of my special debts to Allison Moss, Peter Flemington, Bob Taylor, Gary and Linda Joyce, Wallace Kaufman, Orrin Pilkey, Ben Mieremet, David McCorquodale, Juan and Ray Miller, Peter Rosen, Farley Mowat, Keith and Diane Fisher, David and Stevie Cameron, Stefan Leslie and Stan Riggs. Moira Ross once again served me splendidly as researcher on the project, and the book gained enormously from Susan Girvan's sympathetic but objective scrutiny as editor. Above all, the whole project was driven by the faith, energy and determination of two couples. The other three members of that quartet share the dedication.

Foreword to the Second Edition

June, 2013. The sun jumps swiftly from the Atlantic, continuously repainting the world as it rises. Rose and puce and pastel blue quickly yield to burning white, dancing silver and forest green. My little dogs thunder past me, pelting down the beach at full throttle, chasing birds, teasing each other, yelping defiance at the waves.

It is 5:00 on a calm summer morning. The Shelties and I have the beach to ourselves: life pared down to its elements of sea and sky, air and water, plants and animals. This is the beach I walked on twenty years ago, after a scientist told me that he thought about beaches as living things. At the time I thought it was a vivid metaphor. Now I think it's the truth.

Over the following five years, the conceit that the beach was alive gave me a theme for newspaper and magazine articles, radio and TV shows, a home video, and a book. This book. Published in 1998, *The Living Beach* had a short, brilliant life. It sold well, won several awards and received superb reviews. *The Globe and Mail* selected *The Living Beach* as one of the top 100 books of the year.

And then it was killed.

A few months after the book came out, Macmillan Canada, my original publisher, was purchased by a large US firm with very different interests. The new owners declared the book "out of print" and abandoned it, returning the rights to the author. The book sank with scarcely a bubble.

However, the book had come to the attention of Peter Carver, an editor with Red Deer Press, who suggested a children's book on the same theme. That project never came to fruition—but 15 years later, Peter came across his notes on the project and called to ask whether the children's book still interested me. It did. Soon after that, Red Deer's publisher, Richard Dionne, called to ask whether the rights to the original adult book were available, and whether I'd like it reissued.

Would I? It's probably the most important book I've written. So now here it is, resurrected. The children's book will follow in due course. And I feel more gratitude to Peter and Richard than I can easily express.

The book has aged, I think, remarkably well. The world of 2013 is very different from the world of 1998, but its fundamentals remain the same. In 2013, one can't write about earthquakes and tsunamis without mentioning Fukushima and the 2004 Boxing Day tsunami in Indonesia. Surfers who once thought waves of more than 35 feet "unridable" now plummet down waves 100 feet high. These are spectacular events, but they don't change the forces and constraints that shape the beaches and the world.

I have silently touched up what I wrote about such matters, but overall I was amazed at the continuing freshness—indeed, the prescience—of what I'd learned from scientists, engineers, surfers, conservationists and beach-lovers during my original research for the book. My informants, for instance, pointed out the perilous situation of a city like New Orleans, protected only by dikes from powerful hurricanes borne on rising seas. In 2005, that analysis was tragically confirmed by a storm called Katrina. In 1993, geologist Orrin Pilkey remarked that if human-driven global warming were to have any major effect, "by the year 2100 we won't be worrying about Nags Head, North Carolina. We'll be worrying about Manhattan." Pilkey was wrong only about the timing. Just two decades later, lashed by Hurricane Sandy, the sea was pouring into the subways of Manhattan.

The great change since the book's initial publication concerns global warming, which in the mid-1990s could plausibly be described even by an astute observer like Wallace Kauffman as existing mainly "in the noise zone and in theory." Since then, the Intergovernmental Panel on Climate Change has mustered the science and won a Nobel Prize, Al Gore has won an Oscar and another Nobel Prize, while climate scientists have reached an astonishing 97% consensus that the planet is warming, and that humans are largely responsible. Our political paralysis on the issue is a result of a widespread war on knowledge organized by the fossil fuel industry, which has struck back with the disgraceful disinformation campaign documented so ably by Jim Hoggan and Richard Littlemore in *Climate Cover-up: The Crusade to Deny Global Warming*.

Re-reading the book, I'm also struck by the impact on my own thought of what I learned from coastal geologists. Seeing time through the lens of geology fundamentally changes one's perception of the world. I used to think that Socrates lived a long time ago—but to a geologist, three millennia is barely enough time to clear one's throat. I once believed there was such a thing as "ownership"—in this book I refer to the soil around my home as "my earth"—but in truth we are all tenants, and even that beloved home has already found its next inhabitants. I used to think that some things were permanent— but when a geologist points out a slanting band of ocean sediments embedded in a mountaintop, the very concept of permanence evaporates. As Randy Parkinson remarked to me, in a sentence I particularly cherish, "geological processes are very slow, but they're very persistent—and they have all the time in the world."

All of which drives me to the conclusion that, as environmentalists, we are not "saving the Earth." We may be extending the duration of some species, notably our own, while industrial society also forces innumerable other species into extinction. But even the evolution and decline of mammals is ultimately just an episode in the great epic saga of the Earth.

Still, though we may not save the Earth, we can certainly serve it —and that work is profoundly worth doing. The dazzling beauty and variety of Mother Earth's creatures, of the whole web of life on this planet, is the most magnificent thing we will ever know, and it is evil not to resist its destruction.

So this book is a blend of devotion, learning and resistance. But its casual cancellation at the whim of some distant publishing executive made me so angry and heartsick that I published no more books for a decade. As the internet quickly became the new backdrop to human life, however, my concerns about the future of humankind and the desecration of the planet intensified, and with my friend Chris Beckett I set up a subscription website called *TheGreenInterview.com*, where I conduct uninterrupted hour-long interviews with the people around the planet whose lives and minds represent pin-pricks of light in a darkening world: Vandana Shiva, Paul Watson, Jane Goodall, Satish Kumar, Alanna Mitchell, George Monbiot, David Suzuki and his daughter Sarika, and several dozen more.

Those interviews—particularly the ones with James Lovelock and with Aboriginal thinkers like Greg Cajete, John Borrows and Edmund Metatawabin—have led me to understand, in my bones, that "Mother Earth" is not a metaphor. The Earth really *is* alive, and all other lives are a part of her life, including our own.

Which brings us back to the final chapter of this book on the "living" beach, which contains the seeds not only of *TheGreenInterview.com*, but also of my current project, *GreenRights,* (www.GreenRights.com). This new multimedia project argues that the most important initiative available to North Americans today would be to incorporate in our legal systems not only the human right to a healthy environment, but also the right of Mother Nature to thrive and flourish on her own terms. Of the 193 countries in the United Nations, all but 16 already recognize one or both of those rights. But not Canada, and not the United States.

I first encountered this concept during my research for this book, in Christopher Stone's seminal 1972 essay, "Should Trees Have Standing? Towards Legal Rights for Natural Objects." A little further on I note William Thorsell's suggestion that Canada "might adopt a constitution that included a bill of rights for the environment"—which is the very core of the GreenRights project.

∽

October, 2013. The light slowly fades in the broken slate sky, returning the world to darkness. Towering Pacific seas explode into white foam over the dark rocks that punctuate the wide sands. It is 7:00 on an October evening on one of Canada's most magnificent beaches, at Tofino, BC, on the west coast of Vancouver Island. As Thoreau said: naked nature, inhumanly sincere, wasting no thought on man. But its fury is staggeringly lovely.

I stand watching the boiling surf. Earlier today I was three miles out on the gale-swept waters, tossed around in an outboard-powered Zodiac inflatable, welcoming the Greenpeace ship *Rainbow Warrior III* on her first visit to Canada. Watching these towering breakers, I feel inconspicuous, vulnerable, vividly aware that I, too, am a temporary feature of the beach, a fleeting pattern of the energy of Mother Earth. I too have arisen from her fabric, and like a wave I will dissolve back into her flux.

But for what is left of this lifetime, I am a human being. And tonight, touched by the sacred in this wild, rank place, I am serene, and humbled—and happy.

1. Gaia's Fingernail

"**A** beach stores sand in the dunes behind it," said Bob Taylor. "When it's attacked, it draws material from the dunes for itself and for building a protective shoal or bar offshore. When it's less stressed, it takes sand and gravel from offshore and stores it back on the beach and in the dunes."

"You talk as though the damn thing were alive," I said.

"I think of it that way," said Taylor.

Taylor is a lean, laconic coastal geologist who works for the Geological Survey of Canada in the Bedford Institute of Oceanography in Halifax, Nova Scotia, which has the third-largest concentration of marine scientists in North America. I was interviewing him for a series of 30-second radio spots about Nova Scotia geology, which I was writing for a government agency. And here he was—a tall, bearded, careful scientist—sitting in his tiny, paper-choked office in a brick building on the edge of Halifax Harbour and talking about the beach as though it were a living organism.

The scientists at the BIO were full of surprises. One of them talked about vents in the deep ocean floor, six kilometers below the surface, where liquid rock rises through the Earth's crust, accreting into tall, tubular stacks and precipitating nuggets of minerals. The hot water around the stacks sustains an ecosystem nobody suspected until recently. What could live under the pressure of more than a thousand atmospheres, after all? Answer: huge aberrant clams, twelve-foot eyeless worms and assorted other oddities.

Another scientist told me that most of mainland Nova Scotia was once part of Morocco. You can tell by the rocks, he said. The Meguma terrane was once the shoreline of the ancient proto-African continent. Some was left behind when North America and Africa pulled apart, 180 million years ago. Meguma terrane is common in Morocco and Nova Scotia, but it doesn't occur anywhere else in North America.

A third scientist told me about "mist-puffers" on the continental shelf—bubbles of methane gas that burst up from the seafloor, raising clouds of sediment as they go. Old Mother Earth, farting in the bathtub. A mist-puffer in the Bay of Fundy once eructated with a concussion powerful enough to cause villagers on the Canadian side of Passamaquoddy Bay to call out the militia: they believed they were being invaded by the Americans.

And now Bob Taylor was telling me he thought of the beach as though it were alive.

As it happened, I had just been reading J.E. Lovelock's *Gaia: A New Look at Life on Earth*, which contends that the Earth itself is a single organism that maintains the conditions necessary for its survival. The concept fills many a scientist with horror, but it accords with a nearly universal traditional view of the Earth as mother and sustainer. *Erce, erce, erce, erthen moder,* sang the reverent Saxon poet. Nobody knows exactly what *erce* means, but we get the old bard's drift.

If Lovelock and the Saxon bard are right, if the whole Earth is a living thing, then all its parts must be living, too, the beach among them, just as a liver or a fingernail is a living part of the human body.

That is not quite what Bob Taylor meant. He thought the idea that the beach was alive was a metaphor.

Hmm. A beach, I would learn, behaves in much the same way as a living creature. It changes, moves and adapts; it can be starved or nourished; it advances and retreats according to its circumstances. So why *do* we consider it inanimate? And if we considered it to be a living creature, would we treat it differently?

〜

I had been hanging around beaches all my life without paying much attention to them—seeing them without really *seeing* them. We are all sleepwalkers most of the time anyway, blundering through the world with our minds and senses dozing; when we think we are learning, we are just waking up for a moment.

In a lifetime of somnolence I had seen (without noticing) that the selfsame beach could sometimes be wide and flat and sandy, and at other times narrow and steep and pebbled. I had dimly observed that the shoreline below my house is silt and broken shale, while the house next door is enhanced by a tiny cusp of genuine sandy beach, and I had idly wondered why my property should have been treated thus unjustly. As a sailor, I was aware that sandbars near estuaries and harbor mouths move around, which means that the buoys which mark them have to move, too. Wading along the shore, I had mused over the patterns of ripples on the sandbars; since they mimicked the shape of waves, I speculated that the waves had somehow molded them.

I had absentmindedly perceived that beaches seem to be laid out in horizontal bands, often with pebbles and rock down to the low tide line and a sandy bottom under the water. An inconvenient arrangement for swimmers, I thought, picking my way over barnacled stones only to find comfortable footing once I was in water deep enough for swimming. A proper design would have allowed me to walk on the sand and swim over the rocks. Who designed the beach, anyway? When I was a boy in British Columbia, I often saw cottagers tossing rocks aside to make a smooth path through the stones to the sand. It was an endless job, because the rocks always slowly moved back, as though they, too, were stubbornly alive. How did they move back? Why was the cleared path always choked with rocks again in the spring?

Thinking about these things, I went for a walk on the beach.

∽

The beach I walked on was Pondville Beach, a very pleasant but fairly ordinary gray sand beach near my home on the Atlantic coast of Canada. Beaches, like people, all have features in common, but each is unique. Pondville Beach lies at the head of Baie des Rochers, or Rocky Bay, which looks on the map like a giant bite out of the east side of Isle Madame, Nova Scotia. This is the open Atlantic. If you swam straight east from Pondville for a very long time, you would come ashore just north of Bordeaux, France.

Isle Madame, I now noticed, is a virtual anthology of shorelines. On its north and west sides, where the island snuggles up to Cape Breton Island, the land is protected from the power of the Atlantic surf, and the shores are a mixture of fine clay, mud and broken slate and sandstone. At the southeast corner of the island, facing the Atlantic, bare rock plunges into the water. It looks solid, but it is constantly being split and shattered from the annual cycle of freezing and thawing, and from the explosive power of air compressed into crevices by the surf. The southern and eastern coasts are extremely varied—rounded hills, eroding red cliffs and shelves of solid rock, flaky wafers of stone, turbid ponds, barachois beaches backed by lagoons, beaches with humped dunes, cobble beaches, pebble beaches, gravel beaches, long crescents of sand with Atlantic rollers curling down onto them in a white smother of foam.

If one set out to *collect* beaches, like a geological museologist, one could hardly assemble anything better than Isle Madame.

Pondville Beach, for instance, is a long gunmetal curve of sand between two small rocky headlands. A line of low dunes lies behind it. Near its southern end is a tiny salt marsh, drained by a streamlet too small to reach the sea; it trickles out of the marsh through the dune line and sinks into the beach sand.

At its northern end, Pondville Beach is breached by a creek, which issues from a chain of lakes in the island's interior. The creek meanders toward the beach through a small floodplain, and it is perhaps ten or twelve feet deep where it divides the beach. The creek's banks have been fortified with wooden pilings, and years ago one could find small open fishing boats berthed there. The ocean water beyond the sand is cold, touched by the Labrador Current, and even in July most people prefer to swim in the creek rather than in the sea.

With the help of Bob Taylor and some good reading, I began to comprehend the anatomy of the beach. When most of us talk about "the beach," we mean the strip of dry sand on which we spread our towels and blankets, set up our sun umbrellas, unpack our picnic coolers. Technically, that is the backshore, and it is only one small part of the beach. The beach is a whole ecological and geological system that stretches from the edge of the land—the forest, the cliff, the farmer's field—to the greatest depth at which the water can move sand, silt or other sediments.

On the landward side of our little encampment on the backshore, one or more ridges of sand or gravel dune separate us from an inland body of water, variously called a *lagoon*, a *sound* or a *bay*. Some beaches have no lagoon at all. Elsewhere—on the coast of North Carolina or New York, for instance—the lagoon is a vast, shallow inland sea: Pamlico Sound, Great South Bay. At Pondville the lagoon is represented by both the tiny salt marsh and the estuary of the creek.

We spread our beach towels on the backshore. Immediately behind us is the berm, the ridge that marks the highest point normally reached by the waves. In front of our towels lies the intertidal zone, also known as the *beachface* or *foreshore*, the part of the beach that is exposed at low tide and covered at high tide. Beyond the foreshore is the shoreface, stretching out underwater until the water is so deep the waves can no longer move sand. How far is that? It can be anything from a few feet to several miles; waves can move gravel in 120 feet of water, and very fine sand in as much as 180 feet. Sailors would call that the thirty-fathom line, and at Pondville it lies six and a half miles offshore. Taken as a system, Pondville Beach is about seven miles wide.

It is nice to know the names—backshore, berm, intertidal zone— but, as the Buddhist saying goes, to speak the names is only to point a finger at the moon. The beach—any beach—remains a single entity, a mystery stretching from the spruce woods behind the salt marsh past the dunes and the foreshore into water deep enough for the largest ships ever designed. It may be hundreds of miles long. It is the margin of the continent, at once the edge of the land and the edge of the sea.

The beach also marks the boundary of an illusion—the notion that humanity is somehow separate from nature and in control of the natural world. This is an ancient illusion, dating back at least to the first book of Genesis, where God makes man in His own image, and gives man "dominion over the fish of the sea, and over the fowl of the air, and over the cattle, and over all the Earth, and over every creeping thing that creepeth upon the Earth." As if that were not clear enough, a later verse *instructs* human beings to "be fruitful, and multiply, and replenish the Earth, and subdue it; and have dominion over the fish of the sea, and over the fowl of the air, and over every living thing that moveth upon the Earth."

We have taken that mandate so seriously that we now threaten the Earth's carrying capacity—and we have stewarded our patrimony so poorly that many species of fish and fowl and creeping things have disappeared altogether. And yet the ocean has always made a mockery of our pretensions of dominion. As Thoreau noted, "the ocean is a wilderness reaching round the globe, wilder than a Bengal jungle, and fuller of monsters." Terrestrial creatures may retreat as human settlement advances, but "the most populous and civilized city cannot scare a shark far from its wharves." Byron wrote in similar vein, in *Childe Harold's Pilgrimage*:

Roll on, thou deep and dark blue Ocean—roll!
Ten thousand fleets sweep over thee in vain;
Man marks the Earth with ruin—his control
Stops with the shore ...

Our illusion of dominion leads us to treat the beach as if it were part of the land and similarly vulnerable to our will. But the beach does not belong to the land, nor does it belong to the sea; it is a different reality, submitting for brief periods to human designs on it, but sweeping them away as it yields to the fury of the sea. It is a unity of disunities, a frontier, a paradox, at once stable and volatile. It is more like a dance than a place.

Every beach—like every person—retains its individual character, yet it is constantly changing, chasing itself in the wind, sporting with every wave. The waves we see at the beach fall into two broad categories. *Constructive waves* produce spilling breakers—breakers that simply seem to crumble at their caps. As they tumble forward, spilling breakers nudge sand up the beachface in a slowly dissolving froth called the *swash*. The water curls up the beach and sinks into the beachface, leaving some of its sand burden behind. If you look at the top of the swash zone when the tide is falling, you can often see tiny irregular ridges of sand, which outline the farthest extent to which the highest individual waves have traveled up the beach. The sand ridges look like the castings of some sluggish marine animal.

High-energy waves, which are usually associated with strong winds and storms, produce plunging breakers—surfers' waves, glassy tubes of water that rear up high, curl forward and break straight downward, yielding a strong backwash and very little swash. Plunging breakers are *destructive waves* that pull sand and other sediments back down the beach and out under the water. Beyond the surf zone, the backwash loses its energy. The sand settles, and currents along the shore shape it into a bar.

Like an Asian fighter, the beach is using the energy of the waves to defeat them. "If there's a strong storm coming in, a northeasterly or something, where the waves are very high energy," says Bob Taylor, "then the beachface will be cut down and the sediments will be carried further offshore. That deposition of sediment makes the water shallow, which causes the waves to break and lessens the stress on the actual beachface itself. And then as wave conditions calm down it'll bring the sediment back on the beach and equilibrate for those kinds of conditions."

The power of such a tempest is genuinely awesome. In one day, a winter storm can release as much energy as two dozen hydrogen bombs. In a few hours, a storm can completely resculpt a beach. The howling wind blows sand off the beachface into the backshore, dropping it into a lagoon. Thundering onto the foreshore, storm waves reach into the dunes, carving away the dune faces, dragging sand far into the water. Under the water the shoreface extends itself seaward while the beachface narrows and steepens, left only with coarse gravel and round cobbles. The largest waves may inundate the whole dune, cutting *overwash channels* through the dune ridge and filling the backshore lagoon.

But, as Taylor notes, the migration of the sand is the beach's defense, lengthening and flattening the whole shoreface, forcing the seas to break farther offshore. When the winter storms are over, the spilling breakers patiently resume their work of carrying the sand back up the beach until the bar welds itself to the beachface, restoring the broad and sandy beach of summer. The beach relaxes, sprawling in the sun.

You talk as though the damn thing were alive.
I think of it that way.

"That would make a great documentary," said Charlie Doucet. Charlie is a round-faced, cheerful filmmaker from Halifax, Nova Scotia. I write the shows and he produces them. He is one of my favorite people on the whole round Earth. Good thing, too. As a result of *that* little remark, the two of us were to spend weeks together in a 23-foot motor home, driving down the east coast of the United States and Canada with a payload of cameras and tapes, interviewing geologists and sports fishermen and lawyers and turtle lovers and politicians and surfers and engineers and bureaucrats. Talking about beaches.

You talk as though the damn thing were alive.
I think of it that way.

Bob Taylor said it first. But dozens of people said it later.

A Boy's Beach

The central beach of my boyhood summers is South Beach, in Washington State. South Beach is on the southern face of Point Roberts, an anomalous scrap of U.S. territory created by the international boundary; the 49th parallel cuts straight across the point, leaving four square miles of America at the tip of a Canadian peninsula.*

Isolated on three sides by water and on the fourth side by another country, Point Roberts is psychologically not a point but an island. To reach any other part of the United States, the people of Point Roberts have to transit customs twice, passing from Rainier beer, Congressmen, small gallons and Camel cigarettes to kilometers, Crown lands, "socialized medicine" and vividly colored currency and back again. To attend high school in Blaine, Washington, the teenagers of Point Roberts ride a bus 50 miles each way through Canada. Ironically, the patriotic Americans of Point Roberts are mostly former Canadians, Icelandic families from Manitoba: Gudmundsons, Thorsteinsons, Iwersons and Johanssons. There is—or was—a French-Canadian family, the Peltiers, and a handful of other families bearing names like Culp, Julius and Davis.

---

* I chose to use Imperial measurements because the book is meant to be accessible to a North American audience, not just a Canadian one.

But Point Roberts is, for all practical purposes, a Canadian colony—the only place on Earth where Americans resent Canadian domination. Lying just 20 miles south of booming Vancouver, Point Roberts is cottage country, and the cottagers are Canadian. My parents bought our cottage in 1947, when the postwar boom was only beginning. It was—and is—a primitive clapboard and V-joint affair built between the wars, a single room surrounded by walled-in sleeping porches, with cold running water and no means of heating except a fine beach-stone fireplace. But during my boyhood we could hardly wait for April, when we started going to the cottage for weekends, and it was a melancholy Sunday in November when we drained the plumbing and closed it up for the winter.

The cottage was mainly for sleeping, and for rainy days. As much as possible, we lived on the beach—a long arc of sand sweeping inland from the tall khaki bluffs of Myrdal Point to the east. The shore was steep and pebbled, matted with driftwood logs and other debris, but the sand ran offshore, almost flat, for a quarter of a mile, a wet, gray playground of runnels and ripples ending in a kelp forest just beyond the low tide line.

The beach was a perfect place for forts and castles, a place to run, a place to draw huge faces and messages and pictures of boats, a place to chase and be chased by the family cocker spaniel, a place to play a wet, splashy game of baseball. We buried old tin cans flush with the sand and played golf with rusty discarded clubs and nicked golf balls. We swam and lay on the sand, peered at one another's sisters and wondered what really was under their swimsuits.

One summer the local families—the permanent residents, Wally Vopnford, Mac and Matthew Gudmundson and others—organized a salmon barbecue. They dug pits in the sand, lined the pits with stones and built fires in them. When the stones were white-hot they raked out the fires and threw in layers of seaweed. On the seaweed they placed the carcasses of huge salmon wrapped in muslin bags. They covered the salmon with long streamers of kelp and layers of sand and left them overnight. At noon the next day they dug them up—juicy and sweet, saline and smoky—and sold portions on paper plates with rolls and potato salad to visitors on day trips from Vancouver. I never tasted salmon like it. I swear I can taste it yet.

Salmon that had been swimming toward a Canadian river, caught by American seiners and served by locals who were once Canadians, to Canadian summer people in the United States.

Boundaries. And at South Beach I met a boundary within myself, an internal frontier I knew I could never cross again.

Point Roberts has no natural harbors, though it now has an artificial marina. South Beach lies open to the Strait of Georgia, so we used boats that could be launched off the beach. Our family had a flat-bottomed plywood skiff that my father had bought for $40—light, nimble and handy, an ideal boat for an open shore—and I loved that little boat as I loved little else. It got me into the last fistfight of my life, right at the water's edge.

I don't remember now what started it all, but somehow Louie Jewett hit on the idea of taunting me by pushing the boat off when I was trying to tie it up. I warned him once. I warned him twice.

The third time I hit him, and in seconds we were wrestling in the sand, the waves lapping beside us. A moment later I had his head between my knees. My ankles were locked and I had a red mist in front of my eyes, and I was trying to kill him —*kill him*—concentrating all my strength on crushing his head with my legs, listening icily to his screams, calling up my last reserves of strength and waiting for his skull to crack. I knew exactly how it was going to feel—the dull crack and the sudden yielding as his cranium shattered and his head turned to mush...

But his skull did not crack, and the others pulled us apart, and Louie gave me a hard smack in the face before his friends led him away.

I hardly felt the smack. Chilled and appalled by my savagery, I was absorbing one of the great lessons of my life. You wanted to kill him,

I told myself. If you had been able to do it, you would have murdered him. I stood by the water, the painter of the skiff in my hand, shaking. *You wanted him dead. You wanted to see him lying on the sand with his brains leaking out.* I didn't, I didn't. I'm not like that. *You did. Be honest. That's what you wanted.*

All right. I don't know what happened. And?

You can't handle your own anger. You can't trust yourself.

No. I guess I can't.

Then you can never get into a fight again. Never.

And I never have.

2. The Sea and The Waves

The waves come in slowly; vast and green, curve their
transparent necks, and burst with a surprising uproar;
that runs waxing and waning up and down the long
keyboard of the beach.
　　　　—Robert Louis Stevenson

"There's a Walt Whitman poem, 'Out of the Cradle Endlessly Rocking,' in which Whitman compares the ocean to a great cradle," says Wallace Kaufman. "The poem suggests that this rocking motion of the oceans somehow appeals to a very basic human instinct—that human beings do like to be rocked. And it's associated with the calming effect of what we call white noise. I mean you can now go to a record store and buy a tape of ocean wave sounds, with occasional sea gulls. And people love it. It's powerful."

Kaufman is a friendly, energetic man of 50, an entrepreneur, real estate developer and coauthor of a book called *The Beaches Are Moving*. Like most people who study beaches, he does not live at the beach. Nursing our motor home along a narrow twisting lane, Charlie Doucet and I found him deep in the leafy woods of North Carolina's Piedmont, not far from Chapel Hill. He built his house at the very back of a subdivision with huge lots. He created the subdivision, too.

"I'm a workaholic, I work all the time," Kaufman admits. "I hate to go any place unless I've got a purpose and I'm doing something there. But I happened to be at the beach this past weekend, and I was walking along the beach with a friend, and she stopped and sat down on a sand dune. So I had to stop and wait. And I found myself immediately quite content to listen to the waves come in, go out, watch the different forms. I wasn't trying to learn anything. I wasn't studying anything. It was just a form of semi-hypnosis, which I was quite happy with. I thought at that point, *My God, I'm glad I don't live with this because I might spend half my day just staring at it.*"

༄

Those hypnotic waves begin as wrinkles produced by friction, as the wind drags at the smooth surface of the water and ruffles its film of surface tension into the patches of ripples known as cat's-paws. After lying becalmed for hours or days, a sailor delights in these harbingers of wind. They may be mere playfulness, leaving the sailor to despondency as they fade away—or they may be the beginnings of a true wind, the driving wind the sailor has longed for. Occasionally they are the first tentative notes in the overture to a gale of Wagnerian fury.

As cruising sailors, my family and I have often watched the evolution of the waves from flat calm to rolling seas. On one such occasion, our engineless cutter *Silversark* lay on an afternoon sea of bronze and lead in Northumberland Strait, equidistant from the faint mauve lines that marked the land masses of Nova Scotia, Prince Edward Island and Cape Breton. A jolly little breeze had hurried us out of a Nova Scotia harbor and then left us becalmed all day. Cat's-paws teased us, abrading the surface and fading away. Acres of water heaved slowly and thoughtfully, rising and falling like a sleeper's chest, but the surface was so calm that we leaned over the side and photographed the reflections of our faces on the deep green water.

After four or five hours the cat's-paws strengthened, darkening the whole surface of the sea. The wind continued, pushing on the backs of the ripples, and they melded into one another, growing quickly into wavelets. It was a textbook wind of 12 or 15 knots, frank and steady, and it soon transformed the wavelets into a chop.

A wave is described by three measurements: height, length and period. The height of a wave is measured from the crest to the bottom of the trough, and its length is measured from one crest to the following crest. Its period is the length of time between the passage of two successive crests. The smallest waves have periods of less than a second, while the largest—the tides—have periods of more than 24 hours.

When a wave's height is more than one-seventh of its length, the wave breaks. A two-foot wave, for instance, must be at least 14 feet long, or its top tumbles over in a smother of foam. We saw this now: short, steep waves frothing with whitecaps. New ruffles and ripples emerged and vanished on the backs of the waves, driven this way and that by errant puffs, adding their energy to that of the longer waves.

In a matter of minutes the waves had consolidated, rising and lengthening, and still breaking before the urgency of the wind. It takes no time for the wind to form waves on a glassy sea, though it takes hours and hours for the resulting wave train to dissipate. As the waves rose, their lengths stretched to 15 feet, 20 feet, 25 feet. Each crest caught *Silversark*'s transom, lifted it three or four feet and hurried the little ship forward down its face. Then it left us, rising under the bow and rushing on ahead while the next wave surged up under our stern. I took a photograph that day of Lulu, my late wife, sitting at the tiller in her white oilskins and Tilley hat, grinning into the camera while the blue and white seas marched in ranks behind her. I will treasure that image forever.

That fine little breeze carried us into Pictou Harbor, and by midnight it had died. The seas it had made would be rolling up the strait, subsiding into low mounds of water, which would break at last on shorelines in New Brunswick or Quebec, molding and shifting the beaches as they died.

∽

In the deep ocean, and with a longer, stronger wind, the waves would behave differently. In the absence of nearby land, the character of the waves is determined by three factors. The first is the strength of the wind and the second is the length of time that it blows. The third is the distance over which it blows, *the fetch*. A *fully developed* sea is the largest sea that can be raised by any particular strength of wind, unconstrained by time, fetch and water depth. In such conditions, a 20-knot wind blowing for ten hours will raise a fully developed sea with an average wave height of five feet, and the highest ten percent of the waves will reach ten feet. That is the highest sea that such a wind can raise, no matter how long the fetch or the duration.

The evolving wave form represents the transfer of energy from the wind to the water. When the wind has just begun to blow, the infant waves cannot absorb all its energy. The wave form is short and steep, and the waves break. As the wind continues, the waves grow and gather momentum. Now they can absorb more and more energy. As the waves grow longer and longer, they cease to break, though fresh little wavelets growing on their backs may still be breaking. In a fully developed sea, the energy of wind and waves is in equilibrium: the wave can absorb exactly the amount of energy that the wind can transfer through friction and other types of resistance.

The energy stored in a wave increases in proportion to the *square* of the wind speed. If the wind increases from 20 to 40 knots over a sufficiently long fetch, the fully developed sea will have an average wave height of 28 feet, nearly six times greater, and the highest ten percent will now reach 57 feet. A 50-knot wind blowing for 69 hours over a 1,400-mile fetch can raise maximum seas approaching 100 feet in height.

There is a limit to the possible height of waves. Using a set of extreme but possible assumptions, researchers have shown that it is theoretically possible for the deep ocean to generate waves of 219 feet. That is a wave the height of an office tower. Nobody has ever reported such a wave. On the other hand, roughly 100,000 ships have vanished at sea every century during the 6,000 years that human beings have gone voyaging. Perhaps some of those sailors did see such seas—and those seas were the last thing they ever saw.

⁓

It is the combination of fetch and duration that makes winter nor'easters the most destructive storms of the northern Atlantic coast.

In October 1983, our half-renovated house on Isle Madame only had aluminum storm windows, and they were bulging inward from the terrifying pressure of the northeast wind. I held an upstairs pane in place with my bare hands while Lulu searched for plywood and nails. From the ground floor came the crash and tinkle of splintering glass as another window blew in. Out of the corner of my eye I saw the seas breaking right up into the backyard, carrying away the soil we had just spread behind the new seawall. I mentioned that event to Bob Taylor.

"October 26, 1983." Taylor smiled. "That nor'easter did a lot of damage along the Cape Breton coast."

The nor'easters of the Atlantic coast lack the extraordinary wind speeds and the brief, intense drama of hurricanes, but they cover a much larger area than most hurricanes and they move more slowly, lying along the coast and battering the shore for days at a time. Professors Robert Doland and Robert E. Davis of the University of Virginia examined the records of 1,347 northeast winter storms— defined as generating waves of five feet or more—between 1942 and 1984. They classified each of the storms as Weak, Moderate, Significant, Severe and Extreme. Only seven storms in 42 years could be classed as Extreme, with wave heights of 20 feet and a duration of 96 hours. But those seven storms noticeably reshaped the Atlantic coast.

The typical nor'easter is born between Florida and Cuba and moves up the coast as a low-pressure trough ringed by strong counterclockwise winds. Normally the trough brushes the coast with brief but destructive local gales—like the one that blew in our windows—before swinging out into the Atlantic as it reaches Canadian latitudes. Occasionally, however, the trough's northward movement is blocked by a cell of high pressure. Then the trough stalls just offshore, pounding the coast for days. The longest nor'easter on record, in February 1969, blew for 170 hours—more than a week.

A savage nor'easter in 1991—now known as the Hallowe'en Storm—killed at least seven people and destroyed buildings, beaches, wharves and vessels from Florida to Newfoundland. Pressed against a high-pressure cell over Quebec, the Hallowe'en Storm developed winds of 50 to 70 knots. It had a fetch of 1,000 miles. It later moved seaward, merged with Hurricane Grace near Bermuda and returned to the coast. In all, it blew for 114 hours, nearly five days.

When the waves of the Hallowe'en Storm struck the coast, they were also riding on a "storm surge." A low-pressure system, by definition, lessens the atmospheric pressure on the ocean's surface, allowing the sea to swell upward beneath it. This bulge on the ocean's surface moves as the storm moves; in effect, it is another form of wave, a higher surface on which the wind-generated storm waves arise. The Hallowe'en Storm created a storm surge that raised the water level locally by as much as five feet. Riding on top of the storm surge and high tides, the surf mounted as much as 20 feet above normal sea level, depositing six feet of sand on coastal highways in Virginia and North Carolina and destroying buildings and houses from Key West to the Magdalen Islands in the Gulf of St. Lawrence. At Chezzetcook, near Halifax, Bob Taylor found the storm had torn away nearly 25 feet of a cliff face.

Scientists had predicted that a storm capable of producing even 40-foot waves in the relatively shallow waters of the continental shelf would occur, on average, only once in a century, but this one generated waves accurately measured at 50 feet, fully 25 percent higher. That one storm, says Ralph Bigio of the Canadian Forces meteorological center in Halifax, "simply rewrites the climatology of the region."

∽

Breaking waves are moving bodies of water that release their energy with tremendous force. Paradoxically, waves that are not breaking—and therefore not releasing much energy—do not move very much water. Stand in the surf, and the water tugs and swirls around your ankles. Wade out just beyond the surf, and the waves will lift you, carry you gently forward, move you gently back and deposit you more or less where you started. The wave motion is roughly circular, or orbital, and the water particles in the wave move in exactly the same orbit as your body, a fact first demonstrated by the pioneer German researchers Ernst and Wilhelm Weber, who published a book in 1825 reporting the results of experiments performed in their homemade wave tank.

A wave tank is now a commonplace laboratory fixture. It consists of a long, glass-sided box, like an elongated aquarium. At one end is a device for generating waves, generally an electric motor with paddles or something similar. At the other end is a model beach, which absorbs the energy of the waves. To show the orbital movement within a wave, the demonstrator places drops of gunk in the water—usually a mixture of light oil with weighting and coloring agents that closely replicates the density of water. The wave generator propagates waves down the length of the channel. As each wave arrives, the particles of gunk go forward at the top of the wave and backward at the bottom. The water barely moves as the wave form races on.

Wind-driven waves are peaked, with a steep face and a long sloping back. As they leave the wind that produced them, they become *swell*—long, low, rounded waves, almost symmetrical in shape, sliding quickly outward from their point of origin. Without the wind's steady pressure, their period lengthens and their height diminishes.

They move through the ocean, says Wallace Kaufman, "like a shiver through the skin." In this form they can travel many thousands of miles without much further decay. Swells that become breakers on the west coast may have been generated by storms off the coast of Russia or Japan. The longest swells ever recorded, on the south coast of England, had a wavelength of half a mile and were traveling at 78 miles per hour.

In the open sea, a big swell is truly impressive. The sea heaves in vast rounded hills, and your vessel sails up one side and down the other. In the troughs, the horizon disappears; your little ship glides through a wide shallow valley surrounded by low hills of gray water. Then a smoothly rounded top lifts you calmly into the air, and you can see for miles. Swells are majestic and thrilling, but vast though they are, they pose no danger; they pass harmlessly under the keel and march away on their course.

At sea, as on the coast, the dangerous waves are the breaking seas. Even relatively moderate winds can occasionally raise a very high wave, perhaps two or three times the average wave height. Using a statistical model, Dr. Lawrence Draper of the National Institute of Oceanography in Britain has calculated that in a fully developed 40-knot sea, where the average wave height is 28 feet, one wave in 1,200 may be three times that height, and one in 300,000 may be more than four times higher—or more than 100 feet. Such a wave will exist only momentarily; its unstable peak rears into a fast-moving current of air, which will immediately knock it over, pouring tons of solid water down its steep front. These are the waves that roll yachts over like bottles in the surf, tear away the superstructures of ocean liners, break tankers in two and swallow ships whole.

༄

The appearance of the ocean surface is complicated by the fact that any particular point on the ocean feels the influence of not one but many wave trains, created by winds in different areas. A swell from the east may have smaller wave trains crisscrossing it from north and south, heaping up points of water, racing across the faces of the swells, slapping into one another. In real life the surface of the sea rarely resembles the smooth procession of orderly shapes you see in a wave tank; it is usually a maze of peaks and hollows, crests and depressions, mingled together in ever-changing shapes. Troughs absorb opposing waves, and new waves rise on top of the swells. Small troughs appear in the face of larger waves. Pinnacles of water flicker into being and drop away.

Numerous ships have reported encounters with rogue waves—immense single waves that tower over those around them, breaking continuously as they come, waves beyond even the range of statistical probability. It may be that some such waves occur when the highest waves of a storm happen to arise atop a large underlying swell or when several trains of large waves momentarily coincide, stacking up on top of one another. For whatever reason—and there is still much debate about their origins—rogue waves do arise from time to time, and they are terrifying.

Of all the many accounts of such waves, one in particular has etched itself in my mind. On February 14, 1957, the 46-foot ketch *Tzu Hang* was 1,500 miles west of Chile, 36 days out from New Zealand on a voyage around Cape Horn. The crew consisted of her owners, Miles and Beryl Smeeton, and a young friend, John Guzzwell, who later became a famous sailor, boatbuilder and designer in his own right. The Smeetons were naturalized Canadians described by their biographer, Miles Clark, as "the most accomplished traveling and adventuring couple of the twentieth century." Before their marriage, Beryl had traveled alone through Russia and China, driven across the United States, ridden a horse over the Andes and climbed higher in the Himalayas than any other woman. Miles had been a brigadier in the British Army, fighting in the deserts of Egypt and the jungles of Burma. The two of them climbed the Alps and the Himalayas for fun.

They had already crossed the Atlantic and Pacific oceans in *Tzu Hang*.

The Southern Ocean, where they were sailing, lies just north of Antarctica. It has the longest fetch in the world, a complete circuit of the globe unbroken by land, and its seas build up to heights unknown elsewhere. On that memorable February morning, a powerful storm had been blowing for three days, and the yacht was running before it with her sails furled, driven only by the windage of her masts and rigging, presenting just her narrow stern to the seas and towing ropes to slow her down and keep her under control. Beryl went on deck for her watch at 9:00 a.m. A few minutes later, having slewed slightly on a wave, Beryl corrected course and looked over her shoulder to check that she was square to the next sea. She saw a vertical wall of water stretching from horizon to horizon, towering above *Tzu Hang* and breaking down its face like a waterfall. *I can't do anything about it*, she thought. *I'm absolutely straight.*

The wave lifted *Tzu Hang*'s stern and drove her downward until she tripped on her bows, twisted and fell sideways. When the yacht emerged from the wave she was half full of water, and everything on her deck had been swept away, including her rig and her deckhouse. Miles and John struggled on deck to see Beryl 30 yards away, swimming for the ship with a crushed vertebra, a sprained ankle and a broken toe. Miles and John thought their situation hopeless, but Beryl's first words were, "I know where the buckets are." Together they patched up the damage, constructed a jury rig, and sailed their wounded ship to Coronel, Chile. The full story is told in Smeeton's book, *Once is Enough*.

John Guzzwell believes that the wave which ravaged *Tzu Hang* was created by an uncharted *seamount*, an underwater mountain rising from the deep ocean to within a few hundred meters of the surface. The idea is plausible; the ocean is a big place, and the old sailing-ship routes were largely abandoned by the time oceanography matured.

Rogue waves can damage and destroy much larger ships. Willard Bascom's classic book *Waves and Beaches* shows a 1945 photograph of the aircraft carrier *Bennington* with its normally flat flight deck bent downward like the drooping ears of a dog, the result of a colossal wave crashing down onto it.

The coincidence of several troughs can open a hole in the ocean into which a ship may plunge, burying her bow in the body of the succeeding wave. Here is Bascom's account of one such event:

> In 1966, only eight hundred miles off New York, the Italian liner *Michelangelo* was struck by a huge solitary wave amid a storm. Other ships in the same storm did not observe any especially large waves, nor did the *Michelangelo* encounter more than one. This seems to have been a very deep trough followed by a massive crest. The flare of the ship's bow was crumpled, the inch-thick glass of the bridge windows eighty feet above the waterline was smashed, steel railings on the upper decks were washed away, and some bulkheads collapsed, allowing many tons of water to enter the ship. The liner was carrying hundreds of passengers, many of whom were injured, and three died. Their first terrorized thoughts were that the ship had struck a reef; many commented on the succession of shudders that vibrated through the ship. A few days later the curious onlookers standing on the pier in the calm of New York Harbor had a very hard time believing that a wave could be so large as to rip up steel eight stories above their heads.

Not all waves are on the surface, and not all are generated by wind. Waves can occur at any boundary between two moving fluids of different densities. One such boundary is the surface of the sea, the boundary between the air and the water. Waves *under* the ocean surface occur where two bodies of water lie on top of one another. The ocean is full of different bodies of water: frigid Arctic water carried south by the Labrador Current, fresh water emanating from the great rivers, warm water flowing out of the Mediterranean. The colder, saltier water sinks; warmer or less saline water rides in layers above it. These masses of water can travel intact for thousands of miles, mixing only minimally with the adjacent layers, and any difference in pressure at the surface can generate waves at the interface between the layers. A moving ship can do it; so can a low-pressure weather system on a vastly larger scale. The alternating bands of ripples and slicks one sometimes sees on the surface of the water mark the presence of internal waves.

Waves are also generated by abrupt incidents in the ocean— earthquakes, explosions, landslides and similar events. These extraordinary waves are popularly known as *tidal waves*, but scientists prefer the Japanese term *tsunami.*

One of the most spectacular of all local tsunamis occurred on July 9, 1958, in Alaska. Lituya Bay is an eight-mile-deep fjord surrounded by high mountains and nearly barred by a hilly spit. The entire Pacific basin is seismically active, and Alaskans in particular are accustomed to earthquakes, so the people on three boats anchored in the bay were not unduly alarmed when they felt a mild tremor late that evening. They had no way of knowing that at the head of the fjord a small earthquake had shaken 90 million tons of rock and glacial ice into the bay. Three minutes later, a wall of water 100 feet high came roaring down the fjord. One of the boats was carried high up the mountainside and deposited back in the bay, still afloat. Another was carried completely out of the bay, 80 feet above the treetops on the spit, and dropped in the ocean, shattered and sinking. The occupants escaped in a dinghy. The third vessel vanished, along with its crew.

This was not an isolated event; three such waves had traversed Lituya Bay in 1936, and scientists have found evidence of earlier waves as high as 400 feet. Similar waves have also devastated the Arctic coastal towns of Valdez and Seward.

By contrast, when a major earthquake or landslide occurs in the deep ocean, the tsunamis radiate outward from the epicenter, like ripples from a stone cast into a pond. Their wavelengths can exceed 100 miles, and they travel at speeds of up to 500 miles per hour, killing people thousands of miles from their sources In 1960, for instance, a powerful earthquake on the coast of Chile killed 400 and damaged half a million homes. The resulting tsunami did extensive damage to the waterfronts of Los Angeles and San Diego, and flooded cities in New Zealand, Australia and the Philippines. In Japan, 9,000 miles away, 180 people died.

In the open sea, oddly enough, a tsunami is almost imperceptible; even a ship traveling over the epicenter of an earthquake on the ocean floor may notice nothing unusual. The tsunami simply raises or lowers the surface of the ocean a foot or two. In 1946, the captain of a ship off Hilo, Hawaii, was astonished to see the city's waterfront demolished by a tsunami that had passed under his ship unnoticed.

Nearing the coast, tsunamis react like other waves, growing steeper and shorter as the depth decreases. By the time they reach the shore, they may be more than 100 feet high. One such tsunami, which struck Japan in 1896, killed 27,000 people and destroyed 10,000 homes. Yet the tsunami that wrecks one town may leave another untouched; the effects depend on the configuration and orientation of the coastline or the harbor. The harbor of Hilo is particularly vulnerable because it is perfectly situated to catch and concentrate tsunamis generated off Alaska.

One of the most spectacular tsunamis in historic time was created by the explosion of the Krakatau volcano in the Sunda Straits in 1883. The eruption blew away the entire end of an island, leaving a 900-foot crater where the land had previously stood 700 feet above sea level. It created two new islands and transformed four cubic *miles* of rock into airborne dust, darkening the sky so that people in Jakarta, 100 miles away, had to light their lamps at midday. Pumice covered the sea in a mat thick enough to prevent ships from passing.

The smoke and dust reached 17 miles into the stratosphere, and dust carried on the stratospheric winds caused red sunsets in London. The resulting tsunamis drowned the coasts of Java and Sumatra. Whole villages more than 100 feet above sea level were washed away. In all, more than 36,000 people drowned. The tsunamis flew westward at 400 miles per hour till they burst and died on the coasts in Panama, Chile and South Africa.

The early years of the twenty-first century witnessed the most destructive tsunamis of all time, one created by the 2004 Indian Ocean earthquake, and the other by the 2011 Tohoku earthquake off the coast of Japan.

The Indian Ocean tsunami was triggered by a prolonged 9.1 magnitude quake off the coast of Sumatra, and sent surges all around the Pacific basin, killing more than 230,000 people in 14 countries. In the immediate vicinity, the tsunamis reached 98 feet in height. The 2011 Japanese tsunami, at 133 feet, was much higher, though it killed only about one-tenth as many people as the Indian Ocean disaster. With an economic impact estimated at $235 billion, however, the Tohoku quake and tsunami ranks as the costliest natural disaster in history. The quake actually moved Japan several meters closer to North America, and shifted the Earth's axis by four to ten inches.

∞

The ocean tides are the greatest of all waves, with wavelengths that reach halfway around the world, but they are so different from other waves that it hardly seems reasonable to call them by the same name.

The landsman thinks of the world as a series of continents separated by water. In fact, the Earth is a planet covered with water, interrupted by a few continents. As Arthur C. Clarke remarked, we should not call our planet *Earth,* we should call it *Water.* The planet rotates within a jacket of water, dragging the oceans along in its rotation by friction and inertia. The water is susceptible to the influence of the sun and the moon, each of which exerts a gravitational pull on the surface, drawing the oceans upward and creating a broad hump of water under each of them. Although the sun's gravitational attraction is 150 times greater than the moon's, it is the moon that dominates the tides. The sun's attraction is so great it is felt almost equally all over the globe. The sun is like a floodlight, the moon like a spotlight.

While the Earth rotates, the bulge of water beneath the moon remains more or less stationary, as does the smaller bulge produced by the sun. As each whirling continent collides with a tidal bulge, the tide rises on its shores. As the land rotates away from the bulge, the tide appears to fall. Since the water is moving while the bulge is stationary, the tide is conceptually the mirror image of lesser waves. With normal waves, the wave form moves through the sea; with the tides, the oceans are traveling through the wave form.

As the moon orbits the Earth, however, it slightly outruns the Earth's daily rotation. If the moon is precisely over your home now, the Earth will thus have to make slightly more than one complete revolution to bring your home directly under the moon again. The elapsed time will be 24 hours plus 50 minutes, which is why the tides on most coasts advance by 50 minutes a day. In addition, the orbit of the moon around the Earth is an ellipse, not a perfect circle. Every 27.55 days the moon makes its nearest approach to the Earth—its *perigee*—which increases its gravitational pull, making the tides rise higher and fall lower.

But the Earth is also rotating around the sun, and every 29.53 days the three bodies form a straight line, a position known as *syzygy*. Now the gravitational effects of the sun and moon reinforce one another. The water bulge under the sun is added to the one under the moon, and the tides rise significantly higher—and fall significantly lower— in what are known as *spring* tides. Two weeks later, the sun and the moon are approximately at right angles; the sun's bulge occurs in the trough of the moon's wave, and the two tend to cancel one another out, producing exceptionally low *neap* tides. With mathematical regularity, the cycles of perigee and syzygy coincide, producing perigean spring tides, which may rise 40 percent above normal high tides.

In the open ocean, the great wave that is the tide may rise only a foot or two above normal sea level—which is the tidal range on many Pacific islands. When the great wave arrives at a coast, however (or, more accurately, when a coast arrives at the tide), the slope of the continental shelf forces the tidal wave progressively upward and slows it down. The tidal bulge heaps up on itself. When it arrives at the shore it may raise the water locally by five, ten, fifteen feet.

Where the tidal flow is constricted, the tide surges upward even farther, becoming a *tidal bore.* The sloping floor and narrowing sides of the Gulf of Maine funnel the rising tide into the narrow, steep-sided Bay of Fundy, a flooded rift valley 200 million years old. The bay narrows from 75 miles in width at its mouth to 28 miles at its most constricted point, Cape Chignecto; its floor shelves from 400 feet at the Gulf of Maine to 120 feet at the cape. More than 110 billion tons of water leave and enter the bay on each tide—an amount 2,000 times greater than the discharge of the St. Lawrence River.

With the force of gravity driving it, and with the bay shoaling and narrowing, all that water has nowhere to go but up. The result is the world's highest tide—a foaming wave advancing faster than a man can run and a high tide as much as 50 feet above the low water mark. Tidal bores reach 15 feet in height on China's Tsientang River, and as much as 25 feet on the Amazon, where they penetrate up to 200 miles inland. Because the Amazon Basin is so vast, the tides generate new tidal bores before the earlier ones are spent; at any given moment, several tidal bores are advancing up the river in successive walls of water.

The Fundy tides are enhanced by a phenomenon known as *resonance.* If you slosh water in a half-filled bathtub, the waves move from end to end with a period of about two seconds. If you give them an extra push every time they go by, the waves grow rapidly and eventually overflow the tub. Something similar happens in the Bay of Fundy. In effect, the bay and gulf are like a gigantic bathtub. The outgoing tide takes about 13 hours to travel its length, a period that almost exactly matches the ebb and flow of the tides. The bay's falling tide is met by a new flood tide coming in, which pushes the outgoing water back just as your hand puts extra energy behind the wave in the bathtub.

Resonance within a bay or harbor produces a type of wave known as a *seiche*, which usually starts when ocean disturbances enter the harbor, sending pulses of wave energy into the harbor. The result is a rocking motion within the harbor—not unlike the one in the bathtub—which can go on for days. Los Angeles Harbor is particularly prone to seiches, which can cause large ships to snap their mooring lines in what appears to be an almost calm harbor.

∽

The waves we watch on beaches are among nature's commonplace miracles—miraculous forms that have often traveled thousands of miles to decorate the shore as they break at our feet.

Somewhere out in the Atlantic, an easterly storm generates a wave. The wave becomes a swell and begins a long westward journey. It crosses the range of undersea mountains known as the Mid-Atlantic Ridge, passes over the Newfoundland Basin and kisses the southern edge of the Grand Banks. It rolls north of Sable Island, happily untroubled by rain or ice or snow, which would beat it down. The winds push at it from time to time, but the smooth curvature of the swell flows onward.

The wave moves past the undersea precipice at the edge of the continental shelf and reaches toward the North American mainland. As it approaches the shore the water becomes progressively more shallow and the wave begins to "feel the bottom." The orbiting water molecules start to drag at the bottom of their circuits. The wave slows down and shortens. The wave rises higher and higher in response to the shoaling water, crowded by other waves pushing in behind it. The section of the wave that approaches a point of land—Gros Nez, on Isle Madame—feels the bottom first and slows down. Neighboring sections of the wave sweep in at their old pace until they, too, feel the bottom, and the difference in speed makes the wave bend around the point, shaping itself to the land, closing in on all three sides of the promontory and breaking in a long, progressive curl, which runs up the shore with all the order and beauty of a rising arpeggio.

Farther off, a section of the wave marches inexorably into the Baie des Rochers. At the head of the bay is Pondville Beach, with its long, gentle slope. Now the effect of the bottom has organized the waves into parallel lines of crests, lifting into the air as they approach the shore. The wave rises in direct proportion to the slope, higher and higher, its molecules orbiting ever more rapidly, until the water is roughly 1.3 times as deep as the wave is high.

Now the molecules at the bottom of the wave cannot maintain the orbiting motion of the wave form. The water at the top of the wave races forward, and a deep trough appears in front of it. A frosting of foam erupts from its crest. An offshore breeze catches the broken water on the crest and blows it seaward in skeins of mist and spray—the white mane of a racing green horse, shot with fleeting rainbows where the sunlight shatters among the droplets. The rearing cap leans forward now, curling toward the beach in momentary defiance of gravity, its hollowed face a perfect sculpture in green glass.

The wave is at its most magnificent an instant before its death, and I watch it with a joy that is tinged always with sorrow. For me, these are the most beautiful of all breakers—the combers within which T.S. Eliot imagined the mermaids singing.

∽

And now the wave crashes, a perfect tube of green and white, tossing spray high into the air as it strikes the gray sand of Pondville Beach, its brief swash and backwash a broth of sand that tugs at my rubber boots as its water returns to the sea.

The water remains, but the wave is gone.

And—ever so minutely—the beach has changed because of it.

Oceanographer

On a shelf in an illuminated case stands a glorious, delicate, swirling shell, paper-thin, translucent, perhaps six inches across.

"What is that?" I ask, astounded, staring at it.

"This?" says Willard Bascom, taking it in his hands. He smiles and starts to recite a poem.

> This is that ship of pearl which, poets feign
> > Sails the unshadowed main,
> > The venturous bark that flings
> On the sweet summer wind its purpled wings
> In gulfs enchanted, where the Siren sings
> > And coral reefs lie bare,
> Where the cold sea-maids rise to sun their streaming hair.

On he goes, twelve lines, twenty-four, thirty-six. He speaks the poem well, crisply enunciating the words, savoring the rhythms, relishing the ornate form but letting the grammar ring through to the sense, arriving with measured grace at the conclusion:

> Let each new temple, nobler than the last
> Shut thee from heaven with a dome more vast,

Till thou at length art free,
Leaving thine outgrown shell by life's unresting sea!

"Well?" Bascom looks at me, his eyes merry but intent—lean, sun-browned, his tall head teased with wisps of white hair. This is a test, and I am going to fail it.

"I don't know that poem," I concede unhappily. "It's lovely."

"And you an English professor," says Bascom sadly, shaking his head. He holds the shell up, looking at it with an air of scarcely concealed wonder. "'The Chambered Nautilus.' Oliver Wendell Holmes. This is the shell of a chambered nautilus."

Willard Bascom is among the founders of modern oceanography—a polymath, an autodidact, a maverick. By turns a scientist, an adventurer, a businessman and an author, he is at once unique and typical of his generation—unique in the breadth of his interests and the boldness of his undertakings, typical in having become an oceanographer quite unexpectedly.

Oceanography is not a discipline in the normal sense, of course. As Bascom says, it is "a collection of scientists who find common cause in trying to understand the complex nature of the oceans." The oceans have always been of interest to some scientists—what became the Scripps Institution of Oceanography was established as early as 1912—but its great expansion came only after World War II. After innumerable amphibious landings and extensive casualties on invasion beaches, military planners realized they knew very little about oceans and beaches, and the subsequent growth of oceanographic research was heavily supported by the military.

Oceanography has given Willard Bascom a fairy-tale life, an explorer's life, a Horatio Alger life. When he talks about it, the word he keeps repeating is *fun.* It was "a lot of fun," he writes, "being one of the small group who rode the crest of the wave through the golden years of oceanography."

Born in New York in 1916, Bascom landed a job as a teenager

working as a mucker with the mining crews who were driving the 85-mile Delaware Aqueduct under the Hudson River to supply water to New York City. At 22, an experienced miner, he enrolled in the famous Colorado School of Mines, but left without a degree because "an altercation with the president over my maverick attitude toward the school caused him to expel me a few months before graduation."

By then the United States had entered the war, but Bascom was barred from military service because his jaw had been broken in a mining accident and the two sides worked independently. But in any case he had a job resampling old mines for tungsten and other metals useful to the war effort. It was lonely, cold, dangerous work, traveling the Colorado mountains on snowshoes, accompanied only by a dog.

"During that period," Bascom writes in his autobiography, *The Crest of the Wave*, "I was temporarily blinded by cement dust from a gunite operation in a burning tunnel where the temperature was 120 degrees F, carried out for dead from the Big Thomson tunnel, 4 miles underground, rode aerial tramways for miles in subzero weather while wet from mine water, became involved in a union war underground, where some had sworn to 'get' me, and literally scared a rider to death when an ore truck I was driving ran away on a long steep mountain grade (he was stiff and blue by the time I got it under control). Gradually the idea penetrated my mind that there must be a better way to make a living, in a warmer climate."

In 1945 Bascom went to San Francisco, where he looked up the brother of a friend. John Isaacs turned out to be "one of the greatest people I ever knew, and certainly the smartest—and I've known several dozen Nobel Prize winners." Isaacs had worked for the forest service and fished on the Columbia River; he had just finished an engineering degree, and he casually offered Bascom a job with the U.S. Navy funded Waves Project of the University of California.

Thus it was that Bascom, who had never seen an ocean before, found himself crashing out to sea through 20-foot breakers in an amphibious six-wheel-drive Army truck called a *dukw*, pronounced *duck*. Once beyond the breakers, the dukw would turn and surf back to the beach—cantilevered forward on the crest of a wave as high as a house, moving at 15 knots—while Bascom heaved a weighted line overboard to measure the height of the wave above the sand. It took him a while to notice that Isaacs never went out on the dukws; Bascom assumed that the technique was tested and that others were doing it elsewhere. Wrong on both counts.

As a research methodology, driving dukws through the surf seemed "awfully crude" even at the time, but it got accurate results. By this and other means, Isaacs and Bascom measured waves from Southern California to the Canadian border for five years. They surveyed the beach profile and measured the seasonal movement of sand at Carmel, California. They studied the effects of the great tsunami of April 1, 1946, which killed two men when it wiped away a two-story concrete lighthouse at Scotch Cap, Alaska, 52 feet above the high tide line—and their studies gave rise to a Seismic Sea Wave Warning System. When the United States began testing atomic weapons at Eniwetok Atoll, Bascom and Isaacs measured the waves produced by the explosions. They developed the first electronic wave recording apparatus. They used the new techniques of aerial photography to record the Navy's amphibious exercises. By 1950, the onetime mining engineer was writing the three-volume *Shoreline Atlas of the Pacific Coast of the U.S.*

After joining the Scripps Institution, Bascom took part in a multifaceted 12,000-mile geophysical expedition around the South Pacific. He went diving in some of the first scuba gear and shared an office with the inventor of the wet suit. In 1954 he moved to Washington with the National Academy of Sciences (NAS), taking time off in 1956 to live in Tahiti for some months, reading and writing.

While Bascom was in Tahiti, the Russians launched *Sputnik*, galvanizing the United States into dramatic action on science education. Back with NAS, Bascom became science adviser for a TV series called *Conquest* and was also involved with a series of 100 science books for high schoolers, emanating from MIT. Bascom had written articles for *Scientific American* on waves and beaches, so he was induced to write a book for the series. Thirty years later, *Waves and Beaches*—much revised—is still the standard introduction to the subject. When a group of scientists proposed to drill a hole through the Mohorovicic discontinuity—the boundary between the Earth's crust and its mantle, known to its friends as the Moho—Bascom found himself in charge of what inevitably became known as the Mohole project. The Moho is about 35,000 feet down. At the time, the deepest oil wells were being drilled in 200 feet of water.

Anchoring is impossible in the deep ocean, so Bascom devised a system called "dynamic positioning" to hold the ship in place over the drill site. Dynamic positioning is basically a system of four outboard motors controlled by a joystick, which nudges the ship this way and that as required to hold it in the same position. The invention made deep drilling possible, and it has been widely used ever since. It allowed Bascom's team to drill 600 feet into the sea bottom in 12,000 feet of water before political complications ended the project. Bascom wrote a book about it, *A Hole in the Bottom of the Sea.*

With some colleagues, Bascom next established a private company, Ocean Science and Engineering. OSE went drilling for diamonds on the coast of South West Africa on behalf of the DeBeers diamond interests. DeBeers bought into the company, as did DuPont, Alcoa, Amerada-Hess and Southern Natural Gas. Bascom and his partners had bought their shares at five cents each in 1961; when the company went public in 1969, the shares sold for $12.75, and Bascom found himself wealthy.

OSE developed specialized sensing buoys for the military, configured specialized survey ships for Gulf Oil, surveyed the bottoms of rivers and bays in wartime Vietnam and designed a bridge to cross the Straits of Gibraltar. The company raised wrecked jetliners off the California coast and built underwater dredges and specialized scalloping vessels to work off the coast of Florida.

In 1971 Bascom found himself in Florida with time on his hands;

he had resigned as OSE's president, though he remained chairman. He incorporated a new company, Seafinders Inc., which located and recovered a Spanish treasure galleon on the Little Bahama Bank. But Bascom was much more interested in deeper archaeology—deeper in both time and space. He believed that ships of Homer's era might lie intact on the anoxic bottom of the Black Sea or the Sea of Marmara, where teredos and bacteria cannot live. He published a book on the matter —*Deep Water, Ancient Ships*—and he persuaded Alcoa to build a ship, *Alcoa Seaprobe,* to explore there. Alas, he was unable to finance an expedition, and the ship was later scrapped.

∿

As I learned to my chagrin when I met him, Bascom is a remarkably literary scientist, and his autobiography is full of references to poetry. When he wakes up in hospital after an operation, he finds himself reciting a line from Kipling. When he scuba dives at Bikini, he thinks of Coleridge: "We were the first that ever burst/Into that silent sea." When he contemplates a radioactive tent village on Bikini after the atomic tests, he thinks of *Macbeth,* and the fact that the tests may have simply "lighted fools/The way to dusty death." It is hardly surprising to learn that he edited an anthology, *Great Sea Poetry,* or to realize that *Waves and Beaches* ends with an eclectic collection of excerpts from Homer, Slocum, Darwin, Conrad and Arthur C. Clarke.

As Jonathan Raban notes, Bascom's contemporaries in oceanography write with "a fastidious quantitative analysis while retaining a Romantic sense of wonder at the sea's power and mystery. Bascom, particularly, writes of the sea with such frank passion that his *Waves and Beaches* has the eccentric and engaging character of a monograph by a swaggering adventurer."

Bascom does see himself as an adventurer, an explorer, boldly going where no man had gone before. His generation of oceanographers, he writes, "driven by scientific curiosity ... explored the same seas as the pre-nineteenth century adventurers who used their opportunities to chart previously unknown lands."In pep talks to the crews of his oceanographic vessels, he exhorted them to realize that "we sail in the tradition of Columbus and Magellan, looking for new knowledge that will benefit mankind." As a boy, he wanted to belong to the Explorers Club; in 1980 he won its highest award, the Medal of Exploration.

Oceanography gathered momentum, he says, "because it looked like a fun way to spend one's life." By the end of his career, however, oceanography had been transformed by technology; soon it might be possible to study the sea without even looking at it. In 1980 he chaired a panel on satellite oceanography. He was characteristically enthusiastic about the ability of satellites to record sea surface winds and temperatures, wave heights and current movements, plankton populations and even sea level itself, which it measured to an accuracy of three centimeters from a height of 800 kilometers. He was fascinated by the new information the satellites were providing: Gulf Stream eddies going the wrong way, open holes known as *polynyas* in the polar ice in midwinter, masses of plankton far offshore where they had no business to be. The satellites even discovered a 46-foot depression in the surface of the Atlantic Ocean.

Satellite oceanography, Bascom concluded, was "undoubtedly the most promising new aspect of oceanography," and he was much stimulated by the stream of new and surprising information flowing down from the sky. But in the end, his interest waned. Why? "Probably because this is not a very adventurous form of oceanography."

For Bascom and his contemporaries, oceanography was a mixture of adventure, learning and Yankee ingenuity: finding questions and answering them, finding problems and solving them. As Bascom says, they "had the good fortune to deal with what was, from a scientific and technological point of view, a nearly virginal ocean." When Bascom was writing *Waves and Beaches,* he found the most helpful book on beaches was still *Shorelines and Shoreline Processes,* written by Douglas Johnson in 1919. Nearly half a century later, it had not been superseded.

But the ocean of the pioneers is no longer virginal, their beaches are no longer deserted, and their successors are sitting at computers rather than driving dukws through the surf. One wonders whether oceanography will ever again be dominated by men so intensely human, with such eclectic minds, such gusto, such burning curiosity and soaring imagination.

Willard Bascom sits on the patio behind the ranch house in Long Beach, California, a widower of 78, still lean and tall and brown. He's working on a new book about an undersea treasure find, and he can't talk about it. He smiles.

"I've had a lot of fun," he says. "And I'm still having fun."

3. The Sand
and
The Shore

Come to the window, sweet is the night-air!
Only, from the lone line of spray
Where the sea meets the moon-blanched sand,
Listen! you hear the grating roar
Of pebbles which the waves draw back, and fling,
At their return, up the high strand,
Begin, and cease, and then again begin,
With tremulous cadence slow, and bring
The eternal note of sadness in.
　　　—Matthew Arnold, *Dover Beach*

The sea is volatile, mysterious, beyond human control. The land, we think, is stable. It is not. Slowly, subtly, inexorably, the land is constantly changing, too. At the boundary zone, the land is changing with every passing moment, in tune with the restlessness of the sea. The beach reaches deep into the land and is fed by the land.

The beach begins everywhere. In the melting snowpack high in the Rocky Mountains, a trickle of water rolls down the rock, joins another, becomes a mountain stream. Swinging fast around a curve, the stream dislodges a clump of soil. The soil drops into the water and falls apart.

Its particles are swept away by the rushing water. Their destination may be the Pacific, the Arctic, the Gulf of Mexico. It all depends where the water goes.

Those particles are beach materials. Geologists call them *sediment* —inanimate material that can be moved. Some sediments are silts so fine they can be moved by seeping water or mere breaths of air. Boulders the size of cars or washing machines are also sediments, though it might take a glacier to move them. A beach, says Bob Taylor, "is a collection of materials—it can be sand or pebbles, it can be shells, it can be pop cans—but it's a collection of materials. To understand a beach, you have to think about where it gets its materials from." (There actually *is* a beach, at Fort Bragg, California, composed of tin cans.)

Up in the mountains the particles tumble downward, borne by the mountain stream. The water eddies behind a rock and drops the particles on the streambed. A flowing stream keeps sediments moving along, but when it meets resistance the stream loses energy and drops its larger particles. You can see this on a city street during a heavy rain. Look in the gutter. At any obstruction—a twig, a pebble, a clump of leaves—you'll see a teardrop-shaped deposit of sediments trailing away downstream, marking out the energy shadow of the obstruction. When more energy becomes available, perhaps because it rains harder, those sediments will move on.

Sediments in water are much easier to move than sediments in air, because the buoyancy of the water effectively reduces their weight and thus weakens the power of gravity to resist their movement. The sediments—from your gutter, from the mountains, from gopher holes in the prairies, from everywhere—are all going to the beach, and they will be carried chiefly by water. Ultimately, the beaches are made of sediments shed by the whole continent. On the west coast, beaches are nourished almost entirely by powerful rivers, which bring down sediments liberated by inland erosion. Rushing down the steep Pacific slope, the rivers are met at the shoreline by north-going coastal currents. The currents drag the sand into long spits and bars, which almost block the estuaries, forcing the rivers to make a sharp right turn before exiting through a narrow opening in the north end of the bar. The sand supplied by the greatest of all the western rivers, the Columbia, not only maintains one of the most dangerous river-mouth bars in the world but has also built bay-mouth bars across the coastal indentations to the north, Willapa Bay and Gray's Harbor in Washington state. Without the Columbia's prodigious sand-transport system, Willapa Bay would hardly be a bay at all.

The west coast dune fields, particularly in southern California, could masquerade—and have masqueraded—as deserts. On my desk is a worm-eaten irregular wedge of wood, flecked with white plaster. I picked it out of the Guadalupe dunes near Santa Maria, California. It is part of the set for the original 1923 Cecil B. DeMille production of *The Ten Commandments.* The Santa Maria dunes impersonated the deserts through which Moses led the Chosen People. In 1923, ecology was an unknown word. As late as 1960, only one student in my university grad class was majoring in ecology. Nobody knew what that was, noted the yearbook editors, "but it sounds dirty to us." So when the crew had finished shooting DeMille's epic, the company simply bulldozed a hole in the dunes, pushed the set into it and covered it over.

But dunes are notably unstable. Half a century after the filming of *The Ten Commandments,* the dunes have shifted, and fragments of the set have slowly moved into the sunlight again. I picked my piece of wood off the top of the dune and brought it home as a souvenir.

Farther north, the coasts of Oregon and Washington display the greatest dune fields in North America, stretching up to 50 miles along the coast and penetrating far inland. The innermost dunes do not look like dunes at all; they look like forested hills 100 or 200 feet high. As new dunes have built up in front of them, these old dunes have remained stable for thousands of years, and the forest has colonized them. Driving over a high hill far inland, I was startled to come upon acres and acres of bare brown sand. What I had taken to be one of the foothills of the coastal mountains was an immense dune.

These dune fields are so vast that they defeat your efforts to photograph them. You stand on a dune and slowly turn around. In the distance, pygmy waves are beating on the remote shore. The dunes stretch away to north and south in huge, smooth mounds and irregular hummocks, interrupted by shadows in the valleys and occasional clumps of fir and cedar. The groves of trees stand like islands in an enormous beige oceanic swell. Far behind you the dunes reach into the forest, and fingers of forest probe seaward into the dunes.

A dune buggy appears in the distance, buzzing like an angry bee. It moves over the dunes and drops into the valleys like an insect.

Click.

The photograph shows a brown blur of sand with a small black dot.

❧

On the east coast, from Long Island north into Canada, the beaches are nourished less by rivers than by the glaciers that moved across this landscape more than ten thousand years ago, carrying unimaginable volumes of sediment within them. The weight of the glaciers, which covered almost all of the polar and temperate regions, pressed the Earth's crust downward at the poles and outward near the equator, distorting the Earth's shape like a tennis ball squashed under the weight of a person's foot.

At the same time, the ice sheets absorbed so much ocean water that sea level fell even below the lowered surface of the northern land. Worldwide, sea level dropped about 400 feet. Fifteen thousand years ago, for example, the patch of land that is now Pondville Beach stood high above the ocean, even though it was deep beneath the ice. The shoreline lay nearly four miles to seaward. Cape Breton and Long Island were parts of the mainland. So was the southern half of the Gulf of St. Lawrence, as well as the rich undersea plateau known today as George's Bank.

"We've found teeth of mammoths and mastodons on George's Bank," says Don Forbes, one of Bob Taylor's colleagues at the Geological Survey of Canada. "We've found remnants of spruce and hemlock trees on what is now the ocean floor. Going the other way, we've found old beaches away up in the cliffs above Advocate, on the Bay of Fundy, which tells us that sea level there has sometimes been much higher than today."

As the glaciers grumbled southward, they scoured the bedrock, plucking up sand and stones and boulders and later dropping them as ridges of debris. One such ridge is the north shore of Long Island, New York, the southern limit of the glaciers' travel. The sluggish violence done to the landscape by the glaciers is the factor that gives the northeastern coast its diverse and surprising character—some of the oldest rock formations in the world, and some of the youngest, all overlaid with material carried here by the ice and deposited in a wide array of different forms.

The ice, says Bob Taylor, has given Nova Scotia "headlands in some places, thin blankets of sediment in different areas, and in other cases it's eroded all the sediment and left nothing but a bedrock shore, like Peggy's Cove, our famous tourist landscape.

"Along the Nova Scotia coastline, within a mile you'll go from rocky headlands into an area of glacial deposits, which are a mixture of sand, pebble, clay and boulders, and then you'll go into an embayment where you'll have salt marsh deposits, and then you'll come across pocket beaches of sand or gravel, which have been derived from these eroding headlands. It's a remarkable variety, and it's due to the geological framework of the coastline."

The Audubon Society's guide to the Atlantic coast identifies five distinctive environments between the Gulf of St. Lawrence and the Gulf of Mexico: rocky shores, bays and estuaries, coral reefs, salt marshes, beaches and dunes. Coral reefs excepted, they are all found along the northern coastline, even in a small area like Isle Madame.

We think of geological change as crustal gyrations in deep time—

massive and imponderable, but somehow complete and finished. It is nothing of the kind. The glaciers have not completed their retreat, and you can trace their progress in the character of the landscape as you travel north. In Massachusetts, the land is rounded, smooth, bucolic, covered with trees and grass. Parts of Nova Scotia have similar terrain, but elsewhere in the province the ground has been shaven bare to the Earth's rocky bones, or littered with huge boulders, some of them half the size of a house. Newfoundland is stonier yet, with vast areas of rocky barrens. Although Newfoundland is a huge island, only one cranny of it—the Codroy Valley, on its west coast—is really capable of sustaining traditional agriculture; in Newfoundland gardens elsewhere, the shallow layer of soil is often littered with rocks the size of a lunch box. Under its shallow overlay of soil, the rest of Newfoundland still looks much the way it did when the glaciers withdrew.

Moving north, we find parts of the Arctic are still covered by slowly shrinking glaciers, and the rocky surface of the recently uncovered land is absolutely bare. Here the land is still rebounding after the retreat of the glaciers. In Viking times, Sweden's Lake Malaren was a deep bay reaching inland from the Baltic; today the land has risen enough to make it a freshwater lake well above sea level. Some of the greatest and most interesting beaches of the world are on the Arctic Ocean, though they have precious little attraction for beachniks. In Bathurst Inlet, on Canada's Arctic coast, the rising land has lifted beaches upward from the water and built new ones below them. A dozen beaches ascend from the sea like steps, each one marking another phase in the land's gradual emergence from the water.

Global warming may retard this trend by raising sea level, and in any case we are in a geological interlude of relative warmth. But this is a brief and trivial matter, from a geological perspective. The Earth is thought to be in a long-term cooling cycle, moving toward the next ice age. Over the next few thousand years, the level of the sea will rise and fall again, like a giant tide flooding and ebbing through time.

It is hard for human beings to grasp the true meaning of such a statement because of the truncated nature of our sense of time. To human beings, ten years is a long time, and a century is a very long time. A thousand years is the misty past. In the life of the Earth itself, however, a span of a thousand years, even a million years, is merely an eye blink.

"The thing that separates geology from all other sciences is that sense of time," explains Randy Parkinson, a professor of geology at the Florida Institute of Technology. "Geological processes are very slow—but they're very persistent, and they've got all the time in the world."

The flat beaches of the American southeast—Virginia, Georgia, the Carolinas—originate deep in those echoing reaches of time. South of Long Island, the beach sediments derive not from rivers or glaciers but from the broad, flat continental shelf and from the sandy shoreline itself. Ultimately this sand, too, is derived from the continents, but it is much, much older, and it has been shaped not by one ice age but by dozens.

In each ice age the sea retreats, sometimes beyond the limits of the continental shelf. Plants and animals colonize the newly exposed seafloor. The barrier islands created by a rising sea are abandoned by a falling one, and become sand hills on a flat sandy plain. Georgia's famous pines grow in sandy soil that once lay at the bottom of the ocean.

Then, as the ice melts, the sea refills. Infinitely slowly, the surf creeps higher on the sandy plains, sweeping and spreading across the continental shelf, leveling out the landscape, drowning the vegetation and the animals that once lived in it. The sea nudges grains of sand toward the continent when it rises and takes only a portion of the sand back when it falls. Moving back and forth over unimaginable eons of time, the active edge of the sea has rolled the continent's apron of sand flatter than the prairies. Aside from the salt flats of Utah, the southeastern shoreline is almost the flattest land in North America. The coastal plain stretches inland for many miles, stopping only at the Piedmont fall line where it meets the old mountains of the Appalachian chain.

The sand that survives this prolonged tumbling and sorting is largely quartz and feldspar, which are chemically stable and physically hard. Everything else has been dissolved, ground up, carried away during the millions of years these grains of sand have been milling around together. The result—in New Jersey, Maryland, the Carolinas—is hundreds of miles of beige sandy beaches.

Farther south the sand becomes progressively lighter in color, and by the time one reaches the Florida Keys it is almost pure white. Like the blindingly white beaches of the Caribbean, these are carbonate beaches, composed of the bones and shells of ocean organisms: corals, mollusks, crustaceans and fish. In Sanibel Island, on the west coast of Florida—where the famous naturalist Rachel Carson made her home—the sand is more than 50 percent carbonate. The fine-ground shells that make up the beaches are very old; researchers analyzing the Florida sands have found that their carbonate components may date back as much as 30,000 years.

The coastal plain continues around Florida, through Mississippi and Texas and on down the Mexican and Central American coasts. In all this long shoreline, there are few significant sources of new sediment. Most southeastern rivers are slow and sluggish, lazy wanderers in the level plains. They lack the energy to carry much sediment, and the sediments they do move are normally dropped in tidal bays and lagoons well inland from the ocean.

Some smaller rivers do contribute sediment to the coasts of Alabama, Mississippi, Louisiana and Texas, but the great source of sediment on the Gulf Coast is the Mississippi River, which drains the whole American heartland from Montana and Minnesota to Ohio and North Carolina. Every day, the Mississippi deposits a million tons of sediment in its delta, which covers 12,000 square miles. The delta is several miles thick, and its weight is great enough to depress the Earth's crust below it, slowing the rate at which the river can build new land into the sea. The Mississippi is a prodigious source of sediments, and it is slowly filling up the north side of the Gulf of Mexico from Texas to the Florida Panhandle.

∽

Wherever it comes from, the sand is always moving. Standing on a beach on a windy day you can feel the driven sand stinging your ankles. If the air is still, the waves and ripples are shifting sand from one location to another.

Watch the play of sand and waves on a beachface. Even when the sea is calm, small waves emerge from the placid surface and gently break on the beach, their lips clouded with fine sand. These lazy little waves seem to arise just a few feet out and quickly spill forward, their caps frothing saucily before them.

Now watch their backwash. If the waves come in at an angle, the swash moves diagonally up the beachface. Then the backwash retreats to the sea more or less directly until it meets the next wave coming in. A grain of sand carried up and back by the breaking wave ends its semiparabolic excursion a short distance down the beach from its starting point.

Mingling in the surf zone, the swash and backwash jointly create a longshore current parallel to the beach. The longshore current carries sand along with it in a process known as *beach drifting* or *littoral drift*. The longshore current feeds sediment from nearby estuaries and cliff faces to the beach and carries it on to other destinations. When the wind changes, the longshore current may reverse. On the west coast the predominant direction of the littoral drift is northward; on the east coast it normally runs southward. It is the longshore currents that produce the familiar pattern of alternating bar and channel, bar and channel. Sand moves along the beach as food moves through the body, sustaining and renewing it.

The shape of the land determines whether the sediment stays

nearby or moves on down the shore. On the smooth coastline running south from Long Island to Florida, the moving sand encounters few natural obstacles. As the currents move along the shore, the compliant sand moves with them. The river of sand flows constantly, running for hundreds of miles, blocking inlets and opening new ones, settling around obstructions, making land and removing it.

The sand river slows down only in South Florida, where the coast lies within the energy shadow of the Bahamas. The waves at Jacksonville, near the state's northern border, are twice as high as those at Miami. The littoral drift slows down and loses much of its capacity to carry sand. As a result, many beaches on the southern Florida coast are actually growing.

On the jagged coasts of British Columbia, Atlantic Canada and New England, however, the longshore currents are interrupted by promontories and rocky headlands, which trap most of the moving sediments in closed systems within the bays. Such sediments may move up and down the beachface with the seasons, or they may form a *sediment gyre,* moving sandbars around the bay in a slow circular path, or they may simply migrate up and down between the berm and the offshore bars. But sediment within a deep bay tends to remain inside that bay. On these heavily indented shores, it will form several different kinds of beaches. Some of these are *pocket beaches,* cusps of sand captured between two steep headlands; others are *baymouth beaches*, known in the Maritimes as *barachois beaches*, where sediment has blocked the mouth of a bay or estuary and turned the entrapped water into a lagoon.

In California, where the Pacific coastline becomes more regular, the beaches have other features, which make them particularly susceptible to human interference. The Pacific continental shelf is narrow, and the great Pacific combers, with a fetch that extends for thousands of miles, punish the coastline mercilessly. Off southern California, the shelf is indented by deep underwater canyons, which continually absorb the traveling sand. To survive in these conditions, the beaches need a constant resupply of sediments. The rivers normally provide that steady stream of fresh sand. In California, however, the construction industry mines 23 million tons of sand and gravel from shorelines and waterways every year; at the same time, the state's insensate demand for water and power has prompted the creation of huge dams and reservoirs, which have reduced the supply of sediment from some rivers by as much as 80 percent. The result is a starved beach system that requires frequent nourishment by the U.S. Army Corps of Engineers, at enormous cost to the public.

⤳

The history of the shorelines is the province of coastal geologists, who trace the evolution of beaches in part by drilling *cores* —hollow metal tubes that penetrate the land and the sea bottom and bring up a vertical sample of the underlying layers of sediment. When cores taken 40 miles off the coast of Nova Scotia contain bits of trees, they confirm that the sunken land was once above water. Another layer of sediment in the same core may contain the shells of oysters—which normally live in the brackish lagoons behind the beach—and those shells tell us that the beach once lay to seaward of the site. If the layer above the oysters shows us the shells of clams and quahogs, it tells us that the sea later rose to cover that site, moving the beach back, colonizing the lagoons and finally overwhelming the land itself.

That is how we know that large areas of the Atlantic coastal shelf such as the Grand Banks of Newfoundland were once above water. We find land plants and early Native artifacts buried in the sediments under 40 feet of water, and we can trace the beds of existing rivers running out along the sea bottom across the continental shelf. The story is in the sediments—a vast, mysterious saga of change and renewal—which geologists spend their lives patiently translating.

The modern scientific study of beaches sprang from the complex coastal geology of the northeast, specifically from Nantasket,

Massachusetts. Charlie Doucet and I went out to Nantasket one windy, drizzling morning with Peter Rosen, a youthful professor of marine geology at Northeastern University in Boston. Nantasket consists of a rounded 150-foot hill standing in the ocean and a low, trailing beach, which connects the hill to the mainland. It was once a summer resort for the middle classes of Boston. When the bourgeoisie moved on, working people bought the erstwhile cottages, and the hill and beach were ultimately incorporated as the city of Hull.

To this beach, early in the twentieth century, came a professor from Columbia University named Douglas W. Johnson.

"Douglas Johnson was a pioneer in the understanding of beaches," said Peter Rosen. "He was one of the first to see beaches in terms of evolutionary process. Out here at Nantasket he conducted a pioneering study where he developed the evolution of Nantasket Beach from an earlier time, a time he didn't know, to the present, to show the sequence of evolution of the beach.

"He found abandoned scarps along the beach that he knew had to have been cut by waves. He found ridges of dunes, and he knew that each ridge had to be the position of an ancient shoreline. And by simply sequencing dune ridges and the series of ancient scarps and cliffs, he was able to put together a sequence that *had* to have been the evolution of the shoreline. He couldn't put a date on it. He speculated that it was some considerable time in the past, and he recognized it was associated with rising sea level.

"He had no hard data that sea level was rising, but there was plenty of geological evidence to suggest that sea level rise was driving the process. Of course, what would be taking place is that the entire barrier beach would not only be forming, but would also be driven constantly landward. This led him to predict the future: that Nantasket Beach would ultimately be driven far landward of where it is today."

Rosen paused, looking around him, and grinned.

"Interestingly, at Nantasket all these evidences are gone because the barrier beach has been built over. Johnson couldn't do that study today. The ridges have been bulldozed—they're gone."

With its rounded hill and trailing beach, Nantasket is typical of the topography all the way up the northeastern coast from Long Island. The connective beach is known as a *tombolo*, and it is made up of sediments eroded from the hill. Tombolos often form great V-shaped structures—double tombolos—which protrude into the sea like the prow of a ship, with a rounded hill at the apex. Usually they enclose a lagoon of brackish water. Such a tombolo sometimes includes new land, won by the beach from the sea. Cape La Ronde, on the northeast corner of Isle Madame, is just such a tombolo, and the tracery of beaches around it includes a long trailing spit of cobbles known as the Goulet beach. Here, behind the fringe of cobbles, lie acres of new land—hard-packed sand being slowly colonized by moss, marram grass, spruce trees. At the farthest end of the beach is a field of old, overgrown dunes—evidence that the Goulet beach has been stable for a very long time.

The hills associated with tombolos—like the hill at Nantasket—are called *drumlins.* Drumlins are smooth heaps of glacial detritus, four or five hundred yards across, weathered by wind and rain, overgrown with grasses and trees. They are warehouses of sediments, ranging from boulders the size of cars and sofas to particles of silt so fine they show only as a discoloration in the surf. Drumlins are found all along the New England and Maritime coastlines. The most famous examples are Bunker Hill in Boston and Citadel Hill in Halifax. The term *drumlin* comes from the town of Drumlin in Ireland, where the same basket-of-eggs topography is found. Clusters of drumlins, known as drumlin fields, occur in many parts of Ireland. In Nova Scotia, the islands that speckle Mahone Bay and the islands around Isle Madame are half-submerged drumlin fields.

When a rising sea reaches a drumlin field, it creates an *erosional front,* rather like a cold front in the atmosphere. Since they are simply piles of glacial rubble, drumlins are readily deconstructed by the waves, which easily carry away the light silts and sands. You can see this process any day at the face of a drumlin, where the water is almost always clouded near the shore at high tide; after a rainstorm whole bays may be murky with silt.

The erosional front marches steadily through the drumlins, cutting away their foundations. The destruction of a drumlin may take centuries or it may be accomplished in a single lifetime. Day by day, in fair weather or storm, the sea undercuts the face of the drumlin till the whole cliff slumps. Rising sea level increases the rate of erosion, which is highly distressing to those who own drumlin property and very expensive to prevent. The cliff face in Nantasket is armored with a high cut-stone revetment built by the U.S. Army Corps of Engineers. It cost a million dollars, and the U.S. taxpayer paid for it. It protects three houses.

As the drumlins die, tombolos and other beaches are born. After a drumlin cliff has collapsed, the waves wash through the pile of debris, carrying different types of sediment in different directions, a process known as *sortation*. On beaches where sand occurs along with gravel or cobble, for instance, the larger sediments often come to rest high up on the beach. These are usually high-energy beaches, where plunging breakers strip away the finer sediments and deposit them below the surf line, leaving the cobbles on the upper beach, sometimes with a protected layer of sand underneath them.

Sortation may change with the seasons; the strong winds and waves of winter drag even more fine sand seaward, flattening the overall profile of the shore. Cobbles are much better than sand at absorbing the energy of the waves. As the size of the sediments changes, so does the slope of the beach. A beach of fine sand is normally flat, with a slope of one to five degrees. A pebble beach will have a slope of perhaps 17 degrees, and a coarse cobble beach can slope at 24 degrees. A hill that steep would be about as much as most cars could comfortably climb.

Isle Madame has miles of steep cobble beaches—high-energy beaches with currents and combers strong enough to carry away all the smaller sediments. These beaches are agreeably wild and lonely, but they make miserable walking. The rounded stones roll and capsize, constantly shifting underfoot. Because they are generally deserted, cobble beaches are good spots for beachcombing and bird-watching. The cobbles have an infinite range of textures and colors, being assembled from fragments of parent rock picked up everywhere the glacier traveled. Cobble beaches are hypnotic places, with the swish of the dissolving waves and the deep rumbling and clicking of the cobbles as they roll and collide in the backwash. Here the surf is making sand—abrading the cobbles, smashing the weak ones with the strong ones and compressing the air in the rock's crevices with a force powerful enough to split the solid stone.

The materials from a dissolving drumlin will sort themselves not just up and down the beach, but also along the shore.

"A lot of the drumlin will be mud," explains John Shaw, a colleague of Bob Taylor's at the Geological Survey of Canada, "and that mud will be just carried away in suspension. It'll either go off into deep water further offshore, or it'll go back into a nearby estuary and accumulate on the salt marsh somewhere in that area. Some of the sand will be carried back into the coves to form new beaches. But the boulders, the largest material, will be left right on the beach."

This residue of boulders, right at sea level, forms a *lag shoal* stretching well out to sea in line with the drumlin's spine. Coming home from a cruise, we often sail past Cape La Ronde, the big drumlin with the double tombolo, which is completely exposed to the open Atlantic. A long line of breakers over the lag shoal shows that the cape was once three times its present length. The shoal evokes some poignant memories; an uncle of my sailing mentor, Captain Leonard Pertus, once lost a cargo schooner on that shoal, and my late father-in-law, Arthur Terrio, lived as a boy in the Cape La Ronde lighthouse, which has long since fallen into the sea. The flashing light was moved inland to a skeleton tower, and old photographs reveal that even the land on which the lighthouse stood—the land where Arthur played as a boy—has eroded away. The cape is still retreating; during the winter of 1996-97, the skeleton tower followed its predecessor into the surf. Ultimately the cape will disappear altogether, leaving the tombolos without a source of sediment. The tombolos will vanish, too, and their sediments will be redistributed to make new beaches along the adjacent shore.

Over a period of decades or centuries, erosion appears steady and inexorable, but most of the action occurs in infrequent episodes of spectacular violence.

"Most of the change is associated with storms," says Peter Rosen. "During storms, the most wave energy is expended on the beach in the shortest period of time, and the most sand is transferred over the shortest period of time. Under normal conditions, if there's a supply of sand, generally it will be carried on shore and the beach will build. This is punctuated by short periods during storms when exponentially large amounts of sand are lost.

"If sea level were stable," Rosen continues, "one could assume that equilibrium could be reached, a gradual accumulation of sand to balance the short term loss of sand during storms. But sea level's rising. One foot per century is only a fraction of an inch, a few millimeters a year, and of course storm waves don't notice a few millimeters. But the highest storm waves every year are slightly higher than the highest one the year before, which are slightly higher than the year before that. Over time, the largest waves of the highest storms are continually encroaching at higher and higher elevations—and so at a certain point you'll see great changes."

That is why average rates of erosion are all but meaningless. A shoreline may be stable for decades, even centuries—and then suddenly shrink like melting snow. Statistically, it's eroding slowly. In reality, huge sections of it may have vanished almost instantly.

A patch of coastline 40 miles east of Halifax provides a spectacular example of long-term stability followed by rapid retreat. In 1766, a young naval lieutenant set out to survey and map the coast east of Halifax. His name was James Cook, and he was at the beginning of a magnificent career. His meticulous chart of the coast shows a steep rounded promontory, a half-eroded drumlin within a deep arc of beaches, which was settled and farmed by two families. Part of the promontory became a hay field belonging to the Meisner family.

For nearly 200 years, Cook's chart accurately described Meisner's field. In 1945, in early aerial photos, the whole area appeared almost unchanged. Nine years later, however, Hurricane Edna struck the Nova Scotia coast, and soon afterward the eastern beach began moving landward. It continued to do so for thirty years. John Shaw, Bob Taylor and others have been observing and measuring its retreat.

"Our measurements indicate that the beach there was retreating as much as eight meters a year during the 1960s," Shaw says. "It was probably a much shorter beach at one time, linking together a series of little drumlin headlands. But through time the beach has been overwashed during storms, it's gradually stretched in a large expanding arc, and some of the headlands have been completely eroded away. We predict that some time in the future this beach is going to disappear entirely, and that whole area of coastline will have a much different shape."

Today, nothing remains of Meisner's field but a lag shoal of huge rounded boulders and the remnants of a bridge, which reaches outward from the beach toward the distant horizon of the empty sea.

"Used to be a problem getting enough water from the well out there," remarked a member of the Meisner family, looking out over the tossing waves where his forefathers once plowed. "Plenty of water in that well now."

Le Concours National des Chateaux du Sable

On this beach, a horde of people are watching, talking, swimming, strolling the beach, eating *chiens chauds* and drinking *biere*. This *is* Quebec, after all—a fragment of Quebec way out in the middle of the Gulf of St. Lawrence. This is the beach of Havre Aubert, in the Magdalen Islands. The year-round population of the islands is 15,000, and there are 15,000 people here today—summer people, many of them. There's a big crowd of boats anchored just off the beach, and a drama group is mounting an "ecological fashion show," with actors dressed up as everything from clams and corncobs to seabirds and lobsters.

But the big deal here is the sand castles. This is a whole world of fantasy on a beach—the seventh annual *Concours National des Chateaux du Sable,* the national sand-castle contest, held on the first weekend in August. The sand castles are astonishing—twenty feet across, eight or ten feet high, built in one day by seven-person teams. Some are modernistic, great irregular blocks of "masonry" canted in all directions; others are primitive and basic. But most of the castles boast crenellated battlements, sweeping curved staircases, moats, portcullises, ramparts. More than 70 sand castles are under construction, and they must be completed by four o'clock for the judging.

A young woman does modern dance on a raised wooden stage, and a tiny brass band wanders along the beach playing, oddly enough, "Land of Hope and Glory."

Certain Francophones have an indefinable but utterly enviable style. Such a man is Albert Cummings, the main organizer of this event. Lean, wiry and brown, Cummings wears his white shirt, khaki shorts and shapeless white sunhat with an insouciant grace.

As you enter this beach, a sign welcomes you. In French. Albert Cummings gives the gist of it.

"Now you are coming in the kingdom of castle, house, god, witches, devil," he says. "It's a world of imagination—and you're welcome in this world."

Albert Cummings and his partners started this contest as a logical outgrowth of their business. They call themselves Les Artisans du Sable—the sand artists—and they use sand to make stunning artifacts: bowls and lampshades, clocks and ornaments. They have been working at their craft for ten years, gluing sand particles together with a patented resin developed specifically for them (at considerable cost) by research chemists at Quebec government labs. The mixture hardens slowly, and for three or four days it can be shaped with woodworking tools. Then it sets up as hard as sandstone.

They have invented a whole new artistic metier, and they are still the only ones using it. Different forms, different natural sands—the Magdalens themselves have a variety of sands, and people send them sands from all over the world. They have a whole wall of samples in glass bottles.

The Magdalen Islands are a natural place for the *Concours National;* the chain of islands is only 40 miles long, but it has 150 miles of glorious sandy beaches. The islands are lumps of red sandstone placed in an arc in the middle of the Gulf of St. Lawrence, most of them connected by double tombolos, each pair of sandbars defining an interisland lagoon. The lagoons provide a superb location for sailboarding: the summer westerlies are strong and steady, blowing over a fetch of 150 miles of unbroken ocean, but the landlocked water builds up no chop. Ocean winds over calm water. Perfect.

The ocean is similarly pleasant, but not so safe. The local Coast Guard lifeboat picked up one sailboarder ten miles out on Pleasant Bay, the huge bay defined by the chain of islands. He was used to boarding on lakes, and he had not fully grasped the idea that the other side of this salty-tasting lake was in Newfoundland, 100 miles away. (Admittedly, one man did sailboard to Newfoundland, but that was different: he intended to do it, and he was prepared.)

"This is the nicest sand of the world, that's what the Guinness book says," says Albert Cummings with a Gallic shrug. "It's pure quartz and regular and fine sand, not too much coarse, and a little bit round."

He looks at the sand castles rising all along the length of the beach.

"You know," he says, "the nice time to see them is tomorrow morning at five-thirty when the sun rise over there. There's nobody around. It's a very strange picture. You feel on another planet. They may last two days, three, four days, possibly a week, especially if there is fog and not too much wind and sun. Sun and wind dry them out ver' fast."

There's something very appealing about this—structures lovingly created in the full knowledge that they're ephemeral, that they'll be gone in a week, that no trace of them will remain after the first big storm. Most of us delude ourselves, at least part of the time, into thinking that our works are permanent: that our monuments will endure, our books will be read, our buildings and our cities will stand. They might. Maybe, if we're exceptionally lucky, our works will last for a hundred years. Or a thousand. Or five thousand.

But five thousand years is a mere pulse-beat in the life of the Earth. All we can do is stave off time for a few moments. By the Earth's calendar, all our works are sand castles—and so is the coast itself.

There they stand, those glorious constructions bathed in pearly morning light, already starting to crumble. And built with joy in the knowledge that their destiny was to crumble. There's a liberating acceptance in this gesture, defying chance with order while embracing transience.

Perhaps that is the human glory, the human tragedy: that we are compulsively creative beings who nevertheless are little more than transient creations ourselves.

4. Rising Sea
and
Rolling Islands

There rolls the deep where grew the tree.
O earth, what changes hast thou seen!
There where the long street roars hath been
The stillness of the central sea.

The hills are shadows, and they flow
From form to form, and nothing stands;
They melt like mist the solid lands,
Like clouds they shape themselves and go.
  —Tennyson, *In Memoriam A.H.H.*

Among the Earth's long, slow rhythms is the gradual rise and fall of sea level, the platform on which all beach processes take place. The height, or *stand*, of sea level is in turn driven by the sluggish pulsations of glaciation, the repeated advance and retreat of the polar ice caps during the last two and a half million years. When the glaciers advance, sea level falls. When they retreat, the sea rises.

Sea level is the slowest, the least perceptible and the most important of all the factors that are constantly molding the world's beaches.

On the coast of Turkey, in what was once the ancient land of Lycia, is an indentation known as Asar Bay. Into this bay, one summer day in 1970, sailed the American ketch *Cynthia R*, crewed by its owners, Bob and Cynthia Carter. They were following a nautical chart over which they had laid a map of archaeological sites; the two documents together showed ruins at the head of Asar Bay, and the Carters were curious. The bay proved too exposed for mooring, but they anchored nearby and walked over a low isthmus to the site. They found themselves looking at a ruined town stretching a quarter of a mile up the hillside, with its streets running down to the shore and out under the sea.

A few days later they were back with their fins and snorkels, exploring the site. The ruins on the land were extensive, but under the water they saw "limitless pottery, marble tessera floors, fragments of columns, hundreds of feet of foundation." When they returned to the United States after the sailing season, they asked the scholars what the place had been. Nobody seemed to know.

The charts they were using had been drawn in 1811 by Captain Francis Beaufort of the Royal Navy (later an admiral and the inventor of the Beaufort Scale of wind strengths). Since Beaufort, scarcely any Western scholars or explorers had visited the head of Asar Bay. The Carters sailed back in 1976 and spent three weeks photographing and mapping the site. They paid particular attention to the port, which was entirely submerged. The tops of the wharves and quays were six or seven feet beneath the surface, but the general outline of the port was remarkably complete. In *Sail Far Away*, Carter reports what they saw:

> On the shelf from quayside to shore, which probably nowhere
> exceeded 150 feet in width, we photographed foundations of
> brick and of stone; floors of tile, of large flat stones, and of base-

ball-sized cobbles, which seem to have been the undercourse for tile; apsidal walls; and in one place a wall built across four columns laid horizontally into its footing. What a passage of time is here, for a building with columns to have lived its life and for the columns to have been used as foundation stones for a second building which is now itself sunk a fathom deep beneath the sea!

Home again, they pursued their researches and eventually determined that the sunken city was Apulae, a trading center of some importance and the seat of a bishopric; its ruins had been visited by a German scholar in 1890, and very briefly by a British expert in 1958. It was founded by Doric Greeks around 800 BCE, and captured by both Cyrus and Alexander before ultimately being brought within the empire of Rome. As Rome faded, Attila the Hun swept across Asia Minor, succeeded by Arab raiders who plundered these coasts in the seventh century CE. After perhaps 1,500 years of occupation, the city was abandoned. The Carters' report proved to be the most complete and current account of the site, and—said one expert—"the underwater part in particular is quite new."

No rivers flow into Asar Bay, so Apulae has been spared the process of siltation that has completely filled and closed many harbors of antiquity. Pisa now stands two miles from the sea, as does Patara, a few miles from Asar Bay, and Ostia, once the port of Rome.

In thirteen centuries, abetted by the rivers, the land has claimed those seaports—but the rising sea has claimed many others. Among them is the forgotten city of Apulae.

∽

Since geological time has not stopped, we are still living with the glaciers. Because global temperatures have been rising, they are still retreating and still giving up water to the oceans—and thus raising the level of the sea.

The total volume of water in the world's oceans represents *eustatic* sea level. *Relative* sea level, as opposed to eustatic sea level, is the height of the sea in relation to a particular point on a coastline. Think of an ocean as a half-filled bucket of water. Add water, and you have raised eustatic sea level. Now tilt the bucket and—relative to the rim of the bucket—the water falls on one side and rises on the other, even though the mere act of tilting the bucket has not changed the amount of water in it. The relative water level has risen on one side of the bucket and fallen on the other.

In the Arctic, for instance, the land is rebounding so rapidly from the weight of the glaciers that the rise of the land is outpacing the rise of the sea. In such areas, despite the worldwide rise in eustatic sea level, relative sea level is falling, and the land is emerging from the water. Elsewhere, relative sea level is rising faster than eustatic sea level. In Texas, oil and gas extraction has removed some of the support for the ground, which has slumped into the cavities once filled by hydrocarbon deposits. Relative sea level is rising quickly: the land is going down while the sea is coming up.

Relative sea level is a local concern, but eustatic sea level is a global one. When the glaciers retreat and global temperatures rise, eustatic sea level is affected in two ways. First, of course, melting glaciers physically give up water to the sea. Equally important, the volume of water expands as its temperature increases. That expansion further raises eustatic sea level.

Science is only beginning to deduce long-term trends in glaciation and global temperature change, which may ultimately be governed by fluctuations in the heat the Earth receives from the sun. We do know that in recent centuries the Earth has been warming and eustatic sea level has been rising, though one school of thought maintains that these warm centuries are only a temporary respite in a long-term cooling trend leading to the next ice age. Since the last ice age, about 10,000 years ago, sea level has risen about 400 feet.

The problem of prediction is greatly complicated by human activity. Humans have been burning fossil fuels—and adding to the "greenhouse gases" in the atmosphere—only for 200 years. We may be intensifying the warming trend, which will have disastrous consequences. Or perhaps we are not. What would Gaia be doing about temperature if left to her own devices? Are we really causing a sharp *additional* change in temperature that justifies alarming headlines about global warming?

Wallace Kaufman, coauthor of *The Beaches Are Moving*, doesn't think so.

"The whole global warming scenario exists only in computer models," he says. "Computer models are highly suspect among climatologists who deal with global warming. There may be some general consensus that there could be some global warming—but no scientist that I know about in the field of climatology says, 'I have measured global warming.' It exists in the noise zone and in theory."

If global warming really is taking place, however, new threats will arise—like the danger that the East Antarctic ice pack might break free. That massive glacier contains so much ice that if it ever fell into the ocean, the sheer displacement of water would cause a disastrous world sea level rise—perhaps as much as ten feet—almost instantaneously.

"There was some fear that if global warming occurred, the East Antarctic ice pack *would* break off," Kaufman says, "but now the predictions about global warming have been scaled back so that it doesn't seem to be threatening the ice pack. They've also discovered volcanos under the pack, which actually have a good effect on it; they seem to create a wet sliding path so the pack doesn't cram itself and break. It keeps moving gradually."

Human beings can accommodate a slow rise in sea level, as we have for centuries. We add a little height to the dikes now and then; we build the new wharf slightly higher than the old one; we build seawalls and dump rock and earth along the shore. We are not consciously responding to the rise in sea level; we think the dikes must have settled a bit, and we are just fixing stuff that seems to need it. People have been doing these things for countless generations, unwittingly accommodating themselves to the slow dance between the sea and the shoreline.

A *rapid* rise in sea level would be a completely different challenge. Millions of people live below sea level, protected by dikes and barriers—the city of New Orleans, the southern suburbs of Vancouver and much of the Netherlands, for instance. A ten-foot overnight rise in sea level would be catastrophic. Even a doubling of the historic rate of sea level rise would cost billions of dollars in lost property and dike construction.

Paul Godfrey, an ecologist at the University of Massachusetts, stresses two points: it is absolutely certain that sea level is rising—but it is fiendishly difficult to predict the rate.

"We know eustatic sea level is rising from studying botany in a stable area like the Bahamas, where you have these blue holes—conduits that go down into the sea through the islands," Godfrey says. "The blue holes are like wells. Sea level's coming up in these wells and changing the ecology in them enough that we can actually see changes in the vegetation, a flip-flop where plants that used to live further down in the holes now are growing higher up.

"We know that sea level has been going up here in eastern North America by about a foot a century. That's been determined by tide gauge studies, by carbon dating and so on. About a foot a century. Now we're at a point where that rate can change dramatically. It can start going up much more rapidly, if you accept the scenario of global warming increasing the temperature and melting the ice sheets."

Some scientists do take that scenario seriously; Nova Scotia, for instance, is slipping off a crustal bulge, which means that relative sea level is rising very quickly here. European scientists come here to study the effects of rapid sea level rise in order to predict what might happen when the effects of global warming make themselves felt in Europe.

But, notes Godfrey, a warming trend is not the only plausible prediction.

"You could also say, 'Well, we have other things happening, like light being reflected by the atmosphere. It won't warm up so much.' It might get *colder:* we could predict a trend downward. Even the dust from the volcanic eruption at Mount Pinatubo changed the climate slightly: it gave us a much snowier winter than we normally have here in western Massachusetts. Volcanic dust, smoke, debris—anything that changes the heat balance of the atmosphere will affect the temperature of the sea.

"So it's very hard to make predictions. There are so many variables involved."

Monitoring the effect of greenhouse gas emissions and other human factors in global warming is like trying to filter out a melody obscured by a burst of static. It will take ten years of careful measurement—using satellites, tide gauges, ship reports and sophisticated computer programs—to determine whether sea level is rising faster than the historic rate. Even if it is, the cause may not be human action; it will take further research to answer that question.

All of which places us in the awkward position of being obliged to act in ignorance. Governments, for instance, cannot simply ignore the issue of sea level. The world's shorelines are heavily developed, and in the United States and elsewhere in the developed world people are moving steadily to the coasts.

Rising sea level is not the sort of issue that makes people sit up sweating in the night; precious few are even aware that the sea is rising. Nevertheless, in 1990 the U.S. Congress called on American states and territories participating under the Coastal Zone Management Act to anticipate and plan for sea level rise. It has also participated in various international plans and studies. One of the leading figures in the U.S. effort is Ben Mieremet, an international affairs specialist with the National Oceanic and Atmospheric Administration. Mieremet is a tall, friendly man who sits in a suburban garden near Washington, D.C., and talks quietly and precisely about the prospect of creeping catastrophe.

"It's a multifaceted problem, it's not just a question of erosion," he says. "Based upon the studies that have been done, probably 70 percent of the world's coastlines are vulnerable to sea level rise—erosion, saltwater inundation, saltwater intrusion into rivers, contamination of drinking water and so forth."

How much warming would it take to raise sea level significantly?

"An increase in temperature between one and a half to three and a half degrees centigrade will cause thermal expansion of the oceans," he says. "That's the major effect. Mind you, the rate of sea level rise has not significantly increased during the last century. But according to the models used by the scientists, the accelerated rate of rise due to global warming doesn't start occurring until after the year 2000, somewhere around 2020 or 2030, because of lag factors."

Meanwhile, international organizations are urging all coastal nations to develop plans for coastal zone management. For some nations, the issue is of profound and immediate importance—and the nations most at risk are not necessarily those that caused the problem. Nature has no concept of fair play.

"The Pacific islands are not great greenhouse gas producers," Mieremet explains, "but they'll suffer the consequences. The Marshall Islands, for example: take a look at Majuro, which is an atoll with a highest elevation between eight and nine feet above sea level. In their worst-case scenario, the Intergovernmental Panel on Climate Change is projecting a rise of up to one meter in sea level by the year 2100. If you're projecting a rise like that, you're talking a significant loss of the land on Majuro—probably a third of it, due to inundation and erosion. That would have tremendous effects on the flooding impacts of even lesser storms unless they take measures like elevating the land and protecting it through seawalls and revetments. We estimated that the cost to protect one area of the island would run up to $175 million, a pretty burdensome figure for a small island nation.

"That may be worth doing, because there are more than 20,000 people living on less than one square mile in the Marshalls. But some of the areas that are less populated might have to be abandoned, like some of the outer islands in the Maldives, for instance. The last time I heard, four islands in the Maldives had already been abandoned. You can't afford to defend areas with small populations. In places like that, relocation is one of the major alternatives."

Faced with the inexorable rise of sea level, shorelines respond according to their natures. A rock cliff does nothing at all; the sea simply laps a little higher up its vertical face. A sandstone cliff, like those commonly found in California, remains stable until its base is undercut and then tumbles onto the beach below. Drumlins dissolve, yielding sediments to new beach formations.

Barrier island beaches, on the other hand, just pack their bags and move. These fascinating structures are long, narrow islands of loose, unconsolidated sediment, usually sand, which run parallel to low-lying, sandy coasts. They are called *barriers* because they seem to present a barrier to the sea, preventing the waves from making a direct assault on the mainland.

A typical beach, as we have seen, often looks like a ribbon of sand in front of a bay or lagoon. The strip of sand is usually pierced by one or more channels, or *inlets*, which carry water in and out between the lagoon and the sea. The sandy beach may be low and narrow, frequently inundated and almost without vegetation—or it may be two or three miles wide and tens of miles long, with ridges of high dunes running along its length and stunted maritime forests growing in the valleys between the dunes. If the sand is penetrated by more than one inlet, the segment of barrier beach between the inlets is a barrier island.

Chains of barrier islands run for thousands of miles along the U.S. east coast southward from New York and onward into the Gulf of Mexico. They are also found in the southern Gulf of St. Lawrence, among other places. Almost all the great seaside resorts of the U.S. east coast are built on barrier islands—the Hamptons, Atlantic City, Cape May, Ocean City, Nags Head, Hilton Head, Fort Lauderdale and

Miami Beach.

And barrier islands *move*. That's their nature. They are not really barriers at all; they stand at the edge of the continent, isolated by water that has already flowed inland to drown the land behind them, and as the rising sea assaults them, they yield and move landward.

"Barrier islands are a product of rising sea level," says Orrin Pilkey. A distinguished professor of geology at Duke University, Pilkey is a blocky, bearded, combative man who loves barrier islands and hates to see them bulldozed and paved and populated. He is a hero to environmentalists and anathema to coastal real estate developers.

"No rise in sea level, or a fall in sea level, and you'd have no barrier islands," Pilkey says. "Barrier islands require an unconsolidated coast, sufficient wave energy to move sand and a very flat coastal plain. All coastal plains meeting these criteria have barrier islands.

"Barrier islands originate when sea level starts to rise at the end of a glaciation. The sea is way out on the edge of the continental shelf. As the sea rises it begins to fill the river valleys with water. The valleys become wide estuaries, and the intervening ridges become narrow sandy headlands sticking out to sea, which are susceptible to erosion. As these headlands begin to erode, the longshore currents create spits of sand running up and down the coast from the original headlands. At the same time, sea level continues to rise, and the sea flows in behind the spits. Massive dunes accumulate on those spits because the whole shoreline is basically a linear source of sand.

"Eventually, with the combination of flooding, the breaching of the spits by inlets that open up during storms and so forth, you form actual islands. This all occurs because nature wants to straighten out shorelines. Nature insists on as straight a shoreline as possible."

As the sea continues to rise, the islands and the coastlines behind them retreat, moving shoreward in tandem. This is Bruun's Rule, which states that as sea level rises, the beach changes its position but does not change its shape. It is the same sculpture, shaped by wind and water, though it has moved slightly up the continental shelf.

If the coastline retreats more quickly than the islands, large sounds open up between the islands and the mainland coast—vast shallow lagoons like Albemarle Sound and Pamlico Sound, which lie behind the barrier islands that constitute the Outer Banks of North Carolina. If the islands retreat more rapidly than the shoreline, on the other hand, the lagoons may disappear altogether and the retreating island may weld itself directly to the shoreline behind it. The most stable barrier beaches in North America are on the coast of Georgia, where new barrier islands have collided with sandy hills along the shore—hills that were islands during earlier glaciations. In many places, the two separate components have welded themselves into one fat, sandy island.

"I like to think of beaches as living, barrier islands as living," says Pilkey, "because they do such intelligent and more or less predictable things, things that if you had to sit down and think and design a mechanism for survival during rising sea level or during a storm, these are the very things you would come up with. And barrier islands pick up and move as sea level rises. They're smart enough not to sit there and beat on at the sea. They know the sea's going to win, so they move back and take advantage. The sea overwashes the island and builds up the sand elevation so an island can move up as sea level rises. It's amazing. They really are like intelligent beings. These islands are unique in their flexibility and dynamic nature."

How does an island retreat? Essentially, the sand rolls over backward, toward the land; since the sand is the island, the sand's new position is the island's new position. The sand moves in three ways: wave overwash, dune movement and migration of the inlets that join the lagoon to the ocean.

When storm winds strike a barrier beach, they push water into the bay or lagoon and pin it there at a higher level than the sea. Storm waves crash into the beach, washing right over it—sometimes only in a few locations, sometimes over its entire length—and carrying tons of sand into the lagoon. As always, the greater the energy, the more sediment the water can move and the bigger the particles. So the waves pick up vast amounts of sand as they cascade across the island, but by the time they reach the lagoon they have expended their energy, and they drop the sand on the lagoon floor, often in vast delta-shaped deposits called *overwash fans.*

Eventually the wind loses its power, or the head of water in the bay becomes irresistibly higher than the sea, and the waters pour back into the ocean, cutting channels across the island as they go. But almost all the sand is left behind, and the bay is shallower after the storm. Eventually it is shallow enough for plants to grow in its brackish waters, and their roots bind the bottom together while their leaves and stems disrupt passing currents of air and water, forcing them to drop their silt and sand around the plants. As the plants go through their annual cycles of birth and death, their carcasses fall to the bay floor. The weight of the water and the sand compresses them into peat. More sand washes onto the peat, and the dune slowly grows backward and covers it. New land creeps out across the bay floor.

Sometimes the overwash channels are deep enough to form new inlets, which themselves are constant conveyors of sand. Aerial photographs clearly show deltoid shapes on both sides of any inlet through a barrier beach. These double deltas are called *tidal deltas.*

Tidal deltas are built up by the tides and currents moving across and through the inlets. On a rising tide, the ocean runs inland through the inlet like a river, capturing sand from the littoral drift and carrying it back into the bay. As the water fans out into the bay behind the beach, it dissipates its energy and drops its burden of sand, creating a *flood tidal delta.* The falling tide carries some of the sand back to the sea, depositing it on the beachface, but the energy of the ebbing tide is much less than that of the rising tide. Most of the sand stays in the bay, protected from the surf. The result is a flood tidal delta in the bay that is much larger than the ebb tidal delta on the beachface.

Eventually the inlet has carried enough sand that its own deltas constrict it, and it begins to choke. It may react by shifting its channel slightly to one side, cutting away the barrier island on that side and depositing new sand on the opposite bank. Inlets have been known to migrate this way for miles, constantly renewing their channels and leaving new land behind them, shortening one island and lengthening its neighbor.

Alternatively, the inlet may simply silt up and close. But the tides and the rivers are delivering the same quantity of water to the lagoon, and all that water still has to find its way to the sea. So the cross-sectional area of all the inlets—their carrying capacity—must always be essentially the same because, whatever their configuration, they have to carry the same amount of water to the sea. When one inlet closes, therefore, another must open.

The sudden opening of a barrier island inlet is alarming if your house happens to be built on it, as the residents of Dune Road in Westhampton, New York, learned in the winter of 1992-93, when two fierce winter storms cut new inlets through the Long Island barrier beach, washing away several dozen expensive homes. When I visited Dune Road that April, the breakers were rolling through Pike's Inlet, a gap nearly half a mile wide, and the shore of the inlet was littered with irregular pieces of soft, dark material: peat that had been hidden under the beach, torn away in fragments when the sand above it disappeared.

But though Pike's Inlet was a disaster for the families whose homes were destroyed, it was a routine event in the life of a barrier beach. Inlets come and go, making spits into islands and islands into spits, moving and pausing and moving again. Moriches Inlet, a few miles south of Pike's Inlet, was opened by the great hurricane of 1938; it closed naturally in 1950, opened again in 1953 and has since been kept open only by dredging. Historical research has shown that at least 26 now-vanished inlets have carved their way through the Outer Banks of North Carolina, remained active long enough to be named, then closed again.

The sand that is moved into the bay through the inlets and by wave overwash creates the foundation for the island's new position. When the foundation is built, the island's dunes move back to cover it.

The dunes move chiefly by the energy of the wind, which blows sand off their crests and carries it toward the lagoon. Go to the beach on a fine blustery day and you can see the sand drifting across the damp foreshore like wisps of snow chasing along a winter highway. Onshore breezes blow the fine sediments landward, but they are interrupted by beach grasses, driftwood, pop bottles, animal shells and the bulk of the dunes. In the energy shadows of such obstacles the sand builds up, and the back of the dune grows while the front retreats. The dune eases backward onto the new land created by the overwash fans and the deltas, completing the island's process of retreat.

Like a drumlin cliff, a dune—on a barrier island or anywhere else—may be stable for generations and then suddenly start to move. Whatever lies behind it is buried. Early in my research on beaches, I heard about a wandering dune in Greenwich, Prince Edward Island, and I wanted to see it. The beaches of the island's north shore are among the most glorious in North America, pounded by the warm salt breakers of the Gulf of St. Lawrence, their sand piled up in huge beige dunes. Greenwich, at the mouth of St. Peter's Bay, has perhaps the most extensive dune field on the island. As soon as Lulu and I parked the car we could see that the dunes had been inexorably working their way inland, slowly overwhelming forests and fields as they went. At their innermost fringe, the dunes were spilling into the woods, burying and choking the trees. A few feet into the dune field the trees had died: their bare trunks and branches reached through the brown sand like gray, bleached skeletons.

It took us half an hour to reach the shore through dunes 30 feet high, thinly covered with marram grass. The day was windy, and a coarse blade of marram grass, bent double and twisting, had inscribed a perfect circle around itself in the fine sand. The sand was hunting through the dunes in whirls and sheets, looking like fine snow. In the hollows the sand was damp and seamed with the castings of some small worm or animal. Looking up, one would think oneself in Arabia, completely surrounded by sand hills.

We came through the dunes onto a wide beach where the sea was breaking on a series of underwater bars separated by deep troughs where the longshore currents ran hard. We took off our shoes, alarmed a flight of sandpipers and waded out to the nearest bar. The tips of the breakers were heavy with suspended sand, and they were sculpting the beach as we watched them, moving the sand inward from our right as the wave crumbled against the beach and away to our left in the backwash. Before our eyes, the beach was moving and changing, growing and migrating.

The beach reached in both directions as far as we could see, interrupted only by the entrance to St. Peter's Bay, a mile to the west. To the east, great hills of sand rose like anthills against the distant sky. There was not a soul in sight.

∽

On the southeast U.S. coast, the usual victim of burial by the dunes on the barrier beaches is the maritime forest that has established itself in the valleys between the dunes. A maritime forest is a wiry dwarf ecosystem dominated by gnarled trees whose thick foliage and waxy leaves form a dense canopy, conserving moisture and providing the shade other plants require. When the island moves back, it buries the forest, and most of the trees rot. But not all of them do. When the island retreats still farther, remnants of the dead forest may reappear on the ocean side. On Shackleford Banks, a barrier island in North Carolina, skeletal trees have emerged from the front of the island, a ghost forest of rot-resistant aromatic red cedar washed by the ocean breakers. Fifty years ago, an immense dune known as Penny's Hill began moving backward into the barrier island village of Sea Gull, North Carolina. By 1964, only one house remained visible, and the sand was pouring through its windows. A generation later the village was beginning to reappear on the ocean side of the dune; Penny's Hill was still moving backward.

We have only recently begun to understand the processes that mold barrier islands in particular and beaches in general. All beach processes are affected by the rise of sea level, but science is still probing the implications of sea level rise. Coastal geology is a remarkably young science, and many of its pioneering figures are still alive. As recently as 1919, when Douglas Johnson speculated that the beach at Nantasket must have moved backward over a long period of time, he had no idea how long it had taken or through what processes the move might have taken place. When Peter Rosen was a graduate student in Virginia, he demonstrated statistically that a number of apparently unrelated instances of shoreline change and erosion around Chesapeake Bay were all controlled by rising sea level. That was a major achievement in coastal geology, and Rosen is still in his forties.

The restless movement of barrier islands was first demonstrated 25 years ago by Paul Godfrey, then a young botanist occupying his first job. Today Godfrey is a middle-aged professor in Amherst, Massachusetts. Like most beach scientists, he does not live on the shore; in fact he lives on one of the highest points in western Massachusetts. Perhaps the very fact that he was not trained as a geologist gave Godfrey the fresh perception that led to his discoveries. Here is his account:

> My first job offer after I got my Ph.D. came from the National Parks Service. They wanted me to study the shoreline. I said, well gee, I really know the alpine environment—but then I'm an ecologist, I guess I could go out there. So I asked what the story was and they said, Oh, the Outer Banks are a wreck. They've been destroyed by human beings, the dunes are washed away, it's total disaster.
>
> So we went out and started looking, exploring the islands and digging holes—which is what ecologists do. The first response

of an ecologist is to dig a hole.

The key turned out to be that the Corps of Engineers had set up a series of permanent elevation benchmarks on the island—Core Banks—to measure shoreline erosion. What they didn't plan on was the fact they were going to measure burial, too. We found that many of their benchmarks had been buried since the time they put them in—about 20 years earlier—by varying amounts of sand.

That meant we were able to measure what had happened. Here was the benchmark when they put it in, with its concrete base and its little pipe. Now it's covered by that much sand or this much sand. Well, what's going on? This is not supposed to be the case. It's supposed to be washing away. Why is it piling up? There were many, many of these, a hundred or more; the Corps had installed them in series perpendicular to the shore, going across the island. Some of the benchmarks *had* disappeared in fact. The ones near the ocean had washed away, but all the ones they had put inside hadn't washed away. They were buried instead.

So we figured out how to take shallow cores. Drive a piece of pipe in the ground, put a plug in it, yank it up. Take samples out. Sure enough, we got these beautiful stratigraphic sequences, like a layer cake—layer upon layer upon layer, a soil layer, a shell layer, then soil, then shell, ocean sand, another soil layer and so forth.

My wife is an expert in marine organisms, and she was able to pinpoint those shells. We're in the middle of an island now, maybe 200 meters from the beach. And in the middle of the island those shells were marine, from the ocean, not the bay.

Then we were there for a period of storms and we saw what happened. We saw storms take sand from the beach and wash it over, dump it on these grasslands—and in a year's time the grasses would grow back through it.

So we started doing more experiments, looking at maps, looking at old photographs that showed where the shoreline was in the thirties, and then we got more recent pictures showing how it had moved back and buried part of the old habitat. And once you put this evidence all together it told the whole story of the rolling-over process, the retreat of the island.

We often refer to the changes in a beach as erosion, but the word is misleading. *Erosion* carries a sense of irreparable loss—but that is only a human perspective. Orrin Pilkey particularly dislikes the word, which he sees as an obstacle to understanding.

"Erosion is a lousy term because it implies loss of material," Pilkey remarks. "We speak about a hillside or a farmer's field eroding. That means the soil has gone down the stream and it's lost. The use of that term on beaches is very misleading. It represents an early misunderstanding of beach processes.

"What we think is erosion on a shoreline or beach is simply the beach changing its position. The beach remains the same, but it changes its position in space. If you come back a few years later, you'll find the beach looks the same as it did before, except you might notice it's a little closer to that tree or something. Well, that's not erosion. There's no loss. Much of the same sand is still there.

"The first time I saw this was at the Marconi signal station on Cape Cod where Marconi sent his original wireless message. There was a photo of the beach then and the bluffs, and I went over and looked at the beach and the bluffs. It looks like they're the same, but yet the whole thing has moved back about a hundred feet since that time. That was a startling lesson for me, years ago, about what shoreline retreat really is."

༄

Over the long term, the rise of sea level is *the* most important fact to know about beaches and shores—and it has serious implications for Homo sapiens, the newest of the major influences on the beach. Many of the world's great cities are built on the shore—Lagos and Los Angeles, Shanghai and Singapore, Bremen and Buenos Aires. Over the next century their citizens will face painful and expensive dilemmas. And, of course, the greenhouse effect could bring on major problems much earlier than we might have expected. As Orrin Pilkey says, if human-driven global warming has any major effect, "By the year 2100 we won't be worrying about Nags Head, North Carolina. We'll be worrying about Manhattan."

His prediction arises from the behavior of those intelligent barrier islands.

"When we look around the world," Pilkey says, "we see that most barrier islands that have not been built over are getting thinner, getting narrower—and I think the reason is that they're about to respond to a sea level rise. For two or three thousand years, many of the barrier islands have been building seaward—and now they're starting to thin everywhere. Something very fundamental has happened in the last couple of hundred years. The islands are starting to narrow down, eroding on both the back side and front side. Well, an island has to be pretty narrow in order to overwash on a broad front and to migrate. I look at it as a living thing preparing itself to respond to the coming sea level rise."

If Pilkey is right, the barrier beaches are intelligent enough not only to prepare for a fresh onslaught by the swelling ocean, but also to write a warning in the sands for those who can read it.

I look out my workroom window, where the sea laps against the rough little seawall I built ten years ago. All around the harbor, spruce trees are slipping down the banks and into the swash zone. There are tombstones on the beach below the disused nineteenth-century cemetery. The harbor entrance is widening because the encroaching headlands are washing away. Beyond my seawall there was once a road, and beyond the road there were barns, warehouses, lobster canneries, a school. That was just a hundred years ago. If sea level rose by ten feet, our kitchen would be awash at high tide, and we would need a scuba diver to service the furnace.

One stormy morning last winter, I watched the sea rise over the top of my seawall. A storm surge was passing through, and the water backed up in the little brook that crosses Allen McDonald's lawn next door, the brook that feeds his beach. The water flooded behind the lumps and knolls of his lawn and deposited a whole layer of beach stones in the hollows. I watched, fascinated, as the waves lapped higher and higher on my seawall and finally rose right over the top, flooding the bottom of my lawn—which has been built up two feet higher than Allen's. When the water fell, it carried earth with it. My earth. The water had moved the boundary between the land and the water just slightly farther toward the house.

This house is a sand castle, too. It will not last forever. But then neither will I—and in the tiny space of time that is given to me, I would hate to live anywhere *but* on the shore.

Spanish Horses

"No, suh," said the red-faced, red-haired man at the ferry slip.

"Ain't no more sailin's this evenin'. We been havin' a pile of trouble with the boats. Next one's at seven in the morning."

Charlie Doucet and I had arrived at Cedar Island, North Carolina, early in the evening, in plenty of time to catch the last ferry to Ocracoke, on the Outer Banks. And now we couldn't go. Could we leave the motor home overnight where it stood?

"Oh, yeah. Then you're all set in the mornin'."

"Horses," said Charlie. "Look over there. Horses on the beach."

"Beautiful," I said. "Go get 'em." Like an alcoholic without a drink, Charlie gets morose and fidgety when he doesn't shoot film for a while. It had been hours since he last had his eye to the viewfinder.

"I just want to grab that," he said apologetically. "I won't be long."

"I'll make a few phone calls," I said. "I'll do some bacon and eggs when you get back."

I made my calls at a phone booth across the parking lot and waited. An hour went by. Two hours. No Charlie. It was getting dark: he couldn't still be shooting. What if he was out on a sandbar, caught by the rising tide? What if— . Alarmed, I crossed the road and walked through an empty campsite in the darkness until I came to a stable.

Bold white letters on the unpainted wall said White Sands Trail Rides.

A door opened, and Charlie came out of the stable with his video camera in his hand. A tall man walked beside him, carrying Charlie's tripod: sunburned face, leather Stetson with silver hatband, vest, jeans. A North Carolina cowboy.

"A new friend," Charlie said.

I shook hands with Wayland Cato III.

"You boys take a drink sometimes?" Wayland asked.

"If you knew Nova Scotians," Charlie said, "you wouldn't have to ask."

"Vodka all right?"

"Sure—or we've got some booze in the camper."

Wayland doubled back to the stable and returned with a satchel of little bottles, the type the airlines use.

"I was shooting the horses, but they were too far away," Charlie explained. "Wayland came along. He owns this whole operation. He offered to drive me out to where they were. Drove right out on the sandbars. He made them wait to cross from one sandbar to another till I was all ready to roll. I got some great footage—I can hardly wait to see it."

"Then the damn ol' truck got stuck," said Wayland ruefully. "Big time. Sunk right to the axles. Had to get her towed out."

In the camper we drank vodka and orange juice, snacking on nuts and cookies while Charlie set up the monitor. He was right. It was lovely footage: horses walking over the sand with the sea stretching out behind them to the horizon.

"'Scuse me," said Wayland. He left.

"Amazing guy," Charlie said. "Comes from a wealthy family, he got into horses by playing polo. He's an artist, makes pictures on glass using a diamond-pointed chisel. He got invited to China to show them the technique, and now they're selling the pictures in Europe and giving him a cut of the profits."

There was a knock on the door, and Wayland clambered in.

"You boys feel like a moonlight ride 'n' stuff?" he asked.

Charlie and I looked at each other.

"I've hardly been on a horse in my life," I said.

"I was on one once," Charlie said. "The horse tried to roll over on me."

"Got a couple customers wanna go ridin'," said Wayland, "Love to have y'all come along."

"Sure," we said together.

Wayland's customers included a honeymoon couple. She was infatuated with horses; given the choice, he would have preferred a Harley Davidson. But he loved her, so here they were. Wayland and his two helpers led seven horses out of the stable—he has 22—and saddled them up. Charlie had a white horse named Morgan. I had a brown one called Buck.

"Hold the reins like this," Wayland said. "Yea, that's it. You bring the reins over to one side, like this, and he'll turn his head. Now it's a law of nature, wherever the horse's head goes, the rest of him's gonna follow. To slow him down, just pull back a little. Speed him up, give him a little kick with your heels. And that's bout all there is to it."

We moved out, seven horses and riders crossing the sand in the bright cool moonlight. This is low, flat country: ancient seabed, some of it just above the water, some of it just below. The islands and headlands were little more than sandbars. Pamlico Sound stretched out to our left. The sound is an enormous sheet of water with a horizon as distant as that of the open sea, but nowhere is it much deeper than about 20 feet.

The sand was dark where the water reached it and bright wherever it was dry. Wavelets brushed the shore. The horses' tails swished, and their hooves squeaked in the sand. Lighthouses and buoys flashed far out over the broad, shallow waters. To the right lay a maze of creeks and sand islands, darkened above the high water line by clumps of low bushes.

"We're goin' out to the dining room," Wayland said over his shoulder.

"I got a scheme, I'm gonna offer gourmet dinners away out on the beach. Got lots of beach anyway, I lease 2,000 acres, 18 miles of beach and 15 islands, and it's never gonna be built on 'cause there's no part of it far enough from the water.

"So the deal is, bring your tux and your tent. Bring your own horse, too, if you like. We're building a screened dining room away out on the beach, and we'll ride out there and serve you a gourmet dinner. Plenty of wine, tell some stories, and then you go to sleep in your tent. In the morning we'll give you a gourmet brunch 'n' stuff, and then we'll ride back. Lots of good stories around here. Black-beard was killed just about ten miles from here."

"The pirate?" I said. "Edward Teach?"

"That's him. This was his base, right around here. There's a story that he took his thirteenth wife and a party of pirates ashore with a brass casket, shot the wife and buried her with the treasure, and then shot the pirates, too." He laughed. "Usually when I tell that story there's a wild cow moos at the right time, scares hell out of everybody."

A wild cow?

"There's a herd of wild cattle on this land, descended from Spanish shipwrecks. And a herd of wild horses, too, about 35 of 'em. There used to be wild horses on a lot of these barrier beaches, but I think this is the last herd left on the east coast."

Buck nuzzled against Morgan's rump. He nipped, she whinnied, the two horses scurried apart. I tugged on the reins. We ambled on till we arrived at Wayland's dining room, a wooden structure perhaps 15 feet square, open but screened, with an observation deck on the top. We tied the horses and climbed to the deck. The wide expanse of sand, scrub and sea reached into the distance in every direction. Wayland told us he wanted to put horses on the other islands of the Cape Lookout National Seashore, and he had managed to interest the federal government in the idea.

"Ideal way for people to see these islands," he said. "Leave nothin' behind but hoofprints. The water's shallow for a long ways offshore. In the summer you ride out on the sandbars, away from the bugs. When the wind blows from the northwest and there's no bugs, you ride on the beaches. You can ride every day here, 12 months of the year, and it's always different. There's always something new to see."

There was a sudden flurry of activity in the bushes below us, a dark shape moving.

"Wild cow," said Wayland, and then we could see it: a dark wiry animal with a calf beside it, loping over the sand away from our horses.

We mounted the horses and rode back. Now I saw cattle everywhere, lying on the sand, dark and low as the bushes. Occasionally one would rise to its feet, looking at us warily, sometimes retreating. In the distance, standing in the bushes, I saw the silhouette of an animal that might have been a wild horse. Wayland led us offshore, through deep runnels between the sandbars. The horses waded up to their bellies in the sea, rhythmically sloshing, nodding their heads, and the foam of their passing lay white on the black water.

The moonlight, the soft hoofbeats, the lazy swash of the waves.

Nobody spoke much on the way back.

5. The Animate Beach

"A loaf of bread," the Walrus said,
"Is what we chiefly need:
Pepper and vinegar besides
Are very good indeed—
Now, if you're ready, Oysters dear,
We can begin to feed."

"But not on us!" the Oysters cried,
Turning a little blue.
"After such kindness that would be
A dismal thing to do!"
"The night is fine," the Walrus said,
"Do you admire the view?"
> —Lewis Carroll, "The Walrus and the Carpenter"

The life of the beach is laid out in horizontal stripes, echoing the structure of the beach itself, its life-forms gradually transformed from the obviously terrestrial to the inarguably marine. At the landward edge of the beach, the unique maritime forest that characterizes southern beaches is still a recognizable forest.

Similarly, the mollusks and fish that inhabit the beach's seaward limits are not unlike the mollusks and fish found in much deeper waters.

The horizontal stripes that comprise the beach fall conveniently into three main zones. The backshore is the dry-land beach, above the normal high tide line. The foreshore is the intertidal zone, the boundary zone within the wider boundary zone of the whole beach, alternately covered and revealed as the tides ebb and flow. The shoreface lies seaward of the intertidal zone; under normal conditions, it is always under water.

And over all three zones fly the birds.

ABOVE THE TIDES: THE LIFE OF THE BACKSHORE

The beginning of the backshore is usually defined by vegetation. A spruce or fir tree is not a beach plant, nor is timothy or alfalfa. Salt-meadow cordgrass, on the other hand, grows only in proximity to salt water. The beginning of the backshore, and thus of the beach itself, occurs where the spruce ends and the cordgrass appears.

Cordgrass normally grows along the inland margin of a body of semi-impounded water, which may be called an estuary, a lagoon, a barachois or—if it is very large—a bay or a sound. It may even be called a river; Florida's famous Indian River, fringed with orange groves, is really part of a long chain of lagoons that stretches down the coast behind the barrier islands.

Whatever its official name, the lagoon is a piece of the ocean almost closed off from the open sea by a sandbar, spit or barrier island. The sandbar may be only a few feet wide or, in the case of many barrier islands, it may cover two or three miles between the lagoon and the open sea. Ridges of dunes, sometimes as high as 40 or 50 feet, may run along its length. The dunes closest to the sea are known as the *foredunes*. Between the foredunes and the sea is the dry strip of sand we normally think of when we talk about the beach.

That is the anatomy of the backshore. Go back now to the lagoon. Not all beaches have lagoons, but any account of beach ecosystems has to consider them. The tides reach into them but—except in great storms—the ocean surf does not. Because lagoons are also fed by brooks and rivers, their water is brackish: salt-tainted, but not so salty as the sea. Many of the plants and animals that thrive there could not survive in the sea, and vice versa.

The inland side of the lagoon often provides the conditions needed to create a salt marsh—the most productive biological environment on Earth. Salt marshes develop on flat terrain and in still, shallow water. They are always changing—developing, growing, shrinking. They begin when sediments settle out of the water and slowly raise the bottom. Algae begin to grow on the mud. Then salt-marsh cordgrass takes root, and its stems trap more sediment. The level of the sediment continues to rise, and the marsh develops into a maze of tussocks and muddy islets, drained by tidal creeks and channels that wind through green expanses of salt meadow. Salt-marsh cordgrass remains along the banks of the creeks, but another species, saltmeadow cordgrass, appears on the drier soil behind it. Also known as *salt hay*, the saltmeadow cordgrass was a main food supply for the wild horses that once roamed many of the world's beaches, and it was harvested annually by pioneering coastal farmers.

As the marsh develops, other plants establish themselves, each in its own ecological niche: spike grass, black grass, tall bullrushes. The green color of the marsh is relieved in summer by the mauve flowers of sea lavender and in autumn by the red antlers of glasswort. Strange crabs appear: purple marsh crabs with furry legs; soft-shelled blue crabs hiding in the marsh grass after molting; male fiddler crabs, each one waving a single greatly enlarged pincer, which looks ferocious but has no function except to attract females. Above the mud and through the tall grasses fly masses of biting insects—horseflies, deerflies, golden marsh mosquitoes.

Terrapins work through marsh grasses. Muskrats build dens and feed on the cordgrasses. Raccoons forage for mussels, snails, clams and shrimp. The salt marsh is the home of some exceptionally elusive birds: clapper rails and American bitterns, herons and egrets, harriers and marsh wrens. Bald eagles also favor the salt marsh for its reliable supply of dead and weakened fish washed inland as the tide rises in the shallow marsh creeks.

From birds to microscopic diatoms and dinoflagellates, the salt marsh is a ferment of life, producing far more organic material than its inhabitants can ever use. Its animals—marsh crabs, birds, muskrats—all feed on its plants, but the grasses are almost undiminished by their predations; most grasses die, fall, decay and are washed out to sea by the falling tide. In the open sea, the organic soup from the marsh finds appetites capable of absorbing its vast supply of nutrients: minute fragments of marsh plants feed bacteria, plankton and other basic elements of oceanic life.

Within an estuary or a lagoon the brackishness of the water varies greatly. The nearer to the sea, the more salty the water. The rotation of the Earth creates a force—the Coriolis force—which in the northern hemisphere deflects currents in a clockwise direction. If seawater enters the lagoon from the east, it is pushed south; if river water enters from the west, it moves north. As a result, in the northern hemisphere the south side of an east-coast bay or estuary is normally a bit saltier than the north side.

And, since fresh water is less dense than salt, water from the streams floats on top of the salty ocean water, making higher layers in the water column less saline than the layers below them. The salinity is always changing. The tides bring ocean water in and out of the estuary twice daily, while the fresh water supply from streams and rivers increases dramatically in the spring runoff. Storms and high tides drive salt water far up into the lagoon. Heavy inland rains and neap tides hold it back. Creatures that live within the estuary find their niches according to the salinity of the water, but they must also adapt to rapid and often radical changes. Sea stars—or *starfish,* as most people call them—require salty water, so they are only found close to the seaward inlet. Other animals—various worms, snails and tiny crustaceans, for instance—

persist only in the upper reaches of an estuary. Brackish-water fiddler crabs, which live far up the estuary and in the inland reaches of the salt marsh, can survive for three weeks in water that has no salt in it at all.

Other species adapt differently. When a flood of fresh water enters the lagoon, worms and crustaceans that require salt will burrow deep into the muddy bottom, which remains salty even when fresh water temporarily flows above it. Animals that can move will swim along within the body of water that provides the salinity they need. Mollusks—blue mussels, for instance—will close up shop and stay closed until conditions improve. Cordgrasses have special glands on their stems and leaves that excrete the excess salts that enter the plant through its roots.

The dominant animal in shallow bays is usually the oyster, which can tolerate large variations in salinity. Oysters thrive in water shallow enough to permit light to reach the bottom and produce algae, which feed the oysters. Because they are heavy, oysters need a solid bottom—rock, firm sand, even a bed of discarded shells—with water currents that carry food to adult oysters and also allow their larvae to reach appropriate sites for settlement.

Oysters are a delicacy not only to you and me, but to dozens of predators. Starfish force oyster shells apart; then they extrude their stomachs into the shells and swallow the oyster whole. Several species of snails devour them, most notably a specialist called the Atlantic oyster drill, which bores a hole through the oyster's shell and thrusts its proboscis inside, surprising and eating the oyster in his own home. From Maine south, oysters feed a fish called the black drum, which can grow up to three feet long, weighing a thumping 100 pounds; it has armored crushing plates in its pharynx designed to crunch and grind even the heavy shells of mature oysters. South of Cape Cod lives the oyster toadfish, a creature as repellent as its name, which also has jaws powerful enough to do mischief to a fisherman, let alone an oyster.

When the oyster spawns, it discharges 100 million eggs—and a good thing, too. The tiny larvae, called spat, are borne out into the ocean as plankton. Plankton are the foundation of the ocean's food pyramid, and everything eats them: fish, birds, sea grapes, mollusks, sea cucumbers, whales. There is a jellyfish, Leidy's Comb Jelly, which spawns in huge numbers in east-coast bays specifically to swill up hundreds of thousands of oyster spat.

When the surviving spat arrive in a suitably brackish habitat—in a lagoon, or perhaps along the beach near the mouth of a stream—they attach themselves and start to grow. But more predators are waiting. Blue crabs, rock crabs and turtles eat them. So do such birds as sea ducks, scoters and—of course—oystercatchers. Sea lice, fungi and protozoans infiltrate them. Flatworms invade them. Mud worms build tubes of sediment on the backs of oysters; on occasion these prodigious builders can suffocate an entire oyster bed. Tiny crab larvae penetrate the oyster's shell and grow to adulthood inside, sharing the oyster's food. Algae, anemones and barnacles attach themselves to the outside of the shell.

And then there are men with long wooden tongs like scissors, working their small boats across the lagoons and estuaries, plucking oysters off the bottom. Or there are people like Lulu and Mark and me, drifting in a rubber dinghy across shallow backwaters in the Bras d'Or Lakes, leaning over the side to pick up oysters and taking them to *Silversark* for a feed in the cockpit.

I've never seen a walrus feeding on oysters. But carpenters, from an oyster's point of view, are just another set of predators—and a voracious one, too.

Moving seaward from the lagoon, we find ourselves in the startlingly different world of the dunes. The dunes are unstable, arid, abrasive, salt-sprayed and searingly hot in summer—not an inviting environment. And yet life also pushes into this unpromising terrain with irrepressible determination, adapting to it and shaping it.

The grass on the dunes, for instance, is completely different from the grasses of the salt marsh a few yards away. The marsh grasses, with their roots sunk deep into compacted and airless mud, have developed internal air channels that carry oxygen downward into the root system rather than picking it up from the soil. Beach grass, by contrast, has plenty of air around its roots, but it lives in unstable soil. So it sends out rhizomes both horizontally and vertically. The horizontal rhizomes put out new shoots, and the vertical ones ensure that the plant will survive even if the level of the sand changes dramatically. Beach grasses completely buried by storms under several feet of sand will push through to the surface and reappear the following year.

The grass shapes and stabilizes the dune. Each shoot breaks up the flow of the wind, creating an energy shadow and forcing the wind to drop its burden of sand. The ground rises around the parent stem and also around its nearby offshoots. This process is often the beginning of a new dune. Other plants establish themselves with the grass: sea rocket, beach heather, sea oats, prickly pear, dusty miller. All of these plants are highly tolerant of salt, and all are great conservers of water.

More dunes develop, shaped by the wind, and eventually the dune field stands like a great wave train cast in sand, running parallel to the coast. The sea wind sweeps sand up the dunes' long shallow windward slopes and then, soaring past the crest, loses the solid base that made its airflow coherent. The airstream disintegrates, and the sand falls on the lee side of the dune. Stand in a dune field on a breezy day, and you can watch this happen: sand comes smoking off the tops of the dunes, whirls briefly in the confused air and falls vertically on the back of the dune. Sheltered from the wind, sand on the lee side lies at its natural angle of repose, about 32 degrees from the vertical.

Nutrients and silts wash down into the valleys between the dunes, and new vegetation develops. Waxy-leafed, water-hoarding shrubs take root—myrtles, elders, ivies. Small, tough trees appear: loblolly pine and pitch pine, palmetto, black oak, cherry, red cedar. They form a thick growth of narrow, twisting tree trunks between the dunes, supporting a leafy canopy that protects smaller plants from the full heat of the sun. Hickories, gum trees and magnolia grow high in the shade of the canopy, and other plants grow closer to the ground:

bayberries, sassafras and yaupon holly. This strange, stubby little forest is home to many insects and animals, including rabbits, mice, squirrels, opossums, raccoons, land crabs, even deer.

Maritime forests arise behind the primary dune line and persist toward the back of the barrier beach. In a sense, they are inverted forests, strangely flat and even across the top. The forest canopy is planed level by the sea wind, while below it the trunks stretch down whatever distance is required to reach the ground. If a tree is growing halfway up a dune, it may be ten feet tall; if it grows from the valley floor it may be thirty-five feet tall. But both trees strike the same invisible ceiling defined by the wind, beyond which they cannot grow. This is a forest in hiding. A famous example is the Sunken Forest of Fire Island, New York.

Where the dune valleys have no forest, they are almost intolerable in summer. The dunes act as reflectors, concentrating the heat. Hollows in the dunes become blindingly brilliant, scorching and windless, with temperatures over 125 degrees Fahrenheit even in temperate latitudes. Yet even here, life persists. Insects and spiders that live in the dunes have coatings of silver or dense coats of quasi-fur that reflect the heat or insulate their tiny bodies. Maritime locusts rise high on their fine legs to lift their bodies off the burning sand. Toads hide below bushes and logs during the day and hunt the dunes only at night. So do snakes, lizards, voles and rabbits.

Many insects live above the sand on dune grasses and other plants. Others find bearable temperatures by burrowing into the dune. Sand wasps dig briefly at the hot surface layers, rise momentarily to cool off, then continue until they have reached the cool, damp sand beneath. They paralyze flies, drag them into the burrow and lay eggs on them. When the larvae hatch, they find themselves sitting on a heap of food.

Some of the creatures of the sand are superbly adapted predators. The larva of the Beautiful Tiger Beetle burrows backward into the sand, anchoring itself firmly in its burrow. Its head pops out to seize passing insects in its sickle-like jaws and devour them. Ant lion larvae march backward in circles in the sand, throwing sand with their heads until each has created a conical pit to trap insects. The sides of the pit are at 32 degrees, the very angle of repose that determines the slope of the dune. Just as humans find it difficult to climb the unstable back of a dune with the sand constantly rolling away underfoot, so the ant lion larva's prey finds it impossible to escape from the conical pit. (The larva makes it more difficult by throwing sand above its victim, helping to carry it down.) The hapless victim inexorably slips downward, where the larva pierces it with its hollow jaws and injects an enzyme that dissolves the insect. The larva ingests it on the spot.

On the seaward face of the dune lives a different, smaller community—and some impressive temporary residents. Here the sand is constantly moving, while the temperature is equally relentless. On the mid-Atlantic coast, the most prominent resident is the ghost crab, so called because its coloration makes it almost indistinguishable from the sand. Ghost crabs move swiftly and unexpectedly, appearing from nowhere and vanishing in a twinkling. They are true crabs, born in the water and moving through the usual planktonic stages as larvae—but when they take their adult forms they instantly run up the beach and dig burrows, where they go through a series of molts until they reach their full size. As adults, they visit the sea only occasionally to moisten their gills and to spawn.

Where ghost crabs live on the beach and visit the sea mainly to breed, sea turtles live in the water and visit the beach mainly to breed. Four or five times a year, the turtles come ashore on tropical beaches, dig holes in the sand and deposit their round, leathery eggs. Turtles breed in shallow water, near the shore; the females emerge on summer nights, usually singly, though some species arrive in massed groups numbering in the thousands. They dig cavities in the sand and deposit between 50 and 200 eggs. They cover the eggs, then return to the sea, leaving their eggs to be incubated by the heat of the sand. Female turtles may lay anywhere from one to nine clutches of eggs annually.

"There are four species nesting on Atlantic beaches," says Dick

Ludington of the U.S. Conservation Fund, who grew up in Florida. "The largest numbers are clearly the loggerheads, which make up probably 98 percent of the nesting sea turtles. Green turtles, which used to nest in great numbers, are the next most prolific species. Then you have hawksbill, which are confined to tropical reef areas, mostly in the Florida Keys, and then you have an occasional leatherback that nests as far north as Jacksonville."

The sand protects the eggs, keeping them moist and at a relatively constant temperature. The sex of the hatchlings depends on the sand temperature; if the temperature is unusually high or low, the clutch of eggs produces more males. While the eggs remain in the sand, they are highly vulnerable to predators, man among them. One study showed that 18 percent of the eggs on one beach were eaten by raccoons living in the dunes.

After six to ten weeks the tiny turtles peck through their shells with temporary *caruncles*, or egg teeth, and dig their way up through the sand, which may take several days. Quick and urgent, they waddle and wriggle in their thousands to the sea, let themselves be drawn into the water by the backwash of a wave, and begin a swim frenzy, which may last 24 to 48 hours. Some move around into the lagoon, where they spend their juvenile years, but most move out to sea where they will remain until they, too, return to the beach to spawn.

The temporary residents of the beachface are chiefly large mammals—walrus, seals, sea lions, otters and the like. Manatees— otherwise known as sea cows—survive in the bays and lagoons of Florida, thanks in large part to vigorous conservation measures in recent years. Elsewhere, the large mammals have been driven to remote and isolated shorelines to rest and whelp. We think of the walrus as an Arctic animal, but it once bred as far south in the Atlantic as Cape Cod. It was hunted relentlessly for its oil and its tough hide, and it was extinguished from all the territory south of Labrador as early as 1798.

Near the surf line, just below the surface of the sand, lives a disagreeable little translucent shrimplike crustacean called the beach flea. It is one of more than 3,500 different species of amphipods; one species lives as a parasite on whales and is known as whale lice. Most amphipods look as though their sides have been squeezed in by a vise; their close relatives, the isopods, look as though they were flattened by a truck. More than 4,000 species of isopod have been identified, including such charmers as the Greedy Isopod, which lives on carrion; the Sea Pill Bug, which rolls into a ball when disturbed; and the Sea Roach, which looks like a waterborne cockroach. The most famous of the isopods is the tiny wood-eating Gribble, whose pin-size holes in wood are a sure sign that the wood has been eaten out so that only its shell remains.

To a naturalist or a biologist, the beach is not a geological structure; it is a theater for the ceaseless, ever-changing drama of life. Beach fleas, for instance, bounce and hop across decaying seaweed and other organic matter—and across you, if you happen to be handy. Though they act and even look somewhat like ordinary fleas, they feed not on humans but on seaweeds and other organic material, recycling beach detritus into their bodies. The detritus is heaviest in early fall, when autumn gales tear seaweed from the bottom and pile it in long plaits and windrows at the high tide line.

With this feast before them, beach flea populations explode. As their numbers peak, huge flocks of migrant shorebirds pass down the coast eating the beach fleas. The shorebirds and (in the spring) their eggs feed raccoons, weasels, birds of prey and other predators. The decaying bodies of the predators are recycled by the garbage collectors of the shore: lobsters, crabs, gulls, crows and maggots. The garbage collectors release nutrients into the water, feeding the seaweeds, which are eventually uprooted by the next autumn's storms. The seaweeds come ashore and are eaten once again by the beach fleas.

The beach is the home of Shiva, creator and destroyer of life. There is no pity in it, but there are endless cycles of development and dissolution. To a naturalist, an urban beach, rimmed with condos and created by truckloads of sand, is not a beach. It is a skillful imitation of a beach, but there is no life in it. Exploring such a beach is about as interesting as walking a stuffed dog or sniffing a plastic flower.

BETWEEN THE TIDES: THE LIFE OF THE FORESHORE

The beach fleas and sand hoppers flourish right on the high tide line, the line of demarcation between the backshore and the foreshore. The intertidal community—the community that inhabits the foreshore— has two main populations, residents and commuters. The residents— seaweeds, barnacles, mussels, hydroids—are fixed in place, exposed by the receding water and covered by the rising tide, doing business always in the same location. The commuters come and go as the sea comes and goes: fish, crustaceans, jellies and, most important of all, plankton.

The intertidal zone is truly a kingdom of wonders: plants that look like animals, animals that look like plants, animals that don't move and plants that do, large "plants" that are actually teeming colonies of tiny animals, tiny animals living in glass houses, blind worms and hairy worms and worms with teeth, promiscuous animals that are both male and female, puritanical animals that are sexual only in every second generation, and hermit animals that have no sex at all.

Most of the sponges are residents. They attach themselves to rocks and pilings and grow like plants, but in fact they are animals—though naturalists argued for years over whether a sponge is a single animal or a colony of tiny animals. They are hermaphrodites, releasing sperm and ova at different times; they can also reproduce asexually, by cell division, and some species can reassemble themselves even if they are put through a strainer and reduced to a mere soup of sponge cells.

The jellyfish are commuters, but their offspring sometimes are not. Some jellyfish, at least, are sexual, shedding their eggs and sperm into the water, but their larvae settle to the bottom and develop as small asexual tumbler-shaped "polyps" with tentacles around their rims. Eventually the polyp develops horizontal lines across it, making it look like a stack of disks. Each of these disks in turn peels away from the polyp and floats off as a tiny jellyfish, a sexual creature again.

The plankton are also commuters, carried by the tides and waves. Plankton are the basis of life in the sea, and arguably of life on Earth. They are at the base of the oceanic food chain, supporting everything else that grows in the ocean. The plankton are an unimaginably vast array of tiny plants and animals living in the upper layers of the ocean water. When you rush into a curling wave at the beach, you are running into a veritable soup of life. At certain times and places, the population of plankton in a single wave is probably larger than the human population of the planet.

The phytoplankton, which are microscopic plants, bloom in the spring so profusely that a fine net drawn through a cubic meter of water may capture 40 million individuals. But there may be a thousand times as many additional phytoplankton in sizes too small to be captured in the net. They can be so profuse that they color the water, turning it milky or green or red.

These tiny plants are the grasses of the sea, converting sunlight and dissolved nutrients into organic matter through photosynthesis. That is why they occur only within the upper layers of ocean water: sunlight barely penetrates beyond 360 feet in the ocean, and most ocean life exists above that level. Scientists estimate that phytoplankton produce 4,000 tons of vegetable material annually in a single square mile of the English Channel. Without the plankton, Gaia might suffocate: the process of photosynthesis creates oxygen, and some scientists contend that the oxygen produced by land plants alone would not be enough to sustain life on Earth.*

The phytoplankton occur in a vast range of forms. One set of unicellular plants with external skeletons made of silica are known as *diatoms*. Another huge group propel themselves with infinitely small whips, and are thus known as *flagellates*. Of all the plankton, you

* It turns out that phytoplankton do indeed produce fully half the oxygen produced by nature; they are responsible for every second breath you take.

are most likely to have seen some of the flagellates, because they are normally responsible for *phosphorence*—better called *bioluminescence*—in the water. One such plankter, *Noctiluca scintillans,* lies right on the border between animal and plant. Like animals, these plankters feed on organic debris but, like plants, they also metabolize nutrients directly, by means of photosynthesis. Are they plants or are they animals? Or are they entitled to membership in both clubs?

The second main group of plankters, the zooplankton, are microscopic animals that feed on the phytoplankton, just as all animals ultimately live on plants. Zooplankton includes tiny shrimps and worms and the larvae of crabs, octopus, starfish, clams and anemones, and some are very odd creatures. A transparent amphipod called *Phronima sedentaria* creates a glass-barrel home by chewing and processing other plankton. It uses the home both for shelter and for rearing its young. Another plankter, *Oikopleura,* creates a glass house by secreting the glassy material. It furnishes the house with two grilled windows and uses its tail to draw water in through the windows, from which it strains its food.

Some zooplankton, like the radiolarians and sea gooseberries, capture food on their sticky, entangling arms and tentacles. Others, like the arrow worm, with its bristling jaws, pursue and consume other plankton considerably larger than themselves. Still others, such as the planktonic tunicates, achieve both movement and nourishment by passing water through a set of tubular passages inside their bodies. A zooplankter named *Calanus finmarchicus* feeds on phytoplankton and is the main food of the Atlantic herring—which is eaten by salmon, cod, seals, whales and the Queen of Denmark.

Plankton directly feed some of the largest animals in the sea. The largest animal in the world is the blue whale, which can grow to a length of 100 feet—but it lives on plankton, which it sieves from the seawater with its wiry baleen plates. The basking shark, which weighs seven or eight tons, is the second-largest fish in the sea, and it also feeds exclusively on plankton, which it filters through its gill rakers as it swims along the surface with its mouth open.

The plankton and other mobile life-forms are the commuters in the intertidal community. The resident population is dominated by innumerable species of algae, usually known as seaweed.

Walk along a shoreline at low tide. Those thin emerald-green sheets are sea lettuce—which is perfectly edible, as are most seaweeds. The branching olive fronds with the yellow bubbles are knotted wrack; the similar plants a little above it in the intertidal community are some of the various rockweeds. Look around: you can probably see a dozen more varieties of sea plant nearby—branching tubular plants about the thickness of a fountain pen refill, bristly red weeds, brown plants that resemble bottlebrushes, green cobwebs draped over the rocks.

The Japanese eat more than 20 varieties of algae; North Americans only eat one or two. Purple laver resembles sea lettuce, but it is thinner and reddish-purple in color. It is farmed in the Far East and makes a good soup as well as a garnish for meats. But the most popular seaweed by far is dulse, a burgundy-colored edible seaweed that contains 52 trace minerals and now sells internationally to health-food stores.

Dulse is particularly beloved by people living around the Bay of Fundy, who almost become addicted to it. Expatriate Fundy folk in Boston have been known to wander along the harborfront looking for a Bay of Fundy vessel—and then to hail the crew with "Any dulse?" Connoisseurs insist that the Chateau Lafitte Rothschild of dulse comes from Dark Harbor, on Grand Manan Island, where graceful buff-painted dories depart at low tide to gather it from the exposed rocks.

The texture and flavor of dulse were described by one visitor to Grand Manan as "salted garbage bag." It's not quite that bad—but, like caviar, dulse is unquestionably an acquired taste.

"The best way to eat dulse," says an aficionado in Parrsboro, Nova Scotia, "is to lay it flat on top of a wood stove till it's crisp as a potato chip. And then wash it down with beer. If you've got a couple of good friends around and some good talk—why, dulse makes it a perfect evening."

The most commercially valuable sea plant is Irish moss, which grows just above and just below the low tide line. A profusely branching dark reddish-purple plant, Irish moss grows on shorelines from New Jersey north to the Gulf of St. Lawrence, and also in Europe. Its value derives from a substance called carrageenan, an emulsifier and suspending agent used in soft drinks, jellies, medicines, ice cream, toothpaste and other products. It was traditionally harvested with big rakes drawn by horses through the shallow water, and in some places, notably on Prince Edward Island, it is still harvested that way—not because the farmers couldn't use tractors (some do) but because horses don't mind an uneven footing, don't easily sink in the sand and don't rust when exposed to salt water.

The worms of the shore seem almost infinite—bloodworms, clam worms, paddle worms, worms that live in tubes, worms that live in the gills of crabs, white and green and red worms. Many of them live entirely in the water, below the low tide line, but many inhabit the intertidal zone, often concealed beneath rocks or among barnacles. The simplest are the flatworms, some of which undulate along just above the muddy bottom. Some flatworms reproduce by fission—they just divide—while others are sexual. A few flatworm species, however, are entirely female, and produce young from unfertilized eggs. The more complex nemertean worms all have a hidden proboscis, which they shoot out to impale prey. Some nemerteans have no eyes, while others have two or four or even more eyes.

The most sophisticated worms are *annelids*, or segmented worms. Of these, the most numerous are the *polychaetes*, the bristle worms— most of them flattened, elongate and bristling with *setae*, stubby appendages on either side. A seta is part of the worm's foot, which often includes gills and webbed structures that are especially well developed in swimming worms. More than 300 species of polychaetes have been found on the east coast alone. When you see a Worms For Sale sign along the coast, polychaetes of some kind—bloodworms, clam worms—are very commonly the worms on offer.

Within the bristle worm family there are some strange variations. Some, like the clam worm, are fast-swimming, fierce predators; others, like the lugworm, simply swallow all the sand and mud before them, digest the edible portions and excrete the rest. Their sex lives are astonishing. Some—the palolo worm of the Pacific, for example— engage in virtual orgies, swarming together sexually in huge numbers. In some syllid worms, on the other hand, a group of segments toward the rear of the animal fills up with sperm or eggs, forms a second head and then breaks away as a free-swimming *stolon*. The stolons then mate, sometimes forming entire chains of worms in the process. In the sinistral spiral tube worm, on the other hand, the forward part of the abdomen is female while the rear part is male, which introduces autoerotic possibilities never previously imagined except in obscene phrases.

Some worms—like the sinistral spiral tube worm—build shells for themselves. Others build tubes in the mud or burrow into the bottom. One of the most elegant is known as the ice-cream-cone worm; others include mud worms, bamboo worms, trumpet worms, thread worms, sand-builder worms, T-headed worms and rosy magelonas. The sea mouse is actually a stubby, fat worm—up to six inches long and three inches wide—with a brown furry coat. The "fur" is composed of setae, varying from fine and downy to strong and hairlike. The sea mouse lives below the low tide line and down to considerable depths, so it is very rarely seen by beach walkers.

❧

The mollusks also straddle the foreshore and the beachface. Some— clams, mussels, quahogs—are exposed when the tide falls, while others—scallops, conchs and abalones, for instance—never leave the water.

For some peculiar reason, biologists refer to shells as *valves*, so two-shelled animals like clams are known as *bivalves* while mollusks with one shell are known as *univalves*. Since the univalves are generally snails, however, they are more commonly known as *gastropods,* which means, more or less, an animal that creeps on its stomach. The snail actually moves on a single big foot, often sliding the foot over a sheet of mucus secreted just ahead of the foot. If this sounds to you like the shiny track left by a garden slug, you're right: the slug is a shell-less snail, closely related to the sea snails.

Sea snails range in size from the tiny brown Sargassum snail—an eighth of an inch in height—to the Florida horse conch, which may reach 19 inches. They include limpets, whelks, winkles, olives, tritons, augurs and the wonderfully named Scotch bonnet. All the snails have mantles, from which they extrude their shells, and radulae, toothed tongues that are devastatingly effective in obtaining food. Californian periwinkles known as *littorines* use their radulae to scrape away at siltstone, feeding on nutrients captured in the stone a hundred million years ago. Colonies of littorines are believed capable of eroding 2,200 tons per square mile per year.

Many snails bar the door to their whorl-shaped houses with a tough, leathery plug called an *operculum;* the horse conch preys on smaller snails by holding the operculum of its prey slightly open, then thrusting its radula past the operculum and into the shell, devouring the snail inside. One of the most impressive of the predatory snails is the moon snail, which plows along half-buried in the sandy bottom, looking for clams, which it pierces with its radula. Moon snails can grow as large as five inches, and their shells are exceptionally beautiful.

The shell-less gastropods—sea slugs—are known as nudibranches, and they are often quite elegant and colorful, unlike their landlubber cousins. The leopard nudibranch is speckled like its namesake, and lives on sponges, as does the sea lemon—which looks like a lemon. The hooded nudibranch lives in eelgrass and looks rather like a funnel, with food seeking tentacles around the fringes of its bell.

But the mollusks we all love are the bivalves, which have provided humans with food since time immemorial.

The typical bivalve consists of a soft body encased between two matching shells hinged by a ligament. The body includes two tubes called *siphons*, an *incurrent* siphon, which draws water full of nutrients into the animal, and an *excurrent* siphon, which expels the water once the nutrients have been extracted. Prodigious amounts of water pass through the bivalves; a single oyster can process three and a half gallons per hour. Burrowing bivalves such as clams, cockles and quahogs (pronounced "co-hogs") also have a pronounced foot, which they use for locomotion. They extend the foot in the direction they want to travel, engorge it with blood to form an anchor, and pull themselves to the anchored foot. The jackknife clam can pull itself an inch per second. The cockle also uses its foot to bounce along the bottom in search of new territory or to escape from predators.

The two shells are held together by powerful adductor muscles. In most bivalves, we eat the whole body, but when we eat scallops we are eating only the adductor muscle. Scallops are unique in several ways: they are the only bivalves with eyes—a row of little blue eyes along the edge of the shell—and they are the only ones that can move with any efficiency. They move by opening their shells wide and then quickly clamping them shut, expelling the water and propelling themselves erratically backward. In motion, they look like a set of dentures jetting around the bottom.

One of the most surprising mollusks is a clam called the teredo, or shipworm, the scourge of wooden pilings, log booms and vessels. The name refers to 66 different wood-boring clams, examples of which are found all over the world.

When the teredo enters a piece of wood, it is 1/5,000 of an inch in diameter. It uses its paired shells to cut a hole in the surface of the wood. Once inside, its shells grow, harden and develop rasplike edges. Three months later, it is eating its way through a quarter of an inch a day, using the wood as part of its diet while also filter-feeding through incurrent and excurrent siphons, which reach right back to the original hole. It also develops pads called pallets near the hole, and uses them to plug the hole should the environment become threatening—for example, if someone spreads poison on the outside of the wood. The only sure way to rid a ship of teredos is to run it up a river into fresh water or to remove it from the water altogether, suffocating the teredos.

The crustaceans, like the mollusks, straddle the low tide line—a few even live on the land—and there are more crustaceans than mollusks by far. Crustaceans belong to phylum Arthropoda—the jointed animals—which also includes insects. The phylum includes more than 26,000 marine species alone, ranging from sea spiders and amphipods to shrimp, crabs and lobsters.

One of the oddest of these creatures is the horseshoe crab, which is not a crab at all; it is more closely related to spiders than to crustaceans. It dates back to the very beginning of the age of dinosaurs, and its larvae resemble trilobites. Shaped like a horseshoe, it can measure a foot across its carapace and two feet in length, including its long, spikelike tail.

The horseshoe crab lives on clams, worms and other invertebrates, crunching them up with burr-like sections of its front legs. At the highest tides each spring, the male seizes the female from behind, and the two ride the advancing waves up to the peak of their swash. Then the female scoops out a depression in the sand and lays her eggs, which the male promptly fertilizes. They cover the eggs and retreat into the water. Shorebirds eat many of the tough little eggs, but within two weeks the survivors have become tiny larvae swimming inside a transparent membrane. Now, as the spring tides once again reach the nesting site, the sand abrades the membrane, releasing the larvae into the ocean. Huge numbers are lost once again to the fishes, which lie in wait for them, but enough survive to ensure the persistence of the species.

The true crustaceans have hard, jointed shells that serve both as armor and as skeletons. Mollusks continuously add to their shells as they grow, but a crustacean cannot grow beyond the limits of its complicated shell, and so a crustacean must molt repeatedly as it grows. The things we see on the shoreline, looking like complete crabs with no innards, are *casts* —the abandoned shells of the crab. Crustaceans molt frequently: lobsters, for instance, molt four times in their first three to six weeks of life, growing by 10 percent to 30 percent each time, while Pacific crabs molt 15 times during their life cycle.

In preparation for molting, a crustacean grows a new soft shell inside its existing shell. The old shell splits open and the animal backs out. The molt takes only a matter of minutes, but the animal is then extremely vulnerable, and it hides until the new shell hardens. Some crabs eat the old shell to obtain the lime salts they need to harden the new one. Hermit crabs, by contrast, adopt shells rather than growing them. They are soft-bodied animals shaped to fit inside the abandoned shells of snails, and their claws form the equivalent of an operculum, closing off the entrance.

The largest crab on Earth is the Japanese spider crab, with a spread of 12 feet across its legs. Some crabs are tiny parasites, living inside mussels and sea stars. Some, in the South Pacific, live on land and climb coconut trees. Some Florida crabs camouflage themselves by allowing sponges to grow on them. All true crabs are edible, though many are too small to bother with. Perhaps the most cherished is the west coast *Cancer magister*, the Dungeness crab, which can grow to ten inches across the carapace, supports an important fishery and makes a superb crab cocktail.

If the crab is the queen of the west coast, the lobster is king on the east coast. Shrimp and lobster have powerful tails, which they use for propulsion. Spreading the tips like a fan and pulling the tail vigorously forward sends the animal rapidly backward out of trouble. If it wants to move forward, it walks or jumps. The powerful muscle of the tail is what we eat when we have shrimp or prawns. It is also one of the most succulent parts of the lobster, although the lobster's claw meat is equally delicious.

The lobster family includes flat-bodied slipper lobsters and several species of blind, soft-shelled deep-sea lobsters. Commercially important variants include the spiny lobsters, or sea crayfish (known to French cuisine as the *langouste*), the Cape rock lobster of South Africa (often exported as frozen lobster tails) and the Norway lobster, also known as the Dublin Bay prawn or, when caught in the Adriatic, as *scampi*.

The most important by far is the North American lobster, which can grow to as much as 45 pounds and live to hoary old ages. One famous specimen named Loretta was caught off Lockeport, Nova Scotia, and shipped to Vancouver. She weighed 21 pounds, and fisheries biologists estimated her age at 150 years. Moved by her uniqueness, Vancouver fish dealer Wylie Costain flew to Nova Scotia with her, drove to Lockeport Harbor Fisheries, boarded a fishing boat and returned her to the sea.

Lobsters eat whatever comes along, alive or dead, plant or animal, including clams, crabs, starfish, sea urchins, shrimp, sponges—and even occasional stones and nails. They live in any depth of water from the low tide mark to depths of 1,200 feet. They mate, says one Nova Scotia fisherman, "face to face—just like people." The hen is sexually active just after molting, and if a cock approaches her at that season she whips him with her antennae until he flips her on her back and mounts her. His foremost swimmerets are grooved; placed together, they make a channel through which sperm can flow into a chamber near the base of her tail called the *spermatheca,* where the sperm remain until the hen ovulates, which may be up to a year later. As the eggs pass backward along her body toward her swimmerets, she releases some of the stored sperm and fertilizes them. She carries the eggs glued to her swimmerets for 9 to 12 months. Then she strikes a unique pose on the tips of her walking legs and fans her tail, hatching the eggs and releasing the larvae.

Though barnacles seem more like mollusks, they are true crustaceans, and there are 750 species of them. In their larval stage they much resemble other crustaceans, gobbling up plankton and molting every three or four days. In their adult phase, they take two forms—gooseneck barnacles, which are usually found offshore and only rarely drift in to the beach, and acorn barnacles, the familiar white volcano-shaped critters that cling to rocks and pilings and slash the feet of swimmers on both coasts.

The acorn barnacle's shell consists of six plates around its sides and two that close the crater at the top to prevent the animal from drying out at low tide. In the water, the top plates open and six feathery *cirri* emerge, sweeping around for bits of food and transporting them into the barnacle's body. The cirri are equivalent to legs in other crustaceans, which led a famous biologist to describe the barnacle as "a crustacean fixed by its head kicking food into its mouth with its legs."

To see the intertidal zone properly, a person should see it at high tide, which requires a mask and snorkel or a glass-bottomed boat—or, in some locations, a ride in a glass submarine. As the tide rises, the foreshore comes to life. Crab and lobster mince along the bottom. Algae rise up and undulate in the current. Schools of minnows dart along under the surface. Larger fish drift in, browsing in the shallow water, while barnacles open and scallops or cockles bounce their way along. Snails plow through the mud. It is the same drama we saw on the backshore—creatures spawning, growing, fleeing and pursuing, dying, disintegrating, being eaten. On almost any coastline, the underwater life of the intertidal zone pulses with death and rebirth. It is a scene of ravishing beauty.

BELOW THE TIDES: THE LIFE OF THE SHOREFACE

At low tide, the commuters of the foreshore retreat to the shoreface, where they encounter another group of residents, many of them related to intertidal families—worms, mollusks, crustaceans, algae. But some are unique to the shoreface.

The heavy, rubbery seaweed known as kelp, for instance, seems to thrive especially on the west coast, where it forms huge forests below the low tide line. At South Beach, the other boys and I used our boats mostly when the tide was high—it was a long, hard slog to haul them over the sand flats otherwise—but now and then, when the tide was very low and the tops of the kelp emerged on the surface, we hauled the boats across the sand and rowed out to the kelp forest, where we cut off the round, floating heads of the kelp and used them as cannonballs in epic sea battles between our rowboats. Ecologically appalling, no doubt, but we knew nothing about that at the time.

The hollow heads of the kelp hold the plant up toward the life-giving sun, like the bladders in rockweed and knotted wrack. Algae are nourished from the top, by the water—unlike land plants, which are largely nourished from the soil beneath them. Like other algae, kelp superficially resemble land plants, but they function entirely differently. Their "roots" are simply holdfasts, used to keep the plant positioned. The stem of a land plant carries nutrients and wastes up and down the plant; the stem, or *stipe*, of kelp simply connects the holdfast to the bulb and the fronds, where photosynthesis is going on.

Eelgrass, on the other hand, is structured like the land plants from which it evolved. It is made up of ribbons several feet long and a quarter of an inch wide, sinuously waving in the current. Eelgrass even flowers (very discreetly) underwater, and its threadlike pollen is carried by the currents to other plants. It has true roots, though it hardly needs them for nourishment, since it lives in a bath of nutrients. Like beach grass, its roots are rhizomes running parallel to the surface, which send up new shoots at frequent intervals.

Eelgrass can cover acres of muddy bottom. It shelters small fishes and other marine animals, notably scallops, and it is a major food of the brant, a small goose. It also supports a tiny ecosystem all on its own. The leaves are light green near the roots, gradually darkening as they get older and finally becoming frayed and almost black at the tips. Near the root the leaf is coated with unicellular diatoms accompanied by small crustaceans called copepods, which feed on the diatoms. Farther up, green and red algae grow on the leaf, accompanied by tiny shrimp, which feed on detritus that collects in the algae. Some of these shrimp have the ability to build tubes along the leaf into which they can retreat at moments of danger. Snails—some with shells, some without—browse along the leaves. Hydroids, bryozoans, worms and sea squirts all find niches along the eelgrass blade.

Eelgrass comes ashore in long tangled windrows after autumn storms and is gathered for mulch and fertilizer in gardens. Dried, it has been used as upholstery and mattress stuffing and as house insulation. To this day, it is occasionally used by Maritimers and Newfoundlanders as banking around the foundations of their houses, insulating them against the winter cold. Eelgrass is subject to an occasional killing blight, the most recent episode of which occurred on the Atlantic coast in the 1930s. It was catastrophic not only to the brant and the scallops, but also to a fledgling industry that was planning to produce insulating panels made of pressed eelgrass.

Echinoderms—spiny-skinned creatures—include sea cucumbers, sand dollars, sea urchins and starfish, better described as sea stars. They are radial creatures, for the most part, built around a core that contains their mouths, stomachs and other central functions.

A sea urchin is shaped like a flattened globe covered with spikes and bristles. The spikes are not primarily for defense, but for nourishment. As bits of food drift by—fragments of seaweed, for instance—they catch on the spikes. The spikes hand them along over the surface of the body to the mouth, which is located in the center of the urchin's underside. (The anus is on the top.) Some species grow as large as four inches across. Sea urchin roe is a great delicacy in Japan, where it is believed to enhance sexual powers.

Sand dollars are flattened urchins, in effect, with the bristles reduced to a kind of fuzz. They stand on edge in the current, with two-thirds of their bodies upright, straining organic particles out of the passing water. Their natural enemies are groundfish, like the cod, flounder and haddock. The cast-off shells of sand dollars are beautifully patterned light gray and brown disks much prized by beachcombers.

If sand dollars are flattened urchins, sea cucumbers are elongated ones. Sea cucumbers—one of the smallest is called a sea gherkin—have the same radial pattern expressed horizontally: five rows of tube feet, of which only three are used for locomotion. They are found at all depths in the ocean, from the shallow water just below the tideline all the way to the abyssal deeps. More than half the animals living at 13,000 feet are sea cucumbers, and one has been dredged at a depth of 33,465 feet—farther below sea level than Mount Everest stands above it.

Sea cucumbers have several repellent features. For one thing, their skins contain a poison called holothurin, which Pacific islanders use in fishing. Island fishers mash up the sea cucumber, throw the mash in the water and net the poisoned fish that float to the surface. Sea cucumbers (also known as *trepang* or *beche de mer)* are prized as food in the Orient; they are eviscerated, boiled, smoked, dried and chopped up into gelatinous pieces, which go into soups or stews. The Chinese do something similar with jellyfish; in Shenyang, I once ate something that in texture resembled an onion ring, but which had a distinctly marine flavor. It was delicious, and it proved to be a deep-fried jellyfish.

The sea cucumber makes several quite bizarre uses of its enormous anus, which may shelter a variety of fish and other small creatures. It breathes through its anus, drawing in water and extracting oxygen, then expelling the water. When it is attacked through the anus, the cucumber simply expels all its internal organs through its anus and abandons them. The organs live on their own for some time, while the sea cucumber slowly regenerates the lost organs.

"Look at the starfish, Mommy!" cried the child just before the family sailboat ran aground. It wasn't our boat; it was a friend's in New Brunswick. It had strayed into hip-deep water, and only their daughter was looking over the side.

Most of us have a clear picture of a sea star: five chubby arms smoothly faired into a central core. This is the architecture of the northern sea star of the Atlantic or the purple or ochre star of the

Pacific. Many similar stars exist—slender stars, mud stars, vermilion stars, margined stars and so forth. But not all stars have five arms; the morning sun star looks like an Aztec rendering of the sun, with 8 to 15 arms, usually 12. The spiny sun star has nine or ten legs and spikes all over its body; it has the symmetry and grace of an immense snowflake. The largest sea star is the sunflower star, which can reach three feet in diameter. Adults have 20 to 24 arms and live on worms, snails, crabs, sea urchins and even other stars.

There are more than 1,600 species of sea stars, and most dwell in the deep ocean. All sea stars are predators, usually of mollusks such as oysters, clams and mussels. Unlike most bottom dwellers, they do not provide a home for barnacles, algae, sponges or other creatures. This is not an accident; the upper surface of a star is dotted with *pedicellaria*, tiny pinching organs that crush anything that attempts to settle on the star's back. In addition, stars often exude a mucus that is toxic to fish and other marine animals. (One species is called the slime star.)

A less common family of sea stars is the brittle stars, so called because they are extremely fragile and easily fall apart. In fact, dropping an arm is a common reaction to danger. They have a very distinct central disk and five long, spidery arms, which writhe like snakes as the animal moves. One brittle star—the basket star—hardly resembles a starfish at all. Its five arms repeatedly branch out from the four-inch central disk, leaving it looking like a tangled set of yellow roots detached from some unimaginably complex plant.

Octopus are common in shallow waters all over the world. Octopus and squid are mollusks with skinlike mantles instead of external shells. Eight arms surround the mouth; the squid has two tentacles, as well. Both squid and octopus swim by drawing water into their mantle cavities and then expelling it forcefully, jetting themselves forward or backward. The squid is a fast swimmer, and it captures its prey on the fly, shooting out its two tentacles with their hooks and sucking disks and then pulling in the hapless shrimp or fish with its arms. The octopus stalks its prey slowly, usually at night. Then it drops over lobsters, crabs and other mollusks unexpectedly, like a blanket of death. Both squid and octopus kill their victims with poisonous saliva excreted when they bite their prey with their hard, parrotlike beaks.

Both squid and octopus have well-developed brains and eyes, among the most advanced of the invertebrate animals. They are also the only mollusks that sleep regularly. Both are edible, and both are eaten not only by man but by whales and fishes. Their main defense is concealment; their most famous maneuver is to eject an inky substance that both hides the animal and disables a fish's sense of smell. They can also change their coloration to match their background by expanding or contracting pigmented cells in their mantles.

Squid have always been a popular bait; they swim in schools close to the surface, where they are easily caught. You sometimes find them right along the shore or cast up on the beach. Normally they run a foot or so in length, often less. The giant Pacific octopus has been known to reach 30 feet from the tip of one tentacle to another, but the real monster is the giant squid, which has been reported all around the Atlantic and probably exists in the deep Pacific, as well, since remnants of it have been found in the stomachs of Pacific whales. These squid can grow to 65 feet in length.

You are not likely to see a giant squid on your visit to the beach, nor would you want to. But you could: there has been at least one reported attack on a Newfoundland dory that was fishing in shallow water near the shore.

The Birds

For me, the most visible and striking form of life at the beach is overhead; the air is full of birds. Some are specialists, like the tiny sanderlings that scurry up and down in the backwash, plucking invisible morsels—diatoms, tiny crustaceans—from the wet sand. Others, like the gulls, are tireless gleaners of the entire shoreline, gliding and swooping over remote headlands and seaport waterfronts alike, indiscriminately gobbling down dead fish, terns' eggs, live clams and the remnants of ham sandwiches. Far above them, mere dots against the sky, are the soaring raptors—eagles, falcons and ospreys, monarchs of the coastline, with eyes like spyglasses and talons like scimitars.

Each bird has a niche, and each stretch of coastline has its own rhythm. Look out my workroom window on a sunny summer's day. The back lawn and the trees sustain a variety of land birds: robins and house sparrows, starlings and chickadees, ruby-throated hummingbirds. Perhaps a flicker or a downy woodpecker is at work in the towering old trembling aspens. Swallows zoom over the yard and out across the harbor, picking off insects as they go.

The tide is low, and three or four wading birds are working the land wash. If they are small they are probably spotted sandpipers; in August they could be greater or lesser yellowlegs slowly working their way south. (In French, these bear the dignified names of *le grand chevalier* and *le petit chevalier*; the horned owl carries the resplendent title *le grand duc d'Amerique.*) Or it could be one of the willets, which breed two miles away, in a field of timothy and wild roses beside a shallow inlet. Walk along the shore there and the willets fly at you, diving and wheeling, screeching and scolding—elegant birds with long legs and bills and bright white patches under their wings.

A cormorant swims near the shore, her body low in the water, her neck like a black stick against the silver wavelets. When she takes flight, she runs over the surface of the water, tapping it with her wing tips and her feet, barely rising into the air. Shags, as cormorants are known in Nova Scotia, are everywhere in the summer, flying low and fast over the water, swimming and diving. They nest on old pilings and dead trees; in the Bras d'Or Lakes, not far away, they have nested in the spruce trees of Spectacle Island in such numbers, and for so long, that their droppings have killed the trees and denuded the island.

Ducks are swimming in the harbor—teals and black ducks browsing on aquatic plants, mergansers and eiders farther out, diving for snails and mussels. From time to time a loon appears, almost indistinguishable at first from a cormorant. Beyond the harbor, along the shores of Lennox Passage, are the nests of ospreys and bald eagles.

The ospreys are migratory, returning each spring to their rough, inelegant nests of twigs and branches in dead trees and on power poles. The bald eagle, the American regal symbol, is common on both coasts of Canada; because of settlement and industrial pollution it almost vanished in the United States, and it is still relatively uncommon there. Many eagles winter along the Bras d'Or Lakes a few miles away. We anchored there one night in a long, narrow waterway called the Boom, and all along its banks were eagle nests. Screeching and yelling, the eagles made an amazing din, and whenever they settled down, ten-year-old Mark would restart the chorus with an eerily accurate imitation of their cries.

Eagles look fierce, with their hooked beaks, unblinking eyes and brown pantaloons above yellow legs and curved talons, but they would rather eat carrion than hunt for themselves. We once stayed a couple of days inside a sand spit at another Bras d'Or Lakes anchorage, and each morning we watched a local fisherman dump stale bait and junk fish at the very end of the spit. There the eagles would gather to feed, three or four at a time, just a few yards from our anchored boat. But they will hunt if they must, eating muskrats, cod, herons, hares, cormorants and other prey.

Occasionally I see a gannet in Lennox Passage, though the gannets seem to prefer the wilder shoreline of Point Michaud, 20 miles down the coast. Gannets resemble gulls with black wing tips and buff heads, but they are much bigger, more powerful birds, three or four feet long, with wingspans up to six feet. They are spectacular birds to watch, flying tirelessly along the coast till they discern fish below the surface. Then—50 or 60 feet in the air—they fold their wings and pierce the sea like feathered arrowheads, shooting down several feet below the surface and swallowing their prey on the way up. At Cape St. Mary's, Newfoundland, you can walk to the edge of the cliff and watch a gannet colony on top of a spire of rock just a few yards away.

They build their nests close beside one another and gabble together incessantly. When one of a pair returns from fishing, the two perform an elaborate greeting ceremony, fencing with their bills, bowing with wings and tails raised, grooming one another's heads and necks. Then the bird that is going off watch lifts its wings and jumps into the air, flying off to join the hundreds of others circling over the teeming sea.

The day I visited Cape St. Mary's, the sea stack was a tower of life, with the majestic gannets at its peak, kittiwakes fluttering in and out from narrow ledges along the rock face and uncountable murres, guillemots and razor-billed auks clustered around its base. The surface of the water was heaving as a school of humpback whales moved through a shoal of fish, and the birds were moving through the boundary between air and water as easily as a person walks through an open door.

Great blue herons nest in dozens on an island within sight of my workroom. They seem to work in the early morning and evening, when the water is usually calm. They stand in ankle-deep water, often on one leg, gaunt and meditative, utterly immobile, a study in patience. Then a tiny fish wanders incautiously near what looks to be a tree root. The great neck uncoils, the long bill stabs the water, the fish is gone, and the heron has already resumed its Buddhist state, at once watchful, still and alert. As dusk arrives, the heron stretches its vast broad wings and pulls itself slowly into the air. Its neck is coiled, and its long legs trail behind it like an ungainly tail. As it passes overhead, with its long, slow wing beat, you can hear its feathers creaking. A heron in flight looks more like a pterodactyl than a modern bird—exotic, paleological, otherworldly.

As the herons fly home, the bats come out—not birds but tiny mammals, black oak leaves against the gray ground glass of the sky, fluttering erratically through the cooling air, scooping up flies and mosquitoes, flying so fast and unpredictably that they are almost impossible to watch. On remote islands down the coast the petrels are racing out of their burrows among the tree roots, flying seaward on their nocturnal hunt for small fish and crustaceans. They are daring fliers, fast and abrupt; becalmed off the coast, I listened to them and glimpsed them all one night as they darted past the sails and through the rigging, filling the night with their low cries and the whirring of their flight.

Gulls and crows hang around our harbor all winter. Most of the gulls are the common gray-and-white herring gulls, with vivid yellow beaks, but Iceland gulls winter here. We also have many great black-backed gulls, which nest on a small grassy islet in Lennox Passage. These are the largest gulls in the world, known as *minister birds* or *coffin carriers* because they look, with their icy-white heads and breasts and solid black backs, as though they were bound for some solemn religious occasion.

Watch as my son takes a bowl of organic kitchen scraps down to the shore and throws them in the water. (Our garbage theory is that edible scraps will always be welcomed by some animate neighbor who lives along the shore.) The gulls are elsewhere when he leaves the house, but by the time he reaches the shore a few will be swooping and circling above him; the moment Mark throws the scraps on the water the gulls will be into them, jostling one another, snatching morsels from their neighbors' mouths, muttering insults and screaming obscenities at one another. Look up, and you will see gulls converging from every direction, curious at first and then greedy, dropping into the melee and raucously asserting their claims.

Where do they come from, these clouds of gulls? How do they know there's something going on at our house? They are beautiful birds, gliding motionless through the gales, climbing effortlessly, sideslipping and wheeling in the wind, but their personalities and manners are not a good example for an impressionable young man.

I love birds that fly elegantly and have a sense of drama: swallows, hummingbirds, hawks, falcons. There are peregrine falcons in Cape Breton, though I have never seen one here; but I watched one on Grand Manan Island in the Bay of Fundy playing with a flock of gulls, circling above them and then swooping: plunging down on the gulls like an image of feathered death, only to swerve away at the last moment. In the same way, I love to watch the belted kingfishers sitting on the branches, watching, and then suddenly plunging into the water. But perhaps my favorites among the shorebirds are the terns.

Terns—Nova Scotians call them *mackerel gulls*—resemble gulls, but they are much more finely shaped and distinctly smaller. Three species summer on this stretch of the coast: common, Arctic and roseate. All three have pearly gray backs and wings, white underbodies and black caps, but the most handsome—marginally—is the Arctic tern, with a blood-red bill and legs. They like to sit on pilings and channel buoys, waiting till you have almost reached them and then flitting quickly away. They fish outside my workroom window all summer, circling above the water, flying with easy but urgent beats of their long, narrow wings, occasionally crying *kip-kip-kip.* When they spot something promising under the surface, they rear back and fan their wings, standing up in the air with their wing feathers splayed open, hovering and watching. Then they will dive like a gannet, hitting the water with a splash and immediately taking flight again.

Terns are tireless travelers. The common tern breeds across southern Canada and winters in southern South America. The migrations of the Arctic tern are even more astounding. Nova Scotia is the southern limit of its breeding range, which extends to the high Arctic of Europe and Asia as well as Canada. In the fall this little bird—only 16 inches long—flies not south but east, crossing the Atlantic before flying southward down the coasts of Europe and Africa. One was banded in Labrador on July 23, 1928; it was found on November 14 in Natal, South Africa.

But this was not the end of its voyage. The Arctic tern's winter range is in the Southern Ocean south of Africa, sometimes as far south as the Antarctic Circle. It returns by the same route in the spring—a round trip of as much as 22,000 miles. All this flying must be good for its constitution, since at least one Norwegian tern is known to have lived for 27 years.

When the terns fly south from Nova Scotia, other northern birds take their place—black-bellied plovers from the Arctic, murres and kittiwakes from Newfoundland, dovekies from Greenland, surf scoters from the Ungava Peninsula. Some goldeneye ducks breed in Nova Scotia, but each fall a wave of migrants from the Arctic population passes through to winter farther south, from Maine to the Gulf of Mexico. The long-tails arrive in October and stay till the harbor freezes over, gathering in rafts and gossiping together. (The long-tails' Latin name, *Clangula hyemalis*, means "noisy winter duck.") Long-tails are powerful divers; unlike most ducks, they fly underwater, and they have been caught and drowned in gill nets as much as 200 feet below the surface.

The winter comes and goes. The harbor freezes solid, and the hardiest of the birds—the gulls especially—sit in resignation on the ice. As the winter passes, the ice breaks up and blows out to sea. And the other birds straggle back.

As I write this on a cloudy day in early April, the harbor has filled again with pack ice, small bergs and pieces ranging from 6 feet deep and 20 or 30 feet across to pieces the size of a baseball or a football. This is not local ice but northern ice, carried south on the ocean currents in a sea still cold enough to hold it frozen. The pack moves down the coast every spring; strong easterly winds can push it up against the shoreline and into the bays and inlets, while westerlies will carry it back to sea. Today the wind is doing exactly that; yesterday's easterlies plugged Lennox Passage solid with pack ice, and today's westerly is moving it out. But the sea is still peppered with blocks of white, the falling tide has left a wrack of small fragments around the shore, and a dozen large floes are stranded on the far side of the harbor.

And there they are, the long-tails, the red-breasted mergansers and the goldeneyes, paddling among the white islets of ice, flipping their tails in the air and diving for their dinners. The gulls are gliding over the blocks of ice, the crows are wading in the wavelets, the eagles are soaring high in the distance.

These are, in a sense, my birds: the birds I watch on this particular stretch of northern shoreline as the seasons change around me. But there are birds I never see, birds whose range seldom if ever brings them this far north—flamingos and ibis, rails and stilts and oystercatchers and a dozen more species of gulls. The birds rank high among the pleasures of travel—seeing the brown pelicans of Florida diving behind the surf line or sailing along the updraft from the dunes, huge and dark, never moving a muscle as they come. Seeing a flock of flamingos in the Bahamas was almost a shock: I had scarcely believed that they were really so pink. Laughing gulls are not wholly unknown in Nova Scotia, but I had never seen a flock of them until the morning Charlie Doucet and I took the ferry from Cedar Island to Ocracoke in North Carolina, and a cloud of laughing gulls flew with us all the way.

∽

For me, the life of the beach has two particularly striking features. First, the sheer fecundity of this boundary zone is astonishing. There are millions, even billions, of lives in every little stretch of shoreline, interacting in the most complex and amazing ways. The shoreline is a broth of life, much of it invisible, and it is profoundly vulnerable to human intervention. We cut the shade trees, which raises the water temperature; we flush pollutants into the water; we knock the dunes down and spray oils and insecticides into the marshes to rid ourselves of mosquitoes, and then we wonder where the eagles went, and the little green crabs, and the nesting turtles. The living beach is a fluid but organized whole, a totality, a gestalt: drifting sand, flowing water, all of it permeated with the miracle of life. Living things are as integral to its nature as the sand itself.

The second striking feature is that the plants and animals that live on the shore are hardy, flexible or mobile. Storm waves don't break barnacles; algae lose their fronds, but not their lives. Birds fly inland, mollusks bury themselves, crustaceans retreat to deeper water. This is a violent, plastic environment, and when it erupts in fury, plants go dormant or lie buried, while animals move out of harm's way. When the beach is in fury, its natural life forms do not resist. They yield. They wait. And then, when the storm has passed, they resume their varied and fascinating lives.

Only one species builds elaborate, permanent habitations right in the path of the storm and expects those habitations to survive. Some of the other species that inhabit the shoreline have no brains at all— but in this respect, at least, they are smarter than human beings. And many of them have been hanging around beaches for 50 times as long.

She Sells Sea Shells

Who has not heard how Tyrian shells
Enclosed the blue, that dye of dyes
Whereof one drop worked miracles
And colored like Astarte's eyes
Raw silk the merchant sells?
     —Robert Browning, "Popularity"

"When you're cooped up in a room with five other guys for five months," says Gene Everson, "you get to hate everything about 'em, even the way they part their hair. So just to get out of that room I thought I'd take up scuba diving."

The year was 1966, and Everson was in Guam, flying bombing missions to Vietnam. One of his diving instructors was a shell collector. "He taught me the basics—following a mollusk's trail, turning over stones, that kind of stuff."

After Guam, Everson found himself living in Florida, and he kept on diving and collecting shells. Then, in 1972, "I found out that there were such things as shell clubs. And that changed everything."

Everson had entered the worldwide subculture of conchology, the study of shells. (*Malacology*, once a synonym, now usually denotes the study of mollusks as living animals.) The world of conchology includes competitions and awards, conferences, overseas expeditions, books, specialized collections, newsletters, Web sites and listservs, shell dealers and shell shops. It has its own infrastructure, its own politics, its own heroes. It reaches back to Aristotle and Pliny and forward to technology not yet invented. Its devotees come from every walk of life; the late Emperor Hirohito of Japan was a respected conchologist, author of a study of the shells of Sagami Bay.

In North America, the heart of shell collecting is South Florida, especially Sanibel and Captiva islands, where the shore is thick with whole and broken shells. With an active shell club, a new shell museum and half a dozen shell shops (including one called She Sells Sea Shells), Sanibel and Captiva are natural centers for shell shows, conventions and field trips.

Shell clubs flourish not only in coastal cities but also in such improbable locations as St. Louis and Indianapolis. But then mollusks are not only creatures of the beaches and oceans; many of the estimated 50,000 to 100,000 species thrive on the land, in the trees, in fresh water and inside other animals. For many of its devotees, conchology started on the beach and in the shallow water nearby, but it ultimately led them to the abyssal deeps, the inland swamps and rivers, the jungles of Brazil, West Africa and Ceram.

But it all starts with the urge to pick up beautiful shells. Most of us never even know that the world of conchology exists—but who has not been enthralled by the iridescent mother-of-pearl inside an oyster shell, the delicate pink ruffles of a tiny Florida clam or the patterning and symmetry of a scallop?

The scallop is the classical and prototypical shell, the image most likely to appear in the mind when we hear the word *shell*. As a symbol, the scallop appeared in the arts of the Mayans, the Aztecs and their predecessors, dating back as far as 3000 BCE. The ancient Greek goddess Aphrodite, the goddess of love, was supposed to have been born from a scallop shell, an event often depicted in Greek art and echoed during the Renaissance in paintings by Titian and Botticelli. The Phoenicians had scallop designs on their coins, and the Romans incorporated the shape of the scallop shell in architecture and mosaics and even on coffins. During the Middle Ages, scallops became associated with

St. James, and scallop shells came to be worn as badges showing that the wearer had participated in one of the Crusades. In the thirteenth century, the scallop motif appeared in heraldry; as a Knight of the Garter, Sir Winston Churchill had a coat of arms that included six silver scallops. The scallop is one of the most venerable and elegant of corporate symbols, that of Shell Oil.

It therefore comes as a shock to realize that most conchologists are primarily interested not in scallops, clams, oysters and mussels, but in snails. The next shock is the range and variety of snails. Conchs, periwinkles, poisonous cones, whelks, dogwinkles, abalones, moons, escargots in garlic and butter, garden slugs—they are all snails. The famous purple dye of Tyre came from murex and Thais snails, which the Minoans and Phoenicians crushed and boiled to produce the dye. The cowrie shell, used as money in the Pacific islands and in Africa as recently as the nineteenth century, is a snail; so are the Busycon whelk and the periwinkle, which were often used in the wampum belts of the Iroquois and other First Nations. The aboriginal trumpet was usually a conch shell.

At various times and places shells have been used in medicines and poultry feed, as pots and ladles, in musical instruments and in furniture. Cleopatra is said to have kept her jewelry in shells. But shell collecting as a popular pastime and an organized field of study dates from the European expansion across the world in the seventeenth and eighteenth centuries. Georg Eberhard Rumpf, better known as Rumphius, went to the East Indies in 1627 as a representative of the Dutch East India Company; his collections and publications of Indo-Pacific mollusks made him one of the towering figures in the history of conchology. Captain Cook's voyages to the South Seas in the 1760s brought many new shells to the attention of Europeans. By the 1780s, shell dealers had well-established businesses in London.

The great naturalist Carolus Linnaeus, who devised the standard system of classifying plants and animals, had a superb shell collection, and a regular feature of noble and gracious homes in the eighteenth century was the shell cabinet, where rare and delicate shells were displayed. Many wealthy and powerful people went further; King August II of Poland had an entire room—a shell grotto—decorated with complex murals made entirely of shells.

Building a shell grotto for the king, of course, is not shell collecting but shell craft—and relations between shell crafters and conchologists are not always cordial. Shell craft ranges from the high art of Italian cameos scribed into shells to the slapdash souvenirs found in seaside shops—ugly lamps, dreadful vases, tacky picture frames. Many conchologists, notes *American Conchologist* editor Lynn Scheu, consider such shell craft "a waste of good shells—and the animals' lives."

Perhaps the greatest collector of all time was Hugh Cuming, an English sailmaker who made a fortune in Chile and then built a yacht specifically for research. Cuming made a series of voyages between 1827 and 1840, which covered much of the Pacific basin from the west coasts of South and Central America to the Philippines. He collected thousands of specimens, including nearly 2,000 new species of mollusks, not to mention hundreds of species of birds and plants. Both his motives and his methods have been questioned by later collectors, but nobody denies the scope of his overall achievement.

In Cuming's time, the rarest and most famous shell in the world was *Conus gloriamaris,* the Glory of the Sea. The only specimen in the world had been purchased by a London shell dealer from one of Cook's sailors and was thought to have come from Japan or New Guinea. Cuming found two on a beach in the Philippines; they ended up in the British Museum. For another century, gloriamaris remained extremely rare; even as recently as the 1960s only about 50 had been collected.

Now, says Gene Everson, gloriamaris is almost commonplace. As knowledge and technology expand, fishermen and others discover the habitats of once rare shells. The habitat of gloriamaris was discovered in the 1970s by Philippine fishermen using tangle nets on deep coral reefs, well beyond the reach of scuba divers. Today a really big gloriamaris, says Everson, might fetch $500 to $600, but smaller ones can be bought for $30 or $40.

In recent years, one of the most prized shells has been Fulton's Cowrie, *Cypraea fultoni,* which was known only *ex pisce,* meaning that specimens had been found only in the stomachs of fish, never in their own habitat. In 1987, when a Russian trawler brought up two live specimens off Mozambique, the larger sold to an Italian collector for $24,000. Today, says Florida shell dealer Donald Dan, the most prized shell is *Chimaeria incomparabilis,* a shell long thought to be extinct. Only five specimens are known; two were taken by Somalian fishermen, but the other three have a more complex provenance.

"During the Cold War, the Russians had the largest fleet of 'scientific research' vessels in the world," says Dan. "They were actually mapping the bottom for military purposes, of course, and the Soviet government didn't really care what they found, so the officers and scientists took the shells into their own private collections.

"When the Soviet Union collapsed and the economy fell apart, people were desperate, and these collections became available. Three *Chimaeria incomparabilis* shells came on the market, and I handled all three. I sold one to the Smithsonian and found private donors for the other two. The price was around $20,000."

But someday someone will learn where *Chimaeria incomparabilis* lives and breeds, and the price will plummet immediately.

"Shells are not a good investment," says Gene Everson flatly. "With stamps or coins or something like that, there are only so many of 'em. But the shells are down there every night screwing around making more."

Shells ultimately became Everson's consuming passion. After leaving the military he became a Pan American Airlines pilot and lived for 18 years in Florida, diving extensively in the Caribbean. During layovers between flights and on his vacations, he went on collecting trips. He joined the leading shell collecting organization, the Conchologists of America—which publishes *American Conchologist*—and began entering shows and competitions. The only major mollusk-producing region he has not visited is West Africa, and he plans to go there shortly. In retirement, he moved home to Louisville, Kentucky, with his second wife and bought a house with a basement-level carport; when he prepares for a show, he can load his van straight from the basement—which is completely filled with his shell collection.

After winning numerous awards and competitions, Everson has become "a bit of a celebrity in the shell world," says shell dealer and photographer Richard Goldberg, who discovered several new species on a recent trip to Indonesia. "Gene is very motivated, very determined. He'll go wherever he has to go, do whatever he has to do, in order to expand his collection." Everson spends two or three hours a day working on his shells, 10 to 12 hours when he is preparing for a field trip or a competition, and he frankly confesses that his hobby is good for his ego. On his first trip to Europe, Everson visited a shell shop in Soho, London. The clerk looked at him briefly, then thumbed through an Italian shelling magazine. When he found the page he was looking for, he held up the magazine. Everson found himself confronting a photograph of himself.

"Isn't this you, sir?" asked the clerk. Everson was thrilled.

Conchology is one of the few areas of scholarship where professionals and amateurs meet on respectful terms. Conchology and malacology are not well-supported sciences, and amateurs have been responsible for many discoveries in the field. Dr. Gary Rosenberg of the Academy of Natural Sciences in Philadelphia has estimated that at least 103 of 293 new species in Florida were discovered by amateurs, largely members of the Palm Beach and Broward shell clubs. Christopher Garvie, an amateur, published a scientific monograph in 1996, which described 123 new species of mollusks. Indeed, conchology is one of the few remaining fields in which an amateur can make genuine and significant contributions to the advancement of knowledge. In its own small way, conchology offers its enthusiasts a tiny serving of immortality.

Finding a new species is the naturalist's equivalent of a hole in one in golf or a 29 hand in cribbage, and part of the fun is naming the new species. Species are often named for their discoverer, or for a child, an honored friend, a beloved wife: *Cypraea annettae, Conus juliae, Terebra miranda.* Gary Rosenberg has noted that of 346 western Atlantic species with names ending in the Latin feminine *ae,* 120 are based on the first name of a woman, though only 13 of 1,766 species appear to be named for men. *Bizetiella carmen* was presumably named by an opera lover. Occasionally a venomous or notably ugly species has been named for a special enemy.

The competence of North American amateur conchologists and the camaraderie between the professionals and the amateurs derive from Henry A. Pilsbry, who reigned over the field from a chair at the Academy of Natural Sciences in the early twentieth century. Pilsbry nourished Bill Clench, who wound up at Harvard; Clench in turn taught R. Tucker Abbott, whose students included Jerry Harasewych of the Smithsonian and Gary Rosenberg, who now occupies Pilsbry's old position in Philadelphia. All of them gave freely of their time to amateurs, encouraged them and treated them as colleagues.

Tucker Abbott, who died in 1996, was particularly loved and is openly and frequently mourned. Abbott participated in conventions, judged shell competitions, led collecting expeditions, founded three shell clubs and wrote voluminously both for scientific journals and for lay audiences. His very readable *Kingdom of the Seashell* (1972) is still the best general introduction to the subject. Rosenberg and others are continuing the tradition: they frequently contribute to *American Conchologist* and chime into the electronic conversation on the COA listserv.

"Collecting is not politically correct today," says Richard Goldberg sadly. Environmentalists argue that plants and animals should be left undisturbed, and recent laws on wildlife trade make it difficult to import shells into the United States and illegal to export them from the Philippines. Unquestionably, overcollecting does occur. In some locations, wrote Tucker Abbott, "Even the constant revisiting of biology classes, week after week, has decimated certain small, once-productive spots." Shell watching, he thought, would become an ever-more important activity for the conchologist of the future.

But, as Abbott also pointed out, industrial activity is far more destructive than collecting. One trawler or clam dredge can do more damage in a day than a cluster of conchologists could do in a decade. Beach replenishment is also devastating to mollusks. Worse still are the effects of pollution, which have cleared many a bay of its native mollusk population. All the same, Donald Dan, who administers the prestigious COA Awards, points out that "there is not a single case where a marine mollusk became extinct" through human agency.

Robert Louis Stevenson thought it was "perhaps a more fortunate destiny to have a taste for collecting shells than to be born a millionaire." Gene Everson would probably agree.

"When the airline went bankrupt and the paychecks stopped coming and the wife left, it was a pretty rough time," he says. "I don't know how I would have got through it if I hadn't had the shell collection."

6. The Human Beach

It happened one day about noon going towards my boat, I was exceedingly surprised with the print of a man's naked foot on the shore, which was very plain to be seen in the sand. I stood like one thunderstruck, or as if I had seen an apparition; I listened, I looked round me; I could hear nothing, nor see anything; I went up the shore and down the shore, but it was all one, I could see no impression but that one.
—Daniel Defoe, *Robinson Crusoe*

T he man looked a bit like Robinson Crusoe—or perhaps Ben Gunn, the marooned pirate in Robert Louis Stevenson's *Treasure Island.* He walked the Pacific beach in a pair of ragged, flapping shorts and not much else, and he had an untrimmed gray beard that brushed his sun-browned chest when he turned his head. He might have been 60. He lived in a tiny, basic A-frame cottage built on stones among the trees that fringed the shore; in exceptionally high tides the water surged up the nearby creek and right under his little house. He didn't own the land; he had built there as a squatter, though he had the consent of the owner. I seem to remember that he had originally been a Dane and retained a hint of *dansk* in his soft voice.

There was a woman in the house, perhaps half his age, dark-haired and slender. She had left a husband and children in a city somewhere and she was not the first woman to share his hermitage, nor did she expect to be the last. Shaggy, lean and leathery, he projected an ego-free, Zenlike serenity, which women found magnetically attractive, though presumably not ultimately satisfying. They came to slow down, contemplate their futures, absorb enough of his serenity to restore their spirits. Then they left. He welcomed their arrival and did not mourn them when they resumed their private journeys.

He was a sculptor, he said, and he told me how to reach his workplace, back in the woods across the road. I picked my way through the cut-over land, the huckleberries and alders, till I reached an orange plastic tarpaulin stretched among the trees, which protected his workplace from the west coast rains. Near the tarpaulin were several cedar logs, two or three feet thick, and under the shelter of the tarp lay his current projects. He was carving three enormous totem poles incorporating traditional Native images. Raven, Beaver, Thunderbird: a white man's homage to a great Native culture. The carvings were massive and colorful—red and black paint, fresh tawny wood. I have no idea where, or if, he sold them.

I didn't ask his name. It didn't seem like the kind of detail that would matter to him.

He was an archetype, a modern-day Thoreau who had driven life into a corner and reduced it to its lowest terms. Many men (and some women) have done this, and do it still. Paul Theroux found such men on the beaches of Australia and Oceania; the French stockbroker Paul Gauguin fled to the beaches of Polynesia and spent his life painting; Euell Gibbons spent years on the beaches of Pacific islands, learning to live on what nature provided, living as flexibly as grass.

There are beaches at the edge of the water, and there are beaches in our minds. The dropout—of which the beachcomber is a prime instance—is a well-established fixture in the Western imagination, a staple of film and fiction, the ultimate critic of industrial culture. He lives outside the cash-and-credit economy, purged of the maddening clutter of possessions and obligations. The beachcomber's shanty is a light-duty home, easily built and easily replaced, a house comparable to a Polynesian's thatched hut or a Maine fisherman's seasonal shanty on an offshore islet. His life has ecological virtue; he takes only what he needs and leaves the world much as he found it. By renouncing the whole notion of dominion over land and sea, by accepting that he is simply another animal living at the beach, he attains harmony and freedom. In three years of full-time beachcombing, wrote Euell Gibbons, "I lost the unhealthy urge to battle with nature, and completely recovered from the idea that man should be engaged in the conquest of nature. I found nature full of unexpected kindnesses, mercies, and joys." No other period of his life, he said, was so free of regrets.

The beachcomber lives, to some degree, within most of us. Who does not sometimes feel that the things we claim to own have somehow ended up owning us instead, that we are not living our own lives but being lived by them, that we have been impoverished by wealth? A warm beach with a hut in the trees, seafood and wild vegetables to eat, clean water to drink: does the human animal really need much more than this?

Our hunting and gathering ancestors used the beach in precisely this way. They built few permanent homes or harbor works; they launched their light, small vessels directly from the beach and moved inland in foul weather. The beach was a place to gather food, a base for fishing, whaling and trading, a departure point for travels.

As with so much else, the human relationship with the beach changed dramatically with the Industrial Revolution, which conferred such power to manipulate and shape the world around us. People crowded into towns built around mines and factories; thinkers like Charles Darwin and Herbert Spencer gave intellectual credence to the idea that life—human life included—was a process of vicious competition, in which only the strongest and fittest could survive. Darwinian science and industrial society fostered an outright fear of

"Nature, red in tooth and claw," as Tennyson put it, and an increasing estrangement from the organic world beyond the city limits.

Such a vision of life marginalizes art, religion, friendship, citizenship and love and ignores the realities of cooperation and coevolution in the natural world. It drove other thinkers to despair; resistance to it is one of the driving forces behind socialism, anarchism and literary romanticism. In literature, the sea and the beach began to appear as symbols of untamable wildness, obdurately resistant to human arrogance.

But more and more of the human beings who came to the beach in the nineteenth century were products of industrial society, with its strange division of human life into working time and leisure time, days on and days off. Some of them came for straightforward industrial purposes—mining sand for construction material, for instance—but most of them came in search of amusements to occupy their hours of unfamiliar leisure time. They had no special interest in the beach itself and no notion of its complexity and volatility. They were not looking for food, and if they fished they did so for amusement. They were looking for fun, and the owners of the new resorts and amusement parks were happy to supply it.

The resort beaches of today are directly descended from those of the nineteenth century. The old amusements remain, and new amusements have appeared. We have new beach sports and nude beaches, which would not have been countenanced in the Victorian era. But we still see the beach as a place for human pleasure.

The beachcomber is an atavism, living more like an aboriginal than an industrial-age worker. He comes from the past. But in his sensitivity to the beach—living in it and with it as well as on it—he also comes, we may hope, from the future.

∽

The aboriginal approach to the beach was not particularly reverent or idyllic; those who blanch at the clutter of rubbish around modern shorelines need to remember that shell middens are nothing more than aboriginal garbage dumps and that some Pacific island cultures have always used the beach as a community latrine. Human litter has been part of the shoreline for as long as humans have existed. Today's litter is different, of course. It degrades much more slowly, if at all; some of it is poisonous; and its volume is much greater. We must indeed clean up our act—but when we do, it will be the first time people have ever cleaned up their act on the beach.

In colder climates, the beach was—as it remains—a seasonal habitation. With the temperature at -15°C and a 40-knot gale blowing, a Nova Scotian beach in midwinter is not a cordial venue. The cold goes to your bones. Your cheeks and mouth stiffen, and you have difficulty forming words. Machinery freezes and stops. You want to go inside and stay there until spring.

Nova Scotia's aboriginal people, the Mi'kmaq, did exactly that, spending the most bitter part of the winter in inland valleys, sheltered by the hills and trees from the relentless, piercing ocean winds. In the summer they returned to the shore, dining on shellfish, eggs, berries and a cornucopia of fish—salmon, sturgeon, swordfish, flounder, smelt, shad, skate and eel. Using birchbark canoes, they foraged far offshore, hunting porpoise, seal, walrus and small whales.

For European settlers, as for other animals, the beach was first a place where adaptive specialists found a livelihood. Boat shops and sail lofts, gear sheds and forges, storehouses and smokehouses—these were the structures, usually cheap and temporary, which grew up on the world's beaches. If a raging storm destroyed them, they were easily replaced. In a sense they were not buildings, but tools—artifacts of work, meant to be used hard and replaced. In Newfoundland and Maritime Canada, many beaches were covered with acres of flakes: loose, open, table-height structures on which split codfish were spread to be salted and sun-dried. On cobble beaches, the fish were dried right on the beach stones.

Some fisheries can be pursued only on the beach. Among the most spectacular is the Capelin Scull of Newfoundland. Capelin are small silvery fish, rather like smelts. They live their lives in deep water, where they feed such larger species as cod and haddock. Indeed, part of the reason for the collapse of the North Atlantic cod fishery may have been the development of an offshore fishery for capelin during the 1970s and 1980s.

The capelin move inshore to breed in swarms on the beaches of Newfoundland (and a few other coastlines, including a beach in Isle Madame) in billions every summer. Behind them come their predators—pollock, squid, even whales. The capelin pack into schools dense enough to slow a power boat. They live in sex-segregated herds, and the two sexes meet only on the beach, where they mate in threes. Two males capture a female between them and hustle her up to the tide wash, where she emits ova while the males cloud the water with milt. Most of those that are not caught by fishers or eaten by predators die on the beaches; only a few return to the sea.

The arrival of the capelin creates a frenzy of activity on the shoreline, where people net them and shovel them into wheelbarrows, tubs, Jeeps, pickup trucks—anything that will hold thousands of squirming silver fish. People eat capelin fried when they are fresh; they also preserve them by smoking or *corning* —lightly salting them and drying them in the sun. Uncountable tons are spread on hay fields and gardens, and many tons more are processed into cattle and poultry feeds.

The capelin constitute an enormous annual gift to the people along the shore, but their numbers have greatly diminished since the offshore fishery began—just as the offshore herring seiners have decimated the Gulf of St. Lawrence herring population, whose roe once covered the beaches of New Brunswick to a depth that would mire a horse. Such vast resources always seem inexhaustible. As our generation is learning to its sorrow, they are not.

The same thing happened to the whales that once thrived near the shore. All down the Atlantic coast, the aboriginal people took whales from small vessels launched off the beach, and the European settlers learned the technique from them. By British law, however, whales were the property of the Crown. A seventeenth-century American colonist named Fishhook Mumford went to London to secure the rights of colonists to benefit from such shore-based whaling and described the method used by the Native people, who had told "how he bloweth up the water, and that he is twelve fathoms long; and that they go in company of their king with a multitude of their boats; and strike him with a bone made in the fashion of a harping iron fastened to a rope, which they make great and strong of the bark of trees, which they veer out after him; then all their boats come about him as he riseth above water, with their arrows they shoot him to death; when they have killed him and dragged him to shore, they call all their chief lords together and sing a song of joy ..."

The colonists added a few refinements—a boy perched high in the dunes to serve as lookout and a set of whaling boats always ready, the harpoon gun always nearby. One whale on the Outer Banks of North Carolina was taken by a crew of young boys and went down in oral tradition as "the little children's whale." It took two weeks of hard labor with kettles and driftwood to *try* the whale—to render its blubber into oil.

Ultimately, however, the harvesting became a commercial slaughter, and the whales vanished from the shoreline, along with the walrus, most of the seals, the passenger pigeons and many other species. Whaling became an offshore enterprise, pursued by a world-ranging fleet, which ultimately hunted the whales to the verge of extinction.

The beginnings of industrial activity on the shore often showed the same tentative and makeshift quality as the fishermen's huts and slipways. The early shipyards of North America were not buildings but mere slipways on the beach; wooden ships were built in the open air and skidded directly into the water on launching day. The first coastal engineering works were fortified harbors for deeper ships, which required quays and wharves. But not all coasts possessed harbors.

For those that did not, commerce continued to use the beach, ferrying cargoes back and forth in lighters, whaleboats and other small vessels. Such off-the-beach trading patterns persist in many parts of the world, and even in the developed world beach-based fisheries continue in places without a convenient harbor—on the Oregon coast, for example, and in the Magdalen Islands, where the substantial fishing boats of Old Harry Head are winched in and out of the water every day.

The vessels of early nations—Viking longships, Haida war canoes, Malay praus—were shallow-draft vessels that were meant to be beached, not moored. The great fleet that sailed to conquer Troy was made up of shoal-draft vessels about the size of today's family yacht, and Homer's *Odyssey*, the story of Odysseus's return from Troy—the first great voyaging book of Western culture—is a long string of encounters on beaches.

But the beach was also the scene of heartbreaking disasters, when ships struck the sandy bottom just outside the roaring surf and the crews perished on the very margin of the land. It is only within our lifetimes, with the advent of electronic aids to navigation, that shipwreck has ceased to be routine. For most of human history, shipwreck was a common occurrence, and a catastrophic one.

"The crew was so exhausted after three days of effort that they took to their hammocks," writes a prominent eighteenth-century Quebecois named St. Luc de La Corne, a passenger on the ship *Auguste*, which was carrying civilian and military deportees to France in the fall of 1761 after the British conquest of Quebec. At 50, La Corne was tough and decisive. The fur trade had made him one of the wealthiest men in Canada.

> The mate tried to rouse them and threatened to flog them but his efforts were futile. The men said they preferred to die in their hammocks.
> The mate came to the bridge where I was along with the Captain, the man at the helm and one of my servants. The

mate told the Captain it was impossible to work the ship. "Our mizzen mast is broken, our sails are in a thousand pieces, and we haven't been able to work the sails for 24 hours."

About 11 o'clock we saw a river on the port side about half a cannon-shot away. I had just time to acquaint our people when the ship was aground about 40 yards from the shore.

The ship swiveled and capsized immediately, trapping and drowning most of the passengers and crew below deck. La Corne and six others eventually struggled ashore; the remaining 114 souls aboard perished. The ship broke up and vanished, while the seas carried body after body to the beach. Among them were La Corne's brother, two nephews and two sons.

It was November, and the survivors were alone in the wilderness of northern Cape Breton. They buried the bodies in the sands of Aspy Bay and set out on foot to find help. The others went to Louisbourg, but in the end La Corne walked overland on snowshoes more than 800 miles, all the way to Quebec, where he arrived on February 22, 1762. It had taken him three and a half months, in the dead of a Canadian winter.

"I believe," wrote the governor of Quebec in his official report, "that nothing but main force will get him again on ship board."

The fragments that remained of the *Auguste* and her contents lay undisturbed for more than 200 years, concealed by the shifting sand at the bottom of the bay. They were uncovered and brought to the surface by divers only in 1977. By then everything organic had vanished, and only metal objects remained. The sand yielded a number of cannon and shot, some nautical equipment and some personal effects. The latter included spoons with the family crests of various passengers' families, which confirmed the identity of the wreck. Among the other artifacts were padlocks, a nutcracker, a watch case, sugar tongs, drafting tools, medals and money—the personal treasures of families bound for France but destined for the sands of Aspy Bay.

Among the most famous and eerie of the shipwreck strands is

Sable Island—L'Isle de Sablon, the Island of Sand—lying alone on the edge of the continental shelf 110 miles southeast of Halifax. A 25-mile crescent of sand, barely a mile across, Sable Island has captured more than 500 ships since Sir Humphrey Gilbert's little flotilla lost one of its ships here in 1583. The ships disappear in the sand, perhaps for decades, and then the wind drives the sand away, and the ships reappear, like ghosts.

"Strong winds, blowing sands, exposed forty wrecks in a row," wrote an eighteenth-century visitor, "and when the sand was blown back it uncovered forty more." This is, of course, the nature of sandy islands. The same thing happens—or did happen—in the Magdalens, on the Outer Banks of North Carolina, on the shores of Long Island.

With its herds of wild ponies and breeding seals, its towering dunes and long, lethal offshore bars, Sable remains a wild and eerie place. The sand conceals the makeshift huts of shipwrecked sailors, the foundations of vanished lighthouses and complete buried dwellings. It hides figureheads and trailboards, cannonballs and cod jiggers. In the early twentieth century, when the island was an important radio post, the operators had entire collections of skulls and bones, wooden sabots and belt buckles. As one memorable description puts it, "Sable wears forever round her throat a necklace of men's bones like the grisly souvenirs of a cannibal."

The moment a ship runs aground she comes under the law of salvage, which was always heavily tilted in favor of salvagers. An ancient law of Greenland provided that "whoever finds driftwood or the spoils of a shipwreck on the sand enjoys it as his own, though he does not live there. But he must haul it ashore and lay a stone upon it as a token that someone has taken possession of it, and this stone is the deed of security."

For shore dwellers, a wrecked ship could be a treasure house, yielding trade goods, furnishings, animals, bullion, building materials and anything else a ship or a passenger might carry. Salvagers often stripped the corpses in the surf before burying them, picking up watches and jewelry, cash and clothing. And even if the ship's people survived, the vessel and its contents were there for the taking. At dangerous points on the coast such as Key West and the Bahamas, salvaging was a recognized and rewarding occupation.

Given the larcenous and murderous streak in human nature, it was but a short step from salvage to piracy and to active wrecking—luring ships ashore by showing false navigation lights, known as Judas lights, which were sometimes hung from the necks of grazing cows. Wrecking was honed to a fine art on certain parts of the coasts of England, the Caribbean and Newfoundland, and no doubt on other coasts, as well. The dangerous shoreline of New Jersey claimed nine ships in the month of February, 1846, giving rise to rumors that wreckers were decoying ships onto the beach. The press was full of stories about "the notorious Barnegat pirates" and of "dread deeds of death and depredation upon the unfortunate castaways of the seas, committed with such unparalleled enormities by the lawless wreckers of the Jersey Coast, with whose shocking reports of horrors the land still rings."

The governor appointed a commission to inquire, and the commissioners duly reported that the stories were "utterly untrue; that there are no inhuman and guilty actors therein to be punished, and that the state ought to be relieved from the odium of such barbarity." Maybe so: but in the commission's indignant concern for the good name of the state one discerns a faint tint of whitewash.

Pirates go one step further than wreckers, attacking ships at sea, and they, too, have often operated not from ships but from the beach. Beach-based piracy flourished on the coast of North Africa until quite recently; small, fast-sailing feluccas would overhaul small merchant vessels, board them and rob them, sometimes killing the whole crew. Joshua Slocum, the first man ever to sail single-handed around the world, gives a vivid account of an escape from such a vessel when departing from Gibraltar in 1894. He was similarly threatened by shore-based Patagonian native pirates as he beat his way through the islands around the southern tip of South America.

Small-scale piracy persists in the Caribbean, where wealthy yachtsmen sometimes find their anchored vessels boarded in the night by thugs in dugouts launched from the beach—and piracy positively flourishes in a few areas like the Strait of Malacca, where many incidents are reported each year. "Keep a watch astern," a retired captain once told me. "You always keep a watch forward, but hardly anyone ever looks astern. That's where they get you. They slip up under your stern in fast motorboats, toss a grapnel on the after rail and swarm up the rope. The first you know about it is when they show up on the bridge and take over the ship."

But if there were wreckers and pirates on the one hand, there were guardians and heroic rescuers on the other. Many a sand spit is adorned by a lighthouse, for instance, warning ships away from the beach. The use of lights as warnings to mariners is an ancient practice, but until recent centuries such lights were rare. In the *Odyssey*, Homer mentions hilltop fires that guided mariners, and the Phoenicians are known to have established lighthouses along their trading routes. The most famous early lighthouse was the 440-foot Pharos of Alexandria, one of the Seven Wonders of the World. Built around 280 BCE, it stood for 1,500 years. The first lighthouse in North America was erected at Boston and went into service in 1716; the second, at the French colony of Louisbourg, Cape Breton, followed in 1733.

Ships still went ashore, however, and in the nineteenth century, many maritime nations established shelters for castaways on the more dangerous beaches. In America they were known as Charity Houses, and most were rude and basic. One might survive in them for a while, but without help most castaways would still perish. To Thoreau the Charity House he saw on the beach at Cape Cod in 1864 represented not safety, but merely "a stage to the grave." For Thoreau, the beach was anything but a field of pleasure:

It is a wild, rank place, and there is no flattery in it. Strewn with crabs, horse-shoes and razor-clams, and whatever the sea casts up—a vast morgue where famished dogs may range in packs, and crows come daily to glean the pittance which the tide leaves them. The carcasses of men and beasts together lie stately up upon its shelf, rotting and bleaching in the sun and waves, and each tide turns them in their beds, and tucks fresh sand under them. There is naked Nature, inhumanly sincere, wasting no thought on man, nibbling at the cliffy shore where gulls wheel amid the spray.

By Thoreau's time, the British had already inaugurated a life-saving program. As early as the 1770s a rescue boat was being kept on the beach in Formby, Lancashire, and the Crew Trust of Bamburgh, Northumberland, was patrolling the local beach on horseback during storms, watching for ships in trouble. Perhaps the pivotal moment occurred in 1789, when a ship called *Adventure* was wrecked at the mouth of the River Tyne. Her crew clung to the wreck while their strength lasted and then fell, one by one, into the sea, while spectators on the shore could only watch helplessly. The next year, the Crew Trust bought an "unimmergible" boat designed by an innovative coach builder, Lionel Lukin; this may have been the first lifeboat.

In the following years, various other lifeboats were placed around the country. One of the crewmen on the Isle of Man was Sir William Hillary, who had led a lifeboat crew credited with saving 305 lives. In 1823, Hillary wrote "Appeal to the Nation," which led to the foundation of the National Institution for the Preservation of Life from Shipwreck, with King George IV as patron. The institution established a chain of lifeboat stations around the British coast and became the Royal National Lifeboat Institution in 1854.

In Canada—which was not yet a country—the first Superintendent of the Humane Establishment on Sable Island was appointed in 1801, and crews have been stationed there ever since; the Canadian Coast Guard still maintains a Quonset hut on the island to accommodate shipwreck survivors. In the United States, Congress established the first American lifesaving stations on the Jersey coast in 1848—a direct result of the suspiciously heavy losses of 1846.

The beach-based rescuers developed a variety of techniques. One of the most effective was to fire rockets with light messenger lines out to stranded ships; those aboard would pull a heavy line out to them, and tie it high in the wreckage. The rescuers would send out a *breeches buoy*—a canvas seat, like a pair of pants without legs, hanging from a pulley. Then they could pull the victims ashore one after another, much as a housewife might reel in the clothes from a clothesline.

When possible, surfmen could row out to the wreck in surfboats launched from four-wheeled carts, which could be pushed into the breakers. By the twentieth century, the Australian Surf Lifesaving Association was holding competitions in which crews raced out through the breakers to rescue "patients" acting the role of distressed swimmers; their skills are said to have been responsible for saving 150,000 lives in 50 years.

In storm conditions, of course, the breakers could capsize the boats in a twinkling, and many rescuers became victims. As a grim saying of the American surfmen puts it, "The regulation book says you have to go out. It doesn't say anything about coming back."

~

Attitudes toward the beach began to change in the mid-eighteenth century, when physicians began to take an interest in the health benefits the beach might afford. The seamen of ancient Greece believed that seawater was a useful purgative, and seamen through the ages had followed their example, though most people thought (and still think) that seawater is poisonous and undrinkable.

In our own time, however, that view has been challenged by Dr. Alain Bombard, a French physician whose experience treating sailors and fishermen convinced him that castaways could endure in life rafts for many weeks, if necessary, and that most died not from hunger or thirst, but from fear, ignorance and a lack of determination to survive. Noting that a pint and a half of seawater contains only the amount of salt permitted in a normal diet, Bombard concluded that a healthy person could drink a modest amount of seawater without damage, supplementing it with rainwater and with liquids pressed from fishes. A person can live up to 30 days without food—and the sea can also provide food in the form of fish, plankton and seaweed. But people die in a few days without water.

To prove his theory, Bombard crossed the Atlantic from Tangier to Barbados in a 16-foot inflatable boat, taking only the implements a castaway might have and eating and drinking only what he could glean from the sea. At one point he went three weeks without fresh water. The voyage took 65 days, and Bombard lost 55 pounds in the process. But he was otherwise tolerably healthy, and he had made his point.

The new health-driven attitude toward the beach dates from 1753, when the august Oxford University Press published Dr. Richard Russell's *Glandular Diseases: or a Dissertation on the Use of Sea-Water in Affections of the Glands*. Russell was convinced that drinking moderate amounts of seawater could rectify a wide range of human ailments, including "the consumption [tuberculosis] which greatly afflicts our island, and in the cure of which our physicians find the greatest difficulty."

The book was widely discussed by the medical profession, and the notion that the beach was a healthy place soon became fashionable. Dr. Russell lived in Lewes, Sussex, and as early as 1736 he had suggested that one of his patients "try the waters" at the nearby fishing village of Brighton, on the English Channel. The idea that the seaside was a healthy place caught on. But dunkings and dosages could occupy only part of the day, and the seaside resorts became social gathering places. By 1778, Brighton had been transformed; drawings made that year show a circulating library, and two substantial inns with ballrooms, card rooms and assembly rooms. More than 200 houses had been built, including a mansion for the Duke of Marlborough, and a promenade was covered with elegant strollers. By 1791, the Royal Sea-Bathing Infirmary had been established at the less fashionable east-coast resort of Margate.

Increasing numbers of invalids and health enthusiasts appeared on the beaches, decorously clad in full-length "bathing costumes." They had not come to the beach to swim or tan; they had come to drink the water, to wash in it or to be immersed in it. Victorian bathers did not wade out and swim; they entered the water from small changing rooms on wheels, which were pulled into the water by horses. These were called bathing machines, and they looked somewhat like portable outdoor toilets. The bathing machine concealed the bather and allowed him or her to descend discreetly into the waves, preserved from the observation of vulgar eyes. Diffident bathers might be seized and dunked by "dippers"—husky fishermen or their wives.

Until mid-century, the seaside resort remained an enclave of the privileged classes. The democratization of the beach was achieved by railway lines connecting the seaside resorts to the great industrial cities. In 1841, a railway line joined London and Brighton, and in 1877 a line was built between New York and Coney Island. Pleasure piers were built at seaside resorts on both sides of the Atlantic—at Weymouth, Dorset, in 1812, at Ryde on the Isle of Wight in 1813-14, and later at such watering places as Blackpool and Atlantic City, New Jersey. They are still common at beaches throughout the United States and Britain; in many places, they are primarily fishing platforms.

Music, fireworks, theater, restaurants—all the traditional amusements and pastimes found their way to the beach. Whole traditions sprang up at these amusement centers—rides, vaudeville shows, Punch and Judy puppet theaters, exhibitions, musical comedies. In 1896, a truly bizarre railway, purely a novelty, commenced service between Brighton and Rottingdean; known as the Daddy-Long-Legs, it consisted of a 150-passenger car mounted on 24-foot stilts, with the tracks running right in the water. Resorts like Blackpool and Atlantic City flourished.

Blackpool remains the most visited beach in Britain, attracting 17 million people a year. But probably the most famous—and notorious—of all beach resorts is Coney Island, New York, which has entertained something over two billion visitors in its long history. Its first hotel was erected in 1829, and by the 1840s it was a rather exclusive resort, favored by such celebrities as Daniel Webster, Jenny Lind, Herman Melville, Washington Irving and P.T. Barnum.

By the 1880s, however, Coney Island had become a day excursion by rail from New York. At that time, the U.S. worker was putting in 60-hour weeks; he and his family had little time for recreation, and indeed little notion of how to handle leisure time. Coney Island showed them how. As one writer puts it, "it would not be too much to say that at Coney America learned how to play."

The world's first roller coaster was built at Coney Island in 1884; it was the precursor of a whole host of thrilling rides. The hot dog was invented there. The island's cabarets and theaters saw the first performances of innumerable popular songs; its actors and performers went on to major careers in New York and Hollywood. The whole idea of the amusement park stems from the success of Coney Island. Disneyland is its direct descendant.

Naturally, the teeming mass of carefree humanity that could be found at Coney Island throughout the summer attracted a host of confidence tricksters, gangsters, thieves and charlatans. (The word *coney* means *rabbit*, and an Elizabethan slang term for a con man was *coney catcher*, which seems appropriate. The name was originally Dutch—*Konjn Eiland* —and it may refer to a large rabbit population, which once thrived on the island.) Eventually Coney Island became synonymous with trinkets and illusive romance, tawdry entertainment and small-time corruption. Coney Island and its many imitators had become raucous midways where people, rather than compensating for the squalor of sooty urban life by a brief experience of nature's magnificence, overwhelmed the beach in a tide of industrial ugliness.

༄

The crowds who came to the beaches beginning in the nineteenth century developed new sports to amuse themselves. The first of these was swimming.

As an activity rather than a sport, swimming predates recorded history. Mosaics in Pompeii show people swimming, and an Egyptian bas-relief of 2000 BCE shows a swimmer using something similar to a crawl stroke. Swimming was a part of the curriculum in Greek and Roman military training, and an imperial edict made it part of the Japanese curriculum in 1603. One of the earliest printed books was *The Art of Swimming*, published in 1538.

Before the emergence of the seaside resort, however, swimming was something most Westerners did out of necessity, not for fun. In medieval Europe, conventional wisdom held that seawater was contaminated and caused disease. (People thought the same about night air.) In temperate climates, fishermen commonly could not swim; they argued that anyone who fell overboard would soon die in the cold water in any case, so why prolong the agony?

Other cultures had other ways. Many Natives in North America were accomplished swimmers, and for people on tropical islands swimming was as natural as walking—and almost as useful. One of the earliest world cruisers, Dwight Long, sailing his 32-foot ketch through the South Pacific during the 1930s, noted that Polynesian children could sometimes swim before they could walk. His Polynesian companion Timi thought white men were foolish to fish with lures and lines. Living in a fecund lagoon, the fish weren't hungry: why would they bite? Instead, his people caught fish by diving into the lagoons, swimming underwater and spearing them—a sport that spread around the world after the advent of scuba diving equipment.

In Tahiti, Long met Polynesian pearl divers who could swim to depths of 120 to 150 feet with no equipment at all, staying down for as much as two full minutes. At Thursday Island, Australia, he found Japanese divers working at 300 feet using only a diving helmet, at a time when the U.S. Navy had concluded that humans could not survive such dives below 210 feet.

Swimming contests may have been held in Japan as early as two thousand years ago, but modern competitive swimming began in London around 1837. By then the Romantic poets had brought the appreciation of nature into vogue, and the ocean had become a symbol of power and mystery. Shelley had been drowned at sea, and Lord Byron had swum the Hellespont in 1810 to prove that the Greek hero Leander could indeed have done so. Byron had achieved instantaneous and enormous European popularity with *Childe Harold's Pilgrimage,* with its brooding, misanthropic vision—and he had found magic and mystery on the beach:

> *There is a pleasure in the pathless woods,*
> *There is a rapture on the lonely shore,*
> *There is society where none intrudes,*
> *By the deep Sea, and music in its roar;*
> *I love not man the less, but Nature more ...*

If Byron was a swimmer, lesser mortals could swim, too. Early English swimmers favored the sidestroke and the breaststroke, but in 1844 two Native Americans named Tobacco and Flying Gull amazed Britain by swimming 130 feet in just 30 seconds, using a windmill motion with their arms and an up-and-down kick with their legs. In 1873, J. Arthur Trudgen unveiled a similar stroke, an overhand motion combined with a scissors kick, which became known as the trudgen crawl. Five years later an Englishman named Frederick Cavill observed the flutter kick used by Australian aborigines and married it with Trudgen's overhand stroke to create the Australian crawl. Using the new stroke, he set a world record in 1902 by covering 100 yards in just 58.4 seconds.

Swimming was sufficiently well established to be an Olympic sport from the time of the Games' revival in 1896. It was followed by high diving in 1904 and springboard diving in 1908. By the 1920s, the Victorian bathing costume had shrunk to trunks and a singlet for men and a one-piece swimsuit for women, and the opportunity to swim was helping to lure millions of people to the world's beaches.

By then the first modern surfers were making their appearance, led by the great Olympic swimming champion from Hawaii, Duke Kahanamoku. No wonder: surfing had originated in Hawaii and Tahiti, where Captain Cook had observed the practice during the 1770s. In Hawaii, the nobility once surfed on long wooden boards in connection with their religious observances. European missionaries naturally considered the practice immoral and stifled it for almost a century.

Duke Kahanamoku and a colleague, George Freeth, revived it around 1900. Freeth rediscovered the technique of standing up on a board and brought the sport to Redondo Beach, California, in 1907. Meanwhile the Duke formed the first surfing club, in Waikiki, and used his celebrity to popularize the sport. It grew rapidly after the introduction of lightweight synthetic boards in the 1950s, spreading to such other countries as Australia, New Zealand, South Africa, Peru and Brazil. (A few hardy souls go surfing even in Canadian winters, notably the Maritime author Lesley Choyce.) The first World Amateur Championships took place in Sydney, Australia, in 1964, and a professional series began in 1975.

By the 1960s, the sport had become popular enough to have generated a whole youth culture, centered in Southern California. *Beach Party* (1963), starring Frankie Avalon, Annette Funicello and Bob Cummings, was the first of a series of beach movies, and its release was an important enough event in cultural history for the film to be screened at the Museum of Modern Art. Accompanied by the music of the Beach Boys and others, the California beach culture briefly dominated American styles.

Among the best consistent surfing waves are those at Waimea Bay, Hawaii, rising to what was formerly thought to be the "ridable limit" of 30-35 feet. For many years the highest wave ever ridden was believed to be a 50-footer ridden by a Hawaiian named Holua in 1868. That wave was a tsunami, and Holua was riding for his life. The longest rides took place on tidal bores like the one in the River Severn in England, where surfers could ride almost three miles on the advancing crest of the river's tidal bore.

By 2013, however, all those records had been shattered. Professional surfers had ridden 18 miles on a tidal bore up the Petitcodiac River in Moncton, New Brunswick; extreme surfers were surfing small tsunamis created by calving icebergs, and one, Garrett McNamara, had carved his breath-taking way down a 100-foot monster arising from an underwater canyon at Navaré, Portugal. Surfing, in turn, begat three additional sports, skateboarding, sailboarding (or wind-surfing) and snowboarding. Sailboarding has grown phenomenally since its invention by a Californian named Hoyle Schweitzer, who patented the first sailboard in 1969. Both sailboarding and snowboarding now have complete infrastructures of their own, with international competitions in several classes. Sailboarding became an Olympic sport in 1984, snowboarding in 1998.

Is there any limit to the pleasures human beings can pursue on a beach? Plays and pageants, eating and drinking, concert-going and kite fighting, ball games and board games, pitching horseshoes and riding horses—the beach is a site for an apparently inexhaustible range of arts and pastimes, from painting, surf casting and writing to sand sculpture, gambling and sex.

∽

The beach has also been used for more earnest purposes. When the Wright brothers made their first flights at Kitty Hawk, on the Outer Banks of North Carolina, they inaugurated an industry that has radically reshaped the way human beings live. They chose Kitty Hawk deliberately: its mile-wide hard sand beach ran almost straight for 60 miles, making it the best possible runway in a world without airports.

The Wright brothers were a shrewd and observant pair, watching the comparative flight patterns of hawks and buzzards, measuring wind speeds and noting weather patterns, talking to local people. On his first visit, in 1900, Wilbur Wright remarked on the evidence that the beach was migrating. In a letter, he commented that his tent was pitched on land that "was formerly a fertile valley cultivated by some ancient Kitty Hawker. Now only a few rotten limbs, the topmost branches of the trees that grew in this valley, protrude from the sand." Nearby, a neighbor was tearing down a house that was about to be buried by the retreating dunes.

During those same years, a few hundred miles south at Daytona Beach, the pioneers of the auto industry were using the local beach as a proving ground for their earliest models. "The Most Famous Beach in the World," as local boosters called it, offers 18 miles of hard-packed sand, and it has been closely associated with automobiles for nearly a century. Sig Haugdahl drove his "Wisconsin Special" down the beach at Daytona at 180.27 MPH in 1922, setting a world record, and Sir Malcolm Campbell achieved a later world record of 276.82 MPH there. The State of Florida designated Daytona's beach as a public road, and it was regularly used as a racetrack for stock cars until 1959.

It is still a public road, complete with traffic signs and speed limits. As far as the eye can see, cars, pickups and campers are parked against the seawall, while a long line of cars moves slowly past. Girls in the briefest of bathing suits and portly seniors in Panama hats amble along the promenade past apartment buildings and hotels. Little shops sell sunglasses, ice cream, towels and souvenirs. People lay out their picnics between the parked cars, eloquent testimony to the American love affair with both the automobile and the beach.

The highest altitudes and greatest speeds, of course, are attained by the rockets launched a few miles south of Daytona at Cape Canaveral—

which was located on the beach specifically to give easy access to long test ranges over the ocean. The landmark flights of Alan Shepard, John Glenn and Neil Armstrong all began here, as did the tragic shuttle flight of the Challenger in 1986.

By now, images of rocket launchings are no great novelty, but it is still a heart-stopping sight when you see one in real life—especially with the image of the blazing parabolic curves of the Challenger's falling wreckage burned into your memory. Standing on a beach in Melbourne, just south of Canaveral, I once watched the long silver pencil with the blazing tail tracing a tall, gentle curve into the blue Florida sky, shrinking and vanishing in a couple of minutes, bound for space. You stand with your head tilted back, your feet in the sand, gazing at it: the ship is so big, so fast, and then it is gone, and you think: there are human beings inside that slender metal fuselage, sitting above that blazing fire, and they have just gone right out of this world.

Beaches are also made to serve the purposes of industry. For generations, shallow holding pans on tropical beaches have been used to produce salt. The pans are filled by the rising tide, then sealed off; the water evaporates, leaving the salt behind. Conversely, desalinization plants discard the salt and extract fresh water for human consumption. Nuclear power plants often use ocean water to cool their reactors, and France and Canada have developed electrical generating stations driven by the tides.

Beaches have been drilled for oil and mined for zircon and gold, but the most spectacular mining operation ever conducted on a beach was created on the coast of South-West Africa (now Namibia) by Consolidated Diamond Mines. The diamond-bearing gravels the company was mining along the shore also sloped off under the sea, so the company built a 200-foot dike nearly a quarter of a mile offshore, pumped the enclosure dry and dug diamonds from the former seafloor.

Most beach mining, however, produces a much more humble material: sand. Sand is an essential component of concrete; broken shells are a useful source of lime. For centuries, human beings took material from the beach as though the supply were inexhaustible. As the human population continues to grow, however, and as people continue to migrate to the coasts—especially in the United States—the limits become ever more obvious. In the Los Angeles area, the construction industry mines more than 23 million tons of sand and gravel annually. In the past, most of it has come from beaches, riverbeds and dunes.

Nature cannot replace it that fast. The problem is not new, and it is not limited to California, though—as so often with things Californian—it has perhaps reached its most dramatic level there. There are plenty of examples around the world, in Denmark and the Channel Islands and in northern Australia, among other places. Sand mining on the beaches is still legal in some parts of the United States—in Washington State, for example. Mining always destabilizes the coastline to some extent, and the results are sometimes unexpected and dramatic. In Devon, the village of Hallsands had to be abandoned in 1902 after beach mining had allowed the sea to erode its way right up to the buildings.

In California, of course, the rivers provide almost all the sediment for the beaches—and the rivers have been dammed and diverted for flood control, electrical generation, irrigation and drinking water. The Santa Clara River has lost 37 percent of its sediment; the Ventura has lost 66 percent. And the submarine canyons of the California coast swallow enormous quantities of sand.

Once upon a time—a couple of generations ago—the rivers supplied enough sand to the beaches to compensate for the loss of sand to the canyons and the oceanic abyss beyond the narrow continental shelf. Now the sand budget is badly out of balance; much more goes out than comes in. Meanwhile, much of the missing sediment is accumulating as silt behind the dams, slowly filling the reservoirs and artificial lakes. Eventually—within the next century, in some cases—the reservoirs will become shallow sheets of water over vast plateaus of silt. Nobody really knows what can be done about that. The wealthy cities and irrigated fields of the American southwest could not exist without these elaborate water projects, but their life span is shockingly brief.

Some beach mining is not deliberate. When sand trespasses onto roads and is trucked away by municipal work crews, the very substance of the beach is reduced. Eric Bird, an Australian scientist, points out another striking example of what might be called "accidental mining." Resort beaches, says Bird, "gradually lose sand as it is removed by visitors to the beach, adhering to their skin, clothes or towels, or trapped in their shoes. The quantities are very small, but the losses are cumulative: no one brings sand on to the beach." Mechanical cleaning at resort beaches also picks up sediment along with litter and seaweed; on one Australian beach, Bird reports, scientists estimate that visitors and beach cleaning are removing, every year, half a cubic meter of sand from every 100 square meters of beach.

∽

Since World War II, development on the beach has exploded beyond the wildest dreams of the Victorians. Dick Ludington is a conservationist in North Carolina, but he grew up in Miami, and in his youth even the beaches of Miami were relatively pristine; more of the shoreline was undeveloped than developed. Today, he says, there isn't a single piece of undeveloped ocean frontage on either coast of the contiguous United States large enough to be worth buying for conservation purposes. The United States has set large stretches aside as parkland, wildlife refuges and national seashores, but some unique opportunities have slipped away.

"In 1976-77 the U.S. Fish and Wildlife Service did a sea turtle assessment and figured out that their best chance of having a positive impact on sea turtle nesting was to preserve Hutchinson Island in Florida, between Fort Pierce Inlet and St. Lucie Inlet," Ludington says. "The study determined that the entire island could be acquired for $46 million. That was an enormous number in those days, but today that would be pocket change. The money being spent in Florida today annually on acquisition is about half a billion. Today the cost of Hutchinson Island would be—I don't know, maybe a billion dollars. So it's impossible."

Three factors, says Ludington, have given rise to this assault on the coastline: affluence, air-conditioning and jet travel. Without air-conditioning, "nobody would want to live on the coast of Florida after March. None of the early settlers in Florida wanted to live on the beach. It was a desolate place; you had problems with fresh water; and at sunrise and sunset, if there wasn't a breeze, you got eaten alive by no-see-ums."

Jet travel allows northerners to fly south even for a couple of days and permits affluent people to acquire, develop and occupy beach properties anywhere in the world. Whole condo developments in Florida, for instance, have been created and marketed exclusively to wealthy Germans. Such development has reached well down the coast of Mexico and is racing southward through Central America. The story is the same on any coast near a large population or a major airport: in California and Hawaii, on the Mediterranean coast of Europe, on the Gold Coast of Australia, on the coast of Brazil. Despite the retirement of Fidel Castro, the beaches of Cuba are relatively unscathed, but developers who realize that the regime cannot last forever are already preparing their plans.

And if it is good to be on the shore during one's holidays, why not the rest of the year? Why not live there, work there, retire there? In the United States, the population has migrated steadily out of the center of the country toward the coasts. More than 50 percent of the population lives on the coastal strip that constitutes just ten percent of the land. The same is true elsewhere, though not in Canada. Demographically, Canada is a ribbon of population along the U.S. border; its life has always been dominated by Quebec and Ontario, the provinces in the middle of the ribbon. In Europe, however, 38 percent of the population of the 18 Mediterranean states now lives on the coasts, which represent

15 percent of their land area. In Spain, 12 percent of the population lived on the coast in 1900; today the figure is 35 percent.

In fact, two-thirds of the world's population now lives on the coasts, canalizing river estuaries, dredging barrier island inlets, digging finger canals, fortifying harbors, constructing elaborate buildings and protecting them with seawalls, erecting groins to trap the passing sand, flushing sewage into the sea and dumping bargeloads of garbage into the shallow offshore water. Fly low over a heavily populated coastline on a calm, clear day and you see the discolored plumes of pollution spreading seaward for miles from every major city. A few years ago, residents of Long Island found their shoreline littered with syringes, latex gloves and other medical debris, which had been dumped offshore and carried back in by the tides. Communities on the west coast of Ireland complain about Canadian debris such as empty outboard motor-oil containers, which have migrated clear across the Atlantic on the North Atlantic Drift.

It is easy to deplore such obvious fouling of the beaches. But in the end, is the fouling any worse than the way we have reshaped the beach itself in accordance with our notions of conquest, permanence, dominion? Our holiday beaches are dead beaches, imitation beaches. Smoothed and combed and lifeless, they are as much an affront to nature as an oil spill. Rinsed and agitated by the surf, an open-ocean beach recovers from an oil spill in a decade or two. How long will it take to recover from Coney Island? The oil spill offends us because it messes up our beach. But the beach was never ours in the first place.

⁓

The intense development on low-lying coasts is not only bad for the coast; it also sets the scene for horrific disasters. Lim Vallianos of the Corps of Engineers considers it "a tragedy" that the U.S. east coast did not suffer even a big hurricane—comparable to Hurricane Hazel in 1954, for example—for several decades. Dr. Robert H. Simpson, former director of the U.S. National Hurricane Center in Miami, calls it "a very dangerous thing to go so long between hurricanes. It just causes a larger number of incredulous people—nonbelievers."

The National Hurricane Center rates the intensity of hurricanes on a rising scale from 1 to 5. In the late twentieth century, during a 60-year period, no hurricanes reached the Atlantic coast of North America at Category 5 strength—though several Category 5 storms did reach the US Gulf Coast. Even Hurricane Andrew, in 1992, was only a high 4. It inflicted record levels of property damage largely because there was more property in its path to be damaged.

Almost all the development on the beaches took place during those six decades of relative peace. Many of the new homeowners simply could not imagine the possibilities.

"You can buy a beachfront house when you're sitting in Kansas, and that's part of the problem," says Orrin Pilkey. "Or in Indiana—or even here in Durham, North Carolina. And those buyers don't know anything about ocean processes. They go down on a beautiful calm day when the sun is shining and the lagoon side is dead calm and the open ocean side just has little two-foot waves out there. They don't see the impact of rain, they don't see the impact of wind, they don't know about shoreline erosion rates, and they sure don't know about storms."

A major tropical storm is called a hurricane in the Atlantic, a typhoon in the Pacific and a williwaw in Australia. It begins as a vapor-laden column of air rising over a warm area of the sea about ten degrees north or south of the equator—in effect, a tube in the sky, with wet warm air rising through it. On the surface, the winds are blowing toward the center of the tube. Once the tube is established, if it is far enough from the equator to feel the Coriolis force (the rotary force exerted on moving objects by the Earth's rotation), it begins to spin, just as water spins in a toilet—and for exactly the same reason. The warm air rises into the cooler upper air, and water condenses out of it. The rains begin. The prevailing easterly winds, the trade winds, nudge the whole tube westward.

The release of the energy in the warm moist air is the engine that drives the hurricane. Dry air will stop it, and in areas like the Vietnamese highlands, it does. But continental east coasts in Asia, Africa, Australia, the Caribbean and North America are characterized by warm ocean currents such as the Gulf Stream and the Kuro Shio. These currents carry equatorial water northward as part of the great circulation in the oceans. When the hurricane arrives, the warm moist air on the coasts is sucked inward and upward, feeding the storm.

At the coast the storm's behavior depends on what it encounters in the atmosphere—low-pressure troughs, anticyclones or whatever. In general, the storm tends to turn toward the pole, often curving back out to sea and speeding up as it goes. In the right conditions, a hurricane can also travel immense distances over land. In 1954, Hurricane Carol traveled 400 miles in 12 hours on its way to a destructive rendezvous with New England, while Hurricane Hazel reached into Ontario and battered Toronto. An 1888 hurricane was still a fierce storm when it hit Greenland, and the Galveston hurricane of 1900 recurved across the Atlantic, pummeled Europe and was still a recognizable storm when it reached Siberia. In Washington, Ben Mieremet showed me a map that plotted the tracks of all 793 Atlantic hurricanes that occurred between 1886 and 1980. The whole western Atlantic was solid black, with fingerlike storm tracks streaming eastward into the ocean, northward deep into Canada and westward all across the continent.

One of the rare Category 5 hurricanes of the late twentieth century was Camille, which came ashore on the Gulf Coast in 1969 before curving back to Virginia. Camille was a compact, powerful storm with winds of 125 to 200 miles per hour. When it had passed, 130 people were dead and 4,310 were injured, more than 40,000 homes had been damaged or destroyed, and the area had suffered more than $1 billion in property damage. One of Camille's unexpected side effects was to focus the attention of geologist Orrin Pilkey, whose parents' home in Waveland, Mississippi, had been demolished by the storm. Pilkey was an authority on ocean-bottom sediments; Camille turned him into a coastal geologist.

Climate-change models show an increasing frequency of severe storms as the Earth warms, so it is no surprise that the decade when the most Category 5 storms struck the Gulf Coast is 2000 to 2009, with eight such hurricanes. One of these was Hurricane Katrina, the storm that flooded and flattened New Orleans, killing nearly 2,000 people.

The worst death tolls on record have been caused by Asian hurricanes. In 1737, a 36-foot storm surge described as "a wall of water" crashed into Kolkata and drowned 300,000 people. In 1876, 100,000 died at Chittagong; in 1881, 300,000 died at Haiphong, Vietnam. By comparison with Kolkata and Chittagong, the coasts of North America are sparsely settled, and in recent years the hurricane warning system has greatly reduced the loss of life. All the same, the former director of the National Hurricane Center once told Pilkey and his collaborator, Wallace Kaufman, that horrendous disasters are still possible; he could tick off a dozen places where 10,000 people could die in a single day.

Consider, for example, the nightmare that could easily play out in the Florida Keys. The storm surge from a major hurricane may rise as much as 25 feet above normal sea level, with huge storm waves cresting on its back. The maximum elevation of the Keys is 17 feet. About 65,000 people live there, nearly half of them in Key West, at the very end of the island chain. The Keys have been swept by hurricane seas repeatedly, but not recently. In 1796, for instance, a storm carried ships clear over the Keys, and in 1846 a hurricane sent five feet of water through the streets of Key West.

On Labor Day, 1935, a Level 5 hurricane rampaged across the Keys, raising the water level 20 feet and destroying a railway then under construction. About 760 people were living in the Keys at the time, and 408 were killed. For three years afterward the only way in and out of Key West was by boat, until a highway was built on the old railroad right-of-way. That's the Overseas Highway, a two-lane road that crosses 42 bridges in the process of linking the 34 islands. The Overseas Highway is the only escape route from the Keys. Fodor's Florida guide describes it—under normal conditions—as "a 110-mile traffic jam."

Even today, the National Hurricane Center issues hurricane warnings only 18 to 24 hours before a storm hits the coast, and it can predict the storm's point of arrival only within a 100-mile band. The center is reluctant to issue such warnings, since an evacuation of the coast costs $640,000 per mile of coastline evacuated, and every false alarm increases the likelihood that the next warning may be ignored.

I would not want to be in Key West 18 hours in advance of a Level 5 hurricane, at the end of a 110-mile road that carries 700 vehicles an hour if nobody has broken down and if all the bridges are in service. I am tempted to say that the tempest, the wall of black water sweeping over the Key and the winds that peel bark from the trees are unimaginable. But they are not. They have been imagined by John D. MacDonald, in the novel *Condominium*, published in 1977. MacDonald's account of a hurricane demolishing a crowded key and a bayside city is factually accurate and meticulously imagined. Sooner or later, it will happen. It may have happened by the time you read this.

Dreadful storms can assault northern coastlines, too, of course. In August, 1927, for instance, a storm suddenly formed off the coast of Nova Scotia, with winds of more than 100 miles per hour. Orchards and buildings blew down, wharves were demolished, and numerous fishing schooners foundered off Sable Island with great loss of life. In 2003, Hurricane Juan charged across Nova Scotia and Prince Edward Island, killing eight people and causing $300 million in damage

But on northern coastlines the ground rises higher than 17 feet, and there are no cities 110 miles from the mainland shore.

The Demon Lover

There is something poignant about these two people, carefully upending the cobbles, peering intently into the tidal pools, drifting over the shallows in a skiff they have rented for a shilling an hour and dredging the bottom with sieves and pails.

"What do you say? Shall we try it?" says the man, after they have towed the pail a short distance. He is tall, and he wears a black frock coat. He is the picture of a Victorian gentleman in his mid-forties. The boy, who is eight or nine, is so wrapped in scarves and warm jackets that he looks round as a dumpling.

"Aye, aye, sir!" cries the boy, giving a pull on the line. "'Tis mortal heavy!"

They hoist the bucket and spill its contents onto the floorboards. Sun stars, stones, algae and nut crabs, glistening wet, spill into the bottom of the boat.

At the end of the day they put their treasures into an enormous wicker basket—the son would remember the sound of its creaking all his life, as he would remember the sight of his father's hand darting down to pick up a shell—and they take their best finds home. In the evening they pore over them, the boy seeing all the details with his naked eye, the man using a lens. The father makes drawings of the creatures they have observed. The drawings are accurate, graceful and sometimes oddly frightening.

At the end of the evening, father and son put the living specimens into an aquarium—the first successful aquarium in the world. The father, whose name is Philip Henry Gosse, is a famous naturalist who has already published *Introduction to Zoology* (1843), and he is about to publish other books like *The Aquarium* (1854) and *Evenings at the Microscope* (1859)—which will start a rage for home aquariums; soon thousands of people in England will want them. Perhaps his most influential book will be his account of the things he and his little boy saw together, a book called *A Year at the Shore* (1865).

Having migrated to Newfoundland at 17, farmed in Quebec and taught in Alabama before returning to England, Gosse has recently found himself a widower, breast cancer having taken a wife "to whom he was most tenderly attached," says one source, "and whose intellectual sympathy had become a necessity to him." Left to raise their son alone, Gosse has moved to the coast, to St. Marychurch in Devonshire, where he feels both will find some peace. Like many thinking Victorians, Gosse is a troubled man, suffering from philosophical indigestion, racked by the raging conflict between the consolations of anthropocentric religion on the one hand and the cold, inhuman vistas of time and evolution evoked by such natural historians as Hutton and Darwin on the other.

Philip Gosse is a devout Christian, a lay preacher, a member of the fundamentalist Plymouth Brethren, and he is perhaps the first scientific creationist. He sees at the shoreline the marvels of God's handiwork, not the results of what Darwin will call "evolution." In 1857 he will publish a curious volume, *Omphalos,* which argues that the millions of years posited by evolutionary science were *ideal* time, passed within the mind of God, who only actualized creation when He had envisaged it in its maturity. *Omphalos* will not do much for his reputation as a scientist, but his two-volume *Manual of Marine Zoology* (1855-56) will earn him a niche in the history of science, as will his later book on sea anemones.

He is a curious father—severe, utterly convinced of the ineradicable sinfulness of humanity, firmly hostile to fanciful pursuits like poetry, fiction or drama, and yet filled with childlike wonder at the complex and elegant choreography of life at the shoreline. Frivolous literary writings are no part of his plan for his son's education. The boy will be a thoroughly competent naturalist by early adolescence, but he will know nothing of literature until he is almost a grown man.

The boy's name is Edmund, and in 1925 he will be knighted for his services to English literature. Among his circle of friends Sir Edmund Gosse will include Henry James, Rudyard Kipling, Thomas Hardy and Andre Gide. He will be a minor poet himself, and a well-known literary critic; it will be Gosse whose translations introduce Ibsen to the English-speaking world, exerting a crucial influence on his friend George Bernard Shaw. Gosse will be librarian to the House of Lords, and he will write a biography of Swinburne as well as books on eighteenth-century and modern English literature.

But at the close of the twentieth century Sir Edmund Gosse is remembered primarily for one book, which has been called "a minor classic of autobiography." The book is *Father and Son,* published in 1907. In it Gosse tells the terrible, ironic story of his father's effect on the shorelines he loved so profoundly.

"I never saw my father happy except on the beaches," Sir Edmund wrote.

> It was down on the shore, tramping along the pebbled terraces of the beach, clambering over the great blocks of fallen conglomerate which broke the white curve with rufous promontories that jutted into the sea, or, finally, bending over those shallow tidal pools in the limestone rocks which were our proper hunting-ground—it was in such circumstances as these that my Father became most easy, most happy, most human. That hard look across his brows, which it wearied me

to see, that look that came from sleepless anxiety of conscience, faded away, and left the dark countenance still always stern indeed, but serene and unupbraiding. Those pools were our mirrors, in which, reflected in the dark hyaline and framed by the sleek and shining fronds of oar-weed, there used to appear the shapes of a middle-aged man and a funny little boy, equally eager, and, I almost find the presumption to say, equally well prepared for business.

If any one goes down to those shores now, if man or boy seeks to follow in our traces, let him realise at once, before he takes the trouble to roll up his sleeves, that his zeal will end in labor lost. There is nothing, now, where in our days there was so much. Then the rocks between tide and tide were submarine gardens of a beauty that seemed often to be fabulous, and was positively delusive, since, if we delicately lifted the weed-curtains of a windless pool, though we might for a moment see its sides and floor paven with living blossoms, ivory-white, rosy-red, orange and amethyst, yet all that panoply would melt away, furled into the hollow rock, if we so much as dropped a pebble in to disturb the magic dream.

... the antiquity of these rock-pools, and the infinite succession of the soft and radiant forms, sea-anemones, sea-weeds, shells, fishes, which had inhabited them, undisturbed since the creation of the world, used to occupy my Father's fancy. We burst in, he used to say, where no one had ever thought of intruding before; and if the Garden of Eden had been situate in Devonshire, Adam and Eve, stepping lightly down to bathe in the rainbow-colored spray, would have see the identical sights that we now saw—the great prawns gliding like transparent launches, anthea waving in the twilight its thick white waxen tentacles, and the fronds of the dulse faintly streaming on the water, like huge red banners in some reverted atmosphere.

All this is long over, and done with. The ring of living beauty drawn about our shores was a very thin and fragile one. It had existed all those centuries solely in consequence of the indifference, the blissful ignorance of man. These rock-basins, fringed by corallines, filled with still water almost as pellucid as the upper air itself, thronged with beautiful sensitive forms of life—they exist no longer, they are all profaned, and emptied, and vulgarised. An army of "collectors" has passed over them, and ravaged every corner of them. The fairy paradise has been violated, the exquisite product of centuries of natural selection has been crushed under the rough paw of well-meaning, idle-minded curiosity. That my Father, himself so reverent, so conservative, had by the popularity of his books acquired the direct responsibility for a calamity that he had never anticipated, became clear enough to himself before many years had passed, and cost him great chagrin. No one will see again on the shore of England what I saw in my early childhood, the submarine vision of dark rocks, speckled and starred with an infinite variety of color, and streamed over by silken flags of royal crimson and purple.

7. The Armored Beach

The shattered water made a misty din.
Great waves looked over others coming in,
And thought of doing something to the shore
That water never did to land before.
　　　　—Robert Frost, "Once by the Pacific"

"This is a German pillbox on the coast of France," says Orrin Pilkey, flashing his first slide on the screen. It's a blocky gray concrete structure, lying in the sand at a crazy angle. "I have a French geologist friend who says there are more than 100 of these on the beaches of France. This pillbox, he said, was built 75 yards back from the beach, and now it's 25 yards *onto* the beach. So this is an example of the erosion problem and gives an international flavor to it. Shorelines are eroding everywhere.

"But on shorelines that have no buildings next to them, there is no erosion problem because nobody really cares. Nobody's calling for the Corps of Engineers, nobody's calling for the state or the federal government.

"And what this points out is that *we* are the problem. Shoreline erosion per se is *not* a problem."

Students describe this as Pilkey's little-old-ladies-in-tennis-shoes talk. He adjusts it to accommodate his audiences, but in one form or another he has given it innumerable times. He often gives the talk in east-coast towns where the dunes have washed away, new inlets are forming and properties are in danger. Quite often it is not what the audience wants to hear. The town council of Folly Beach, South Carolina, once passed a special motion declaring Pilkey's opinions to be "insulting, uninformed and radical both in content and intent."

Energetic, irrepressible, unrelenting, Pilkey is James B. Duke Professor of Geology at Duke University in Durham, North Carolina, director of the Program for the Study of Developed Shorelines and a ruthless realist about the inevitability of geological change. As one of his colleagues put it: "Not only is he built like a little bulldog, he takes hold of something as if it were a rag doll and just keeps shaking it until there's nothing left." A writer for *The Smithsonian* once described the stocky, bearded Pilkey, who carries 220 pounds on a 5'4" frame, as "built like a grenade," and many coastal engineers and beach residents consider him just as dangerous. Almost single-handedly, Pilkey has put the whole issue of shoreline retreat and the human response—or at least the American response—on the political and social map.

What *are* Pilkey's shocking opinions? When sea level is rising and shorelines are moving inland, human beings must choose from among four possible responses. They may do nothing, in which case their dwellings will eventually be swept away. They may adapt—for example, by putting their dwellings on stilts, so that storm waves can pass harmlessly below them. They may try to resist the sea by armoring the shore with seawalls, groins and revetments, or by "nourishing the beach," adding sand to replace what has been carried away. Or they may retreat by moving their shoreline structures or abandoning them.

We have been resisting for thousands of years, says Pilkey, but ultimately resistance is stupid, expensive and futile. On the shore, he says, "Nature always bats last." He is an outspoken advocate of retreat, even if it means destroying or abandoning buildings. He is also a trenchant critic of the alternatives, especially of armoring. And he is relentless in his reminders that sea level is rising *now,* that the shore is retreating *now* and that decision time is *now,* in some urgent cases, and soon, in most others.

∾

Today, in a cluttered meeting room in one of Duke's stately stone buildings, Pilkey is giving his talk privately for Charlie Doucet and me. The slides flash by, a catalogue of hubris and innocence. Long Beach, North Carolina, where a single storm in the mid-1950s, Hurricane Hazel, drove the beach inland 25 to 50 feet. A good many houses were washed away, which no doubt was a problem for the owners—but not for the beach. "The beach simply moved back in space," Pilkey says. "Look at this beach today: it's wide and healthy and handsome and everybody can use it. Shoreline retreat per se is not a problem—for the beach."

Shorelines retreat at different rates and in different ways. At Indialantic-Melbourne, Florida, the beach moves landward in abrupt jumps. At Nag's Head, North Carolina, the beach moves back six feet a year in "a steady drumbeat of retreat."

In the face of such evidence, we persist in erecting buildings on the sand, right at the edge of the water. One of Pilkey's slides shows construction workers fishing from the windows of an unfinished high-rise tower in Garden City, South Carolina. It is a bizarre image. "One of the things we've learned," Pilkey says dryly, "is that you shouldn't be able to fish from your condo window."

Pilkey has a whole sequence on the fabled Cape Hatteras lighthouse, 193 feet high, the tallest brick lighthouse in the United States. In 1870, when it was built, it was 1,500 feet from the water's edge. By 1898 the water was all around the buildings and grounds. By 1935, high tides were lapping at the base of the lighthouse. The building was abandoned and the light moved to a steel tower farther inland. Sand fencing and grass planting helped to restore the sand in front of the lighthouse. (Pilkey thinks it was natural accretion—"But why? Nobody knows.") By 1950 the lighthouse was considered stable, and the light was moved back from the steel tower to the historic lighthouse. In the 1960s, the new sand was going away, and the Corps was building groins and pumping more sand onto the beach. By 1982 the sand was gone, and the sea was knocking at the door again, occasioning a loud public debate about the future of the lighthouse. As a temporary measure it was protected by sandbags.

"They've already replenished the sand three times, so now they've decided to move it back," Pilkey says. "It's a tough structure, and it has a foundation that's only six feet deep, so it's capable of being moved. If it stays where it is, it's going to be undermined. Here's a shot of the lighthouse during the Hallowe'en Storm in 1991. Look at it—it's just being held in place by three groins. It could go tomorrow with the right storm.

"Now my view is we should either move it or let it fall in—but if we let it fall in, it should not be due to an 'accident' or 'a tragic act of God.' We should state that our policy is to let this lighthouse fall in when its time comes. And then it becomes a coastal zone management act, which would set the example for other buildings and other lighthouses."

He puts up another slide: three small, cheap concrete-block houses on the south shore of Puerto Rico, standing behind a small seawall.

"Now I think anyone would agree that cheap buildings are not worth losing a beach for. It gets more complex with 25-story condos—at least it does for other people. It doesn't for me. To save a beach, I'd bulldoze an apartment tower in the wink of an eye."

Pilkey is trying to cure human beings of a very old habit. In the book he co-authored with Wallace Kaufman, *The Beaches Are Moving*, Pilkey gives examples of shoreline engineering dating back to the Romans. Tiring of moving goods through the port of Naples, a hundred miles away, the Romans decided in the third century BCE to use the small port of Ostia, at the mouth of the Tiber. But the harbor was small, exposed and in constant need of dredging. In the year 42 CE, the Emperor Claudius decreed the creation of a new harbor two and a half miles north along the coast from the old port. The new port was 150 acres in area, protected by two huge breakwaters and connected to the Tiber (and thus to Rome) by canal.

Fifty years after its construction, the harbor was so badly silted up that it was useless, and the Emperor Trajan built an entirely new harbor behind it, entered by means of a canal through the old harbor. It was a magnificent stone-walled harbor, surrounded with warehouses, markets and public buildings, but it, too, silted up.

Ironically, the problems of Ostia and its successors were exacerbated if not caused by an earlier Roman project, the canalization of the Tiber. Engineers in the first century BCE had captured the river within a narrow set of stone walls, which meant that it flowed faster, whisking sediment downstream and obviating the need for dredging. The sediment that would otherwise have settled on the Tiber's floodplain was carried to the coast. Longshore currents conveyed it north, where it built the shore out and filled the new harbors.

Today Trajan's harbor stands two miles inland from the coast. An even worse case was the Roman harbor of Utica, in North Africa, also built at the mouth of a fast-flowing river. Today the harbor of Utica stands 12 miles from the sea.

࿓

When a rising sea drives a beach back into the shoreline, we have a simple choice. We can protect the shoreline, or we can preserve the beach. In an earlier age, a more naive age, when ecology had not taught us that nature responds to our actions in complex and subtle ways, we thought we could do both. So we built seawalls and revetments along the edge of the land, like dikes along the shore, designed to thwart the besieging sea. The seawalls were intended to prevent the beach from retreating. But we found to our consternation that after we built the seawalls, the beach disappeared altogether.

Seawalls destroy beaches. Sometimes, of course, it is a rational choice to build the seawall and lose the beach; even Orrin Pilkey would concede that certain shoreline structures should be defended by seawalls—major harbors, for example, and urban centers like New Orleans or Manhattan Island. A one-meter rise in sea level during the next century, which some scientists think possible, would threaten the existence of half a dozen sovereign nations, chiefly island republics in the Pacific and Indian oceans. Living on coral atolls, they have no possibility of retreat. In such situations, people have little choice but to build seawalls, protecting the shoreline and relinquishing the beach.

In normal situations, seawalls usually begin as modest structures, created to deal with what seem to be rare and minor incursions by the ocean. Bring in the dozer, push up a line of artificial dunes or a bank of earth. Oddly enough, the problem becomes worse and the incursions become more frequent. The modest little seawall is breached or washed away, to be replaced with something more solid, perhaps built of rocks, steel or wood. In my part of the country, old railway ties are often knitted into neat and rather handsome structures.

But the problem seems to keep pace with the attempts to solve it: the waves hit harder, the beach continues to shrink, the seawall is undermined. Perhaps the seawall is abandoned and a heavier one is built a little farther inland. On a breezy day at The Glades, near Scituate, Massachusetts, you can watch the waves rolling right over two successive seawalls before smashing into a third one, sending spray into the windows of houses across the road. A risky spot, one might think, but a new house is going up almost within the spray zone.

Seawalls are "the typical solution for dealing with the problem of erosion," says Peter Rosen of Northeastern University, looking at the triple seawalls of The Glades on a wet, cold April afternoon. "And people often do this because they want the beach, they want access to the beach. But the solution to providing stability at the beach leads to the destruction of the beach.

"Interestingly, nobody's really pinned down exactly what a seawall does to a beach. We know seawalls are associated with losing a beach, but there's a lot of myth. The popular opinion is—and there may be truth to it—that waves hit the seawall, and their energy doesn't dissipate. The waves *reflect* off the seawall, which you can see, and carry the sand seaward. But there's never been any scientific measurement of this.

"Another hypothesis is that when you build a seawall, very often the seawall is pushed as far seaward as possible, because waterfront real estate is very valuable. Maybe the beach doesn't move inland as much as seawalls tend to push seaward. And then beaches erode by themselves, due to rising sea level. If you put a seawall up, the beach would have eroded back to the seawall anyway." Orrin Pilkey calls this *passive erosion*. Anything static next to a beach, he says, "will result in narrowing and loss as the beach moves back into it."

There are other theories. The smooth, sculpted face of a seawall may increase the intensity of longshore currents, thus hurrying the sand away down the shore. Seawalls also prevent the exchange of sand between the dunes and the shoreface; during severe storms, the beach would normally move dune sand out to sea, flattening itself and forcing the waves to break farther offshore. Cut off from the dune, the beach is helpless. As the beach profile becomes steeper and steeper in front of the seawall, heavy seas can come closer and closer to the shore before they break, exposing the seawall to ever larger and more destructive wave impacts.

"Really, it doesn't matter where you put the blame," says Peter Rosen with a shrug. "If you put up a seawall, you end up without a beach."

And, he might have added, ultimately without a seawall, too. As the seawalls collapse and new ones are built, ever more massive structures arise on the shore. The predictable result is what Orrin Pilkey calls *Newjerseyization*—the construction of seawalls so massive that the sea cannot even be seen from a second-story window. Even if one could see it, the beach view is not very pretty. I scaled the 15-foot masonry wall in Sea Bright, New Jersey in 1993 and found myself atop an enormous structure, as wide as a roadway, stretching for miles down the coast. On the shore side, on the alleged beach, there was hardly a pailful of sand to be seen. Instead, the surf washed through the ruins of earlier structures, long since overwhelmed by the sea—twisted, rusty steel plates and broken pilings, heaps of rock and toppled concrete. That beach has since been replenished, and no doubt it looks better at the moment, but sooner or later the sand will migrate, uncovering the garbage beneath it once again.

This is a sad end to what was once a pleasant seaside resort. And, monumental though it is, the seawall *still* does not provide security. The sea has broken through it repeatedly. Eventually, I thought, it will be undermined and toppled – and indeed, just 19 years later, Hurricane Sandy completely overwhelmed it.

This is one of the great lessons about shoreline engineering: it is a process that, once begun, never ends. History shows us, write Pilkey and his collaborators in a book on the North Carolina coast, "that there are two situations that may terminate shoreline engineering. First, a civilization may fail and no longer build and maintain its structures. This was the case with the Romans, who built mighty seawalls. Second, a large storm may destroy a shoreline-stabilization system so thoroughly that people decide to 'throw in the towel.'"

Engineers have devised alternatives to seawalls, of course, but many of them are equally depressing. At Lepe, on the Solent in southern England, the beach has been divided into corral-like compartments defined by solid walls of vertical pilings. The arrangement promises all the pleasure of suntanning in a cattle pen. At Minehead, Somerset, a low sheet-metal roof has been built over the beach. If you are less than two feet tall and happy to lie on pebbles under a steel roof, the Minehead beach may be your cup of tea. At Hel Spit, Poland, the beach has been replaced by a sloping lattice of concrete blocks interspersed with hardy plants. The shoreline is stable, but as a beach it is a Polish joke. In Honshu, Japan, miles of beaches are protected by grotesque four-legged concrete devices called *tetrapods,* developed by the Neyrpic Hydraulics Laboratory at Grenoble, France. Willard Bascom describes them as "a sort of sea monster with four tentacles." They make the Japanese shoreline look like an elongated concrete hedgehog.

Not surprisingly, seawalls have increasingly fallen into disfavor, although some defenders persist. Even the defenders are not exuberant proponents of seawalls, however. One of them is a tall, white-haired man with a soft voice and an easy smile. Robert Dean is chairman of Coastal and Oceanographic Engineering at the University of Florida in Gainesville. Pure scientists—biologists, geologists—sometimes portray engineers as brutish pragmatists, bulldozers of the intellectual landscape, he-men who get things done no matter what gets crushed or broken. Nobody speaks that way about Bob Dean.

Dean has, writes John McPhee, "an extraordinary affection for water. On his days off, he liked nothing more than to dive into one or another of Florida's limestone sinks, scuba gear on his back, and swim upstream into the total darkness of an underground river, carrying a light and seeing albino crayfish that had no functioning eyes. He had found stone knives from the Ice Age, when the water table was lower and such caverns were dry. He had to watch his oxygen supply closely, and turn back when it was not quite half gone. And now he strode through the ocean in long rubber boots ..."

The ocean through which Dean was striding when McPhee met him was a model built in a huge metal building on a 12,000-square-foot concrete floor. When I was there, parts of the floor were dammed off and filled with sand and water. Wave generators pulsed wavelets out across the floor, rippling the sand. A long, clear-sided Plexiglas wave tank ran across one end of the lab, giving the visitor a cross-sectional view of the passing waves.

Florida has such an intimate connection with water—the whole southern section of the state, the Everglades, is really a vast, slow-flowing river—and so much pressure for coastal development, that this lab is constantly occupied with modeling harbors, inlets, jetties and breakwaters. What would happen if we put a breakwater off the inlet? Would the sand build up behind it? Would sand still bypass the inlet? Would the inlet silt up? The planners and politicians bring such questions to this lab, and the engineers build models.

Bob Dean stood smiling at the edge of a model inlet and talked about seawalls.

"Seawalls have an adverse effect on the beach, but I think the prevailing view is not correct," he said. "I think that seawalls are much maligned, myself. I was over at the beach yesterday, in Volusia County, where the county is litigating with a property owner who wants to build her own sand fence out on the beach. But we walked back in the dune, and there, buried in the dune, I'd say maybe 100 feet back from the dry sandy beach, all vegetated, we found an old seawall. There were aluminum handrails and steps that went down—but they didn't go anywhere, because the seawall was buried.

"Well, you know that seawall was built at a time when the beach was in much worse condition. That happens pretty often. When we have a major storm here, people may find that they have a seawall they didn't know they had. They bought the house maybe ten years ago, but at one time the beach was much more threatened than it is today. That's not due to beach nourishment. It's just that nature goes through some swings. We had some bad storms in the sixties here, for instance, but not so many recently.

"Now those seawalls, I think, are like an insurance policy. You keep your insurance policy in a drawer when you don't need it: well, a seawall like this you keep buried under the dune when you don't need it. But when you need it, you know it's there. When we have that 100-year storm, the people that have those seawalls will have some protection.

"I'm not wildly in favor of seawalls, but I think they have their place. And if you compare a seawall to a jetty or a groin that protrudes out, there are orders of magnitude of difference in their impact."

Groins and jetties are structures built out into the water perpendicular to the beach. They may be made of wood, steel, stones, concrete, sandbags, anything that will hold back sand. They are dams, in effect, designed to intercept the river of sand flowing along the beach. (A breakwater, on the other hand, is a similar structure with a completely different purpose. It thrusts into the water, often in an arc, and parts of it, at least, run parallel to the shore. Its function is to protect the boats behind it. Its effect on the beach in front of it, if there is one, is incidental.)

Groins are relatively short and attached directly to the beach. Jetties are similar but much larger structures, which are built along the sides of inlets and extended into the sea to keep the sand from choking the passage and to keep the currents from moving the inlet laterally along the beach. Like all hard structures, groins and jetties attempt to prevent change, to stabilize an inherently unstable natural system.

To the extent that they succeed, both jetties and groins intercept sand. The updrift beach *progrades;* expands into the ocean. The downdrift beach erodes. Orrin Pilkey points out a dramatic case, a jetty built to protect a harbor entrance at Ocean City, Maryland. It had a drastic effect on neighboring Assateague Island.

"In 1933 a hurricane formed an inlet here," says Pilkey, flicking to another slide. "It was immediately jettied to provide access to the lagoon for development purposes. Well, the sand flows from north to south, and the jetties trapped sand and starved the northern end of Assateague Island to the south. Since 1933, the northern four miles of Assateague Island have migrated completely off their location. They've gone back 1,750 feet. The surf zone of the island is now behind where the lagoon shoreline was in 1933.

"I mean, that's amazing, isn't it? Talk about a living—talk about doing something sensible! In this case the beach is starved for sand, so it moves back because it doesn't have enough sand to sustain itself."

Bob Dean wouldn't argue much.

"A good starting point on structures is that they don't add any more sand to the beach," he says. "Structures don't manufacture sand. If the structure causes sand to deposit in one location, it's going to cause a deficit elsewhere."

That is, of course, the point: I want the sand on *my* beach, so I build a groin. Now your beach starves, so you build one, too. Thus the groin field slowly propagates itself all up and down the beach. Pity the poor chap at the end of the line, with his shrinking, sand-starved beach. Such compartmentalized beaches can be found all over the world: on the east and west coastline of the United States; on the English Channel at Felixstowe; on the Tasman Sea near Melbourne; on the Adriatic at Rimini; on the Sea of Japan at Niigata; on the Black Sea at Sochi, to name a few. Even where they seemed to succeed, they have probably been irrelevant, at best.

"In 1926, Miami suffered a major hurricane," says Bob Dean. "It took all of their beaches away. The city engineer built groins, and over the next five years or maybe a decade, the beach came back. And he swore that it was his groins that brought the beach back. But I think we all know that it was just natural recovery.

"Another example: In Holland they've discovered what they call *sand waves*, underwater bars that move along at an oblique angle to the shore. As the bars migrate along the coast, there are phases of erosion and accretion.

"Back in the forties, they had one section that had very bad erosion, so they built groins. And within the next couple of decades the groins filled up, and they assumed it was just the groins filling with the littoral drift. But now they're starting to empty again, and a number of Dutch coastal engineers have concluded that the groins had no effect at all; it was just a sand wave moving by. I don't know whether that's correct, but it's an interesting observation."

It might seem that a groin would simply deflect the longshore current outward; once the groin filled, the current would continue as before. Sometimes it does, but more commonly it does not. The very existence of the groin changes the orientation and force of the longshore current, and the groin also moves the current into deeper water, where its capacity to move sand is much diminished.

Jetties are much larger structures, sometimes as much as two miles long, and they have a much more profound effect. Normally, an inlet warps the longshore current outward or inward as the tide ebbs and flows. The inward-flowing current pulls sand into the inlet and deposits it on the flood-tidal deltas inside the bay; the outward-flowing current creates much smaller deltas of material carried out from the bay and also pushes the longshore current seaward. As the deflected current spreads out and slows down in deeper water, it drops its sand. The result is the familiar banana-shaped bar or *ebb-tidal shoal* that typically forms at river mouths and outside the entrances to inlets. In many locations, the shoal is a well-recognized hazard for navigators.

"In their natural state, inlets would bypass the sand around them," explains Bob Dean. "The flow of sand on the east coast of Florida is from north to south, and the sand would work its way around the inlets across the ebb-tidal shoal. In its natural condition, the water was quite shallow there, so in order to improve those inlets for navigation, a deep channel was incised through the shoal, and also jetties were built to block the sand. But the ebb-tidal shoal really served as a sand bridge, a bridge across which the sand moved to nourish the beaches to the south.

"To compound that problem, for about five or six decades all the sand that was dredged from these inlets was taken offshore and dumped in about 200 feet of water. It was good quality sand, and it was actually taken out of our natural system.

"My students and I have studied the shoreline changes on the east coast of Florida," says Dean, "and our estimate is that the inlets which have been modified for navigation are responsible for approximately 80 to 85 percent of the beach erosion on the east coast of Florida. There's very little doubt about that."

Orrin Pilkey tells of an entire Oregon resort community destroyed by jetties. In 1907, Bay Ocean resort was built on a sand spit on the southern side of the mouth of Tillamook Inlet. The developer laid out more than 3,000 lots, selling for $500 to $1,800 each, and built a grand hotel with bowling alleys, tennis courts and a dance hall.

But in 1917 the U.S. Army Corps of Engineers built a mile-long jetty on the opposite side of the inlet, and in 1932 they extended it. The shores of Bay Ocean, which had been retreating at a sedate one foot per year, suddenly started washing away at an annual rate of six feet. The seafront sidewalk fell into the sea, and in 1936 the hotel followed it. In 1939, a fierce winter storm made two breaches through the spit, severing the road and the water line. Storms in the 1940s opened two more gaps, and in 1952 another great storm wrecked 4,000 feet of the beach ridge, leaving a gap three-quarters of a mile in width at high tide. Far from being a posh playground, Bay Ocean had become an unserviced island, stranded in the waves.

∽

It is hardly surprising that such man-made structures as seawalls, groins, jetties and breakwaters fail on the shoreline; the amount of energy that assaults the coast every day is colossal. In 1872, a pioneer lighthouse engineer named Thomas Stevenson reported on the destruction of the breakwater at Wick Bay, Scotland. At that moment, Stevenson might well have been preoccupied by the difficulties he was having with his rebellious 22-year-old son. The young man had flatly refused to become a lighthouse engineer like his father and his grandfather and had only grudgingly agreed to study law—but now the lad had taken up a bohemian life-style and was saying he wanted to become a writer. Robert Louis Stevenson, writer! What kind of a profession was that?

Addressing himself to his professional responsibilities, Thomas Stevenson bent to his desk in Edinburgh and wrote:

The end of the breakwater was composed of three courses of blocks weighing 80 to 100 tons each which were deposited as a foundation in a trench made in cement rubble. Above this foundation there were three courses of large stones carefully set in cement, and the whole was surmounted by a large monolith of cement rubble, measuring about 26 by 45 feet by 11 feet in thickness, weighing upward of 800 tons. As a further precaution, iron rods 3.5 inches in diameter were fixed in the uppermost of the foundation courses of cement rubble. These rods were carried through the courses of stonework by holes cut in the stone, and were finally embedded in the monolithic mass, which formed the upper portion of the pier.

Incredible as it may seem, this huge mass succumbed to the force of the waves, and Mr. McDonald, the resident engineer, actually watched from the adjacent cliff as it was gradually slewed round by successive strokes until it was finally removed and deposited inside the pier. It was several days before an examination could be made of this singular phenomenon, but the result of the examination only gave rise to increased amazement at the feat which the waves had actually achieved. Divers found that the 800-ton monolith forming the upper portion of the pier, which the resident engineer had seen in the act of being washed away, had carried with it the whole of the lower courses, which were attached to it by the iron bolts, and that this enormous mass, weighing not less than 1,350 tons, had been removed in one piece and was resting on the rubble at the side of the pier, having sustained no damage but a slight fracture at the edges.

The determined Scots replaced the 800-ton cap with another weighing 2,600 tons—and this one, too, was carried away in a storm five years later. The power of the crashing water was later calculated by a U.S. Army engineer as being on the order of 6,340 pounds *per square foot*. And yet waves have been recorded that exerted more than twice that power; for 1/100 of a second, a French engineer observed a force of 12,700 pounds per square foot during a storm at Dieppe.

At East London, South Africa, in 1963, a storm ripped away 60 percent of the breakwater's armor. The armor consisted of 40-ton blocks, and the fact that they went walkabout led Eric Merrifield, the harbor engineer, to wonder whether it was a mistake to put solid blocks in the ocean. Maybe some other shape might work better—something porous, something that would absorb and scatter the energy of waves rather than resisting it. He thought about tetrapods. They would be effective, but they required careful placement. Eric Merrifield wanted something much less fussy.

Eventually, Merrifield noticed children playing with *dolosse*—the knucklebones of sheep and goats, used as toys by generations of South African children. A *dolos*—*dolosse* is the plural—is roughly what you would get if you took the letter H and twisted one upright by ninety degrees, so that one upright was horizontal and the other vertical. Merrifield made *dolosse* weighing 20 tons each and sprinkled them on his breakwater. The result delighted him: the *dolosse* deconstructed the waves and dissipated their energy. Breakers crashed into them and vanished.

The first *dolosse* in North America were emplaced on the breakwater at Cap-aux-Meules in Quebec's Magdalen Islands in 1971. They shook down into place during the storms of their first winter, and they have never moved since. Today *dolosse* are used all over the world. They are a remarkably durable and effective form of armor. But, like all armor, they only stabilize the shoreline. They don't preserve the beach.

⁓

The most exuberant armorers of the beach have been the U.S. Army Corps of Engineers, whose *National Shoreline Study*, published in 1970, proposed almost two billion dollars' worth of engineering works to counter the effects of erosion all around the American coast. In 1970, two billion dollars was a lot of money. One of the unexpected consequences of the *National Shoreline Study* was the priming and charging of Orrin Pilkey, who was already an ardent lover of the wild beaches of North Carolina. He read the Corps' proposals with rising alarm and resolved to look into the matter.

How did the U.S. Army come to be in charge of the republic's beaches, anyway? Lim Vallianos explains. Vallianos is a retired senior policy analyst with the U.S. Army Corps of Engineers. He is sitting in a white turtleneck and dark jacket on a patio in McLean, Virginia. The patio is overhung with flowering magnolia trees and carpeted with white petals. Vallianos is a veteran of much combat with Orrin Pilkey. Upstairs in his library is one of Pilkey's books, and on the flyleaf is inscribed, *To Lim Vallianos. Stop deprogramming my audiences. Orrin Pilkey.*

"The Corps' responsibility for water resources goes back to the beginnings of the nation, after independence," says Vallianos. "George Washington, having been elected as the first president, looked around for a group of engineers who could help in developing the country, with the emphasis being on the development of commerce. Waterways being the principal means of transportation at that time, he sought engineers with waterways experience. He couldn't find any in what we now call the private sector. He then went to the military engineers— who were practically the only engineers with public works experience in the United States at that time—and from that point onward the responsibilities for waterways resources in the United States have been primarily vested in the U.S. Army Corps of Engineers."

In 1794, the Corps was divided into military and civilian branches. The civilian branch began by clearing wrecks, sandbanks and detritus from harbors, and as the new nation expanded westward it took part in the exploration and surveying of the new territory. Late in the nineteenth century, its ambitions expanded to include reshaping the great rivers to make them more suitable for barge and ship traffic.

The Corps dredged channels and built levees and dikes. It went on to construct such massive navigational structures as the Red River, Tennessee-Tombigbee and Arkansas River projects. After spending a billion dollars, it has—so far—even prevented the Mississippi from cutting a new main channel to the sea via the Atchafalaya, which the Mississippi would very much like to do.

Moving into the west, the Corps built something like 600 dams in 60 years, providing flood control and reservoirs for irrigation. It is fair to say that the American southwest in its present form could not exist without the work of the Corps. In *Cadillac Desert,* Marc Reisner questions whether the southwest *can* exist for long, given its exponential growth in a land of limited water. But even Reisner is impressed by the scope of the Corps' activities:

> The Army Engineers have so many hands in so many different types of work that their various activities sometimes cancel each other out. The Corps drains and channels wetlands— it has ruined more wetlands than anyone in history, except perhaps its counterpart in the Soviet Union—yet sometimes prohibits the draining and dredging of wetlands by private developers and other interests ... Its dams control flooding, while its stream channelization and wetlands-drainage programs cause it. Its subsidization of intensive agriculture— which it does by turning wetlands into dryland, so they may then become soybean fields—increases soil erosion, which pours into the nations rivers, which the Corps then has to dredge more frequently.
>
> Cynics say this is all done by design, because the Corps of Engineers' motto, "Building Tomorrow Today," really ought to be "Keep Busy." Its range of activities is breathtaking: the Corps dams rivers, deepens rivers, straightens rivers, ripraps rivers, builds bridges across rivers, builds huge navigation locks and dams, builds groins on rivers and beaches, builds hatcheries,

builds breakwaters, builds piers and repairs beach erosion (finally fulfilling the first stage of a destiny conservationists have long wished on it: carrying sandpiles from one end of the country to the other and back again).

The Corps has few if any counterparts; in Canada, for instance, these responsibilities are spread among several separate agencies. The Corps is a monster agency with about 35,000 employees, mostly civilian; it is the largest construction organization in the United States. Given the "free enterprise" rhetoric of which American politicians are so fond, it is amusing to regard the Corps as perhaps the largest socialized construction company in the world, and also as the source of unacknowledged government handouts to sturdily independent freedom-loving western farmers, some of whom pay as little as $7.50 for water that costs the government $97 to capture, transport and deliver. Its critics consider it a government within a government, arrogant and powerful enough to defy even the president—which on several occasions it has done. Harold Ickes, Franklin Roosevelt's Secretary of the Interior, raged against the Corps as a "self-serving clique," contemptuous of the public welfare, and a spectacular wastrel of public money. "No more lawless or irresponsible group than the Corps of Army Engineers," said Ickes, "has ever attempted to operate in the United States either outside of or within the law."

In concert with other agencies, the Corps has made possible an agricultural civilization in the western deserts, but Reisner and others question the longevity of that civilization, given the slow massing of catastrophic problems—dam siltation, soil salinization, heightened erosion by rivers that no longer nourish their floodplains and so forth. Two thousand years ago, an irrigation-based agricultural culture, the Hohokam, flourished in what is now Arizona. Then they vanished, as most irrigating cultures had vanished before them—the Sumerians, the Assyrians and many others. Could the same thing happen to

Arizona and California? Bet on it, says Reisner. In the desert, as on the coast, nature always bats last.

∽

In his attacks on the Corps, Orrin Pilkey likes to cite the case of Cape May, New Jersey, a favored seaside retreat of several early presidents. The entrance to the town's harbor was jettied in 1911, and by the 1920s the beach was eroding 20 to 30 feet annually. The town built groins and seawalls, floating one bond issue after another to pay for them, but to no avail. The Ash Wednesday storm of 1962 flooded the town, and by 1968 Cape May was broke, hiding behind seawalls. It had, said the mayor, "finally reached the point where we no longer have beaches to erode." In 1974 the seawalls trapped heavy rains within the town, turning it into a lake and causing $2 million in damage. The town used sewage pumps to clear the water, but the pumps carried the sewage out, as well, and Cape May spent the summer rimmed with its own effluent, its wholly artificial beaches closed.

All this started with the jetties in 1911. By engineering standards, however, the jetties were probably a success: the harbor entrance stayed open.

The fundamental problem with engineering solutions in a geologically active context—a river, a shoreline—is the measurement of success: a calculation of costs and benefits only in dollars and only over very short periods of time. Lim Vallianos, for example, explains that "the planning horizons usually used not only by the engineer but by society in general are one or two generations—25 to 50 years. The alternatives are evaluated in terms of engineering economics, usually in terms of benefits and costs over that 25 or 50 years."

Reasonable enough, one might think, but rivers, beaches and societies endure far beyond those short horizons. One might build a $10 million system of seawalls and groins in front of a set of hotels, for instance, calculating that the cost would be recovered from taxes paid by the hotel owners over 25 years. The calculation may well be correct, and within the context of a 25-year horizon, the project may be a success, though late-coming swimmers and boaters picking their way through the wreckage in the surf might disagree. Beyond the horizon, after all, what are you left with? A shoreline littered with broken fortifications, a vanished beach and a set of hotel owners who *still* insist that their investment be protected. Do you now do it again? In terms of the ocean's planning horizon, the engineering is temporary, but the problem is permanent—and the natural defenses of the beach have been destroyed.

Lim Vallianos is a hospitable, almost courtly man whose thinking, one suspects, has been much influenced by the onslaught of the conservationists. He is not much worried by any projected rise in sea level; "for the next two to four hundred years, there isn't a crisis," because in the case of storm tides and hurricane surges "we deal with extremely large differences in water level now." Still, the only places where heroic defenses of the shoreline can be justified, he says, are densely populated urbanized shorelines. Otherwise, "relocation is the better option." And new development should be planned to avoid erosion problems.

The solutions proposed by the Corps have also changed. Seawalls, revetments, groins and breakwaters are known to professionals as *hard solutions,* and their failures—or at best their highly uncertain prospects of success—have led to a worldwide preference for *soft solutions.*

Throughout the world, says Vallianos, "probably the most common method along extended shorelines is simply to replenish sediments which the sea has deposited somewhere else, and which has caused a narrowing of the beach. It's a kind of treatment which is very similar to continued medication versus radical surgery."

Replenishment—beach nourishment—along with such techniques as sand bypassing and dewatering, represent soft solutions to the erosion problem. Sand bypassing means moving sand across the mouth of an inlet, using pumps or trucks to do what the ebb-tidal shoal once did naturally and automatically. It is perhaps as innocuous a technique as any in the engineer's bag of tricks—though it does underline the point that when we interfere in the natural system, we can never stop. As long as the inlet is jettied and the ebb-tidal shoal is dredged, the sand will have to be artificially bypassed.

Beach dewatering is a fascinating technique, discovered by accident in Denmark in 1984. The Sea Life Center at Hirtshals on the Baltic coast needed seawater for its aquariums, and the Danish Geotechnical Center suggested that it be pumped from under the beach rather than running a pipe beyond the surf. Geologists had known that wet beaches erode more rapidly than dry ones, because wet sand moves in water while dry sand absorbs it. Still, nobody was quite prepared to see the beach at Hirtshals broaden by 90 feet, adding a yard to the depth of sand directly over the perforated pipe drain. In 1985, the Danes tried the technique again at Thorsminde, on the North Sea coast, with similar results. When the pumping was stopped, the new sand washed away again.

In 1988 and 1993 the same results occurred on beaches in Florida, at Hutchinson Island and Englewood. In 1995, drains and pumps were installed under Towan Beach, near Newquay, Cornwall, as an experiment, using a pipe high on the beach to divert groundwater and another mid-beach to capture swash water. The system seems to be both effective and cheap. A British consulting firm estimates the cost at £500 ($1,145 Canadian) per meter of beach. Beach nourishment could cost twice as much and rock armoring five times as much, while solid concrete walls would be ten times as costly. Dewatering may be a system with a future—although, as Pilkey points out, no engineering technique produces sand; engineers simply move sand around. If a dewatering system traps sand in one place, it will create a sand deficit somewhere else.

Meanwhile replenishment is certainly in vogue everywhere in the world. The concept is straightforward: the sea has taken sand away from the beach, so we will put it back.

Nothing about beaches is as simple as that, of course. Where will the sand come from? Sometimes it is pumped or dredged from offshore, sometimes it is trucked from inland quarries, sometimes it comes from the lagoon, sometimes from rivers or other beaches. Sometimes it consists of completely alien materials—mine tailings, for example, or spoilings from harbor dredging.

Not any old sediment will do. The size and character of the grains are important: too fine and the sand immediately drifts away, for instance. The sand is also important to the ecology of the particular beach. Do birds nest in it? Turtles? Will the new sand be too heavy, or pack too hard, for a turtle or a bird to dig in it?

When replenishment works, it works very well. It results in a sandy beach, not a pile of stones or *dolosse.* And it interposes a reasonable imitation of a natural barrier between the sea and the roads and buildings on the shoreline. Its disadvantages are the usual problems of shoreline engineering: it is expensive, and it has to be done again and again. It may last fifteen years or fifteen hours, depending on the weather. One of Orrin Pilkey's slides shows a beach at Ocean City, Maryland, which was replenished in 1982 at a cost of $5.2 million. Most of the new sand disappeared in about 75 days. The Corps of Engineers disputes Pilkey's claim, contending that most of the sand has moved underwater, where it helps to protect the beach from storms. Wherever it may be, however, the sand is not above the high tide line, where the citizens had expected it to be.

The new sand is more vulnerable than the old sand because replenishment renews only the berm, not the whole shoreface. The beach, after all, is a dynamic system, which may stretch a mile or more into the ocean, into water 100 feet deep. Storm waves crash onto the new sand and carry it away in the backwash, sending it off down the beach in the longshore current or dropping it in deeper water beyond the surf line. These adjustments flatten the shoreface—which is, after all, a beach's normal reaction to wave attack. The sand has not evaporated: it has simply migrated. But the laboriously rebuilt berm has disappeared again.

Conservationist Dick Ludington thinks that replenishment is an ideal activity for the Corps of Engineers; it will keep them busy forever. As long as this harmless game continues, Ludington says with a smile, the Corps will be too busy to cause more damage elsewhere.

From an engineering perspective, of course, if the renourished beach lasts long enough to generate economic benefits that cover its costs, it has succeeded. By that standard, and by standards of durability, the replenishment of Miami Beach has been "the premiere example of a successful beach restoration project," says Brian Flynn, Chief of the Restoration and Enhancement Section of Dade County's Department of Environmental Resources Management. Young, vigorous and articulate, Flynn stands amid the palmettos of South Miami Beach, his dark hair flying in the warm wind, and explains why this particular project has worked so well.

"This project has all the elements," he says, ticking them off on his fingers. "We've got very dense development, we've got a local economy that has tourism at its heart, and we've got a climate that makes beaches very attractive to tourists and residents. The need had developed from the 1930s to the mid-1950s, where the beach was disappearing at a faster and faster rate. We had tried various things like groin fields, and they canceled one another out. By the 1940s, about 40 percent of the shoreline was seawalls or bulkheads.

"The original project took place from 1977 to 1982 and covered 10.5 miles. It was designed and constructed by the U.S. Army Corps of Engineers as a federal shore-protection project. It incorporates two basic elements. One is recreation benefits, but the main thing that the project is based on is storm protection. The cost of the initial restoration was about $60 million. The federal government pays half, and the state government pays 37 percent, so the cost to the local government is relatively low.

"There are two parts to a beach restoration project: there's the initial cost of the project and—just as with any other capital project—there's a need to maintain it. What a beach restoration does is to put a beach back; it doesn't stop the erosion or the original causes of the erosion. We've only had to do two maintenance projects, and only a little less than three miles of beaches had to be addressed at all."

In 1988, the project was extended 2.5 miles. It now stretches from an inlet on the north to the jettied entrance to Miami Harbor on the south. Its very length is part of the reason for the success of the project. Most of the loss of sand from a replenished beach occurs at the ends, says Bob Dean, so the life span of a replenishment project is directly related to its length. In Dean's lab at Gainesville, students have calculated that the longevity of a project increases exponentially with its length: if a one-mile nourishment project in a certain location lasts two years, a two-mile project will last eight years, and a three-mile project would last 18 years.

Codswallop, says Orrin Pilkey; Dean's equations derive from wave tanks and computer models rather than real-life observations. "The basic assumptions behind the models are simplified to the point of absurdity," he says. "The physical basis of the models is nonexistent." Reality is too complex, and beaches are too individual, for models to predict their behavior. Far from being helpful, "mathematical modeling of beaches becomes an impediment to progress in understanding coastal evolution."

But even Pilkey concedes that "in South Florida, where there has been much experience with beach nourishment, estimates of beach life spans are often reasonable." Miami's project had some specific advantages, too. For one thing, it ends with a jetty at the down drift end, so only one end of the beach is really exposed to erosion. In addition, South Florida has a low-energy coast, since it is protected by the shallow Bahamian plateau 50 miles offshore.

The replenished sand at Miami is unusual, too. Drawn from offshore gullies between coral ridges, it is primarily calcium carbonate—the shells of millions of tiny sea animals. The shells crack, break, nest and interlock, settling into a hard-packed surface—"like rock or concrete," grumbles Pilkey, who concedes all the facts that Brian Flynn cites but still considers the result to be something less than a beach.

Economically and socially, however, the Miami project has been a great success; its $60 million cost generated recreational benefits which alone were estimated at $16 million a year. And the restoration of the beach has had remarkable indirect benefits, Flynn says.

"Ten to twelve years ago, you wouldn't have wanted to stand in the portion of South Beach which we're standing in, because you'd have had a very good chance of being mugged." A once elegant district of 1930s Art Deco hotels, the area had become a low-income neighborhood with little appeal to tourists. The beach restoration revived it. Today the Art Deco district is delightful, a fantasy of swirling curves, pastel stucco, seafront sidewalk cafes and beachfront parks. At the crowded beach, fighting kites attack one another; inline skaters do elaborate pirouettes; sailboarders fly over the aquamarine water. The area is such a favorite of fashion photographers that one entire hotel has been converted to a photo lab.

The renovations are now pushing back behind the seafront, upgrading this entire quarter of the city. Capitalizing on the changes, the city fathers have been rebuilding dunes, revegetating the upper beach and constructing a two-mile boardwalk, which gives public access to a beach that was once almost totally blocked by exclusive high-rise hotels that treated the beach as their private fief.

In the particular circumstances of Miami, beach nourishment has worked well. But every case is different.

"In many ways beaches are *animistic*," says Lim Vallianos, voicing the sense of mystery and wonder that beaches evoke in almost everyone who studies them closely. "They display characteristics of almost *living* things. And beyond even that, they each have very peculiar circumstances—things that are unique to a specific beach. One beach may have a different rate of erosion from an immediately adjacent beach. Some seem to be rolling over on themselves, but others don't display this behavior at all. We may see dune lines that are very robust; close by, for no apparent reason, there are very low or nonexistent dunes. In fact I've found that there's very little generalization that you can make."

For some beaches, then, beach nourishment is a workable strategy. But we have only been nourishing beaches for a few decades, and over the longer term it is probably not a sustainable practice because— within the time horizons that matter to human beings—sand is not a renewable resource. Sand that goes away is not lost forever, of course. Sand may be dumped offshore, lost to submarine canyons or locked up in concrete buildings, but it will return somehow. It may come back in 50 or 60 thousand years as part of the soil in the great inland plains of a newborn continent, or it may be upthrust in a hillside as part of a band of sandstone—with fossilized shirt buttons and surfboards encapsulated in it, a bizarre thought. But your descendants and mine will never see it again.

And if the overall supply of sand is diminishing, the supply of *convenient, appropriate* and *affordable* sand is diminishing much faster. We can take some sand from the lagoons, but dredging eventually will cause erosion along their shores. We can pump up sand from the seafloor or quarry sand in the back lands, but the seafloor is not infinite, either, and the new hollows on the bottom will change the movement of water and sand in ways we cannot foresee. Quarries will eventually collide with other things we value—woodlands, cities, highways. Replenishment will have a good long vogue, but eventually it, too, will become impossible.

Meanwhile, as seawalls and groins have fallen increasingly out of favor—they are now prohibited outright by many coastal governments—the search for alternatives continues. Offshore breakwaters, cement bags, artificial headlands, reefs made of buoyant Frisbees, tubes buried in the sand to imitate offshore bars—"there are lots of strange devices," reports Orrin Pilkey, putting up another slide.

"Here's one of them—an artificial seaweed, plastic, which absolutely doesn't work. If these guys were selling bridges and they had all failed, they'd be out of business. But it's much more complex to determine the success of something like this because there are so many factors."

∽

The world's great experts in shoreline engineering are the Dutch—and their experience in 1953 demonstrates that even a well-tested system can fail when a really exceptional storm hits the coast. The Dutch have been dealing with the incursions of the sea since the beginning of European history; they were living on raised mounds called *terpen* when the Romans arrived in the Low Countries two millennia ago, and they have been building dikes since the twelfth century. But their most ambitious projects have been completed only in this century. Before 1953, their most extensive project was the Afsluitdijk, which cut off the southern part of the Zuider Zee—an abandoned estuary of the Rhine—from the North Sea. Though it had been proposed as early as 1667, the 19-mile dam was completed only in 1932.

The Dutch had suffered severe floods many times in their history, but by 1953 they were living behind their dikes with some confidence; even the attempts by the retreating Germans to flood the country had failed. On January 31, 1953, however, the North Sea spawned a storm of a severity to be expected only once in 700 years. Riding on spring tides, the storm surge rose 11 feet above mean high tide level, attacking the Dutch dunes and dikes with unprecedented ferocity. The water broke through in 500 places, flooding 600,000 acres of land, demolishing 26,000 homes and killing 1,835 people. Without a well-developed warning system, the death toll would have been much higher. In England, the same storm flooded large areas of the southeast, threatened the center of London and killed 300.

As Pilkey likes to point out, such "natural" disasters are in a sense man-made; the flood is natural and predictable, but it is not a disaster unless people have chosen to live in the path of the floodwaters. Holland—the name means *hollow land*, the land behind the dikes— exists only because of the skill and the stubborn determination of its people. Without their dikes and pumps, 38 percent of their land would already be under water, and 20 percent already has been; over the years, 3,000 of their 15,000 square miles have been captured from the sea. In England, says Ian Whittle, Flood Defence Manager of the National Rivers Authority, "demand for developable land has meant extension into zones where risk of flooding is high." Translation: we are building in dangerous places.

The 1953 flood was a traumatic shock to England as well as Holland, and it resulted in some of the most massive and ingenious structures ever erected on or near the coast. The English bolstered 650 miles of dikes, embankments and seawalls and created the Thames Barrier, a set of lens-shaped gates that lie in the bottom of the river but can be swung into a vertical position to resist a storm tide. The water will overtop the barrier, but the tide will fall again before the water fills the natural reservoir created by the 28-mile tidal length of the Thames Valley.

But the British have defended their shores largely by destroying them. A geologist friend recently returned from a conference in Europe to report that almost the entire British shoreline is now armored, with "hardly a scrap of natural beach left."

The Dutch, meanwhile, responded with a truly massive project, the Delta Plan, an 18-mile system of dams designed to block completely the estuaries of three great rivers—the Rhine, the Maas and the Schelde— which allowed storm waves to penetrate far inland. The project took 25 years to complete and is gradually turning the area behind the dams into a freshwater lake.

But the Dutch have little choice; with half their prosperous and highly developed country threatened, they have no place to retreat. And—tellingly—these consummate coastal engineers rely on their natural defenses whenever they can. Of their 220 miles of coastline, 160 miles consists of beaches and dunes, and for most of those shorelines the new Coastal Defence Policy of 1990 calls for simple maintenance, with replenishment of the sand as required. The dunes of Holland are protected by stringent laws. People are not even allowed to walk on them without acceptable reasons and valid permits.

Yet the 1990 policy commits the Dutch to defending, for the foreseeable future, the position of the 1990 shoreline. They will respectfully use the beach to help them, where it can. But in the end, if they have to choose between the beach and the shoreline, they will choose the shoreline. The beach is a valued ally, but it is ultimately dispensable.

∽

The fourth and final option on an eroding shore—Pilkey's solution—is retreat. Pilkey's argument is powerful and seductive: nothing else works over the long term, and the alternatives destroy the character and utility of the beach. The beach is magic, an infinitely complex and beautiful ballet of the shore and the land, a pas de deux between change and resistance. Caught up in the dance are the animals and plants that live there. The beach is not just a strip of sand: it is a community, a wild and living thing. To focus on keeping the sand in one place is to miss the point. When you replenish, have you protected the beach and the life that goes with it, or have you simply fixed the current position of the shoreline?

For Pilkey, the wild beach is like an endangered species of animal. In much of the developed world, we have destroyed its habitat, cut off its food supply, domesticated it, weakened it, left it exposed to its enemies. And we have done so out of arrogance and hubris and selfishness. In the end, Pilkey's argument—widely shared among geologists—is at once a well-buttressed scientific position, a practical criticism and a moral passion. *There is no erosion problem until we build things on the beach, and the things we build on the beach usually increase the erosion rate. Trying to save the beach, we destroy it, and the property we save is worth less than the cost of saving it. Shoreline engineering is a treadmill: once you start it, you can never stop. Leave the beach alone.*

But then one hears the quiet, moderate voice of Bob Dean, gently taking issue with Pilkey.

"The issue of coastal zone management is a very difficult one," Dean says, "because there's an element in the United States, a mentality, that says the people that build on the coast really should bear the responsibility of their actions, and we should just let their houses fall in. And maybe that's okay, but I think we have to be a little bit compassionate about it, and I think we have to consider beyond that immediate question. If there is an erosive beach, eventually that erosion will get back to the road. And it's a public highway: are we *then* going to armor? Those are the questions that I think we have to consider all at one time. It can't be a short-term coastal management plan or protocol."

In the end, perhaps the difference is between the geologist's time sense and the engineer's. For an engineer, 100 years is a long time. For a geologist, 1,000 years does not register on the dial. But geologists are citizens and parents, as well, and in those roles they think that vain attempts to halt the inevitable are a waste of our resources and a terrible legacy for our children. What Raphael Kazmann says in *Modern Hydrology* about the water management system of the west— great dams, reservoirs, irrigation—applies equally well to shoreline engineering:

> ... objectively considered, [it] is really a program for the continued and endless expenditure of ever-increasing sums of public money to combat the effects of geologic forces, as these forces strive to reach positions of relative equilibrium ... It may be that future research ... will be primarily to find a method of extricating ourselves from this unequal struggle with minimum loss to the nation ... The forces involved ... are

comparable to those met by a boy who builds a castle on the sandy ocean beach, next to the water, at low tide ... It is not pessimism, merely an objective evaluation, to predict the destruction of the castle.

The Spicy Shores of Araby

Off at sea northeast winds blow
Sabaean odours from the spicy shore
Of Araby the blest.
　　— John Milton, *Paradise Lost*, IV, i, lines 161-163

"The Gulf War spill was 40 times as big as the *Exxon Valdez*," said Miles O. Hayes. "In that area of Saudi Arabia there's a large amount of sheltered marshes and sheltered tidal flats, which are the most sensitive habitats in the intertidal zone as far as oil is concerned. It penetrates the sediments there, it stays there, there's no natural process to clean it up.

"Two years later, you can dig trenches on that site and the oil just pours out, looks like chocolate syrup. Everything is dead. From the mid-tide level up, in all those marshes, there's nothing alive. In places, because it's so hot, it's turning into a pavement. Looks like a parkin' lot. I'm talking about a tidal flat that's 400 to 500 meters wide, and as far as you can see it's just like a parkin' lot. You can walk on it and your footprints don't even dent it."

Miles O. Hayes is a near-legendary figure, fondly remembered by some of his colleagues from years gone by as "a wild man in a red bandanna surrounded by admiring grad students." He was then a professor at the University of South Carolina doing research projects such as measuring the beach erosion that occurred when Hurricane Carla struck the Matagorda Peninsula on the Texas coast in 1961. He calculated that the beach had uniformly retreated 800 feet.

By 1993 Hayes was a grizzled, soberly dressed consultant, president of Research Planning, Inc., sitting in a nicely appointed boardroom in downtown Columbia, South Carolina. Having accepted that human beings *would* use the beach, no matter what, Hayes and RPI have carved out a niche for themselves as experts on oil spills and advisers on beach development planning. Responsible planning and action, Hayes points out, requires that you know not only the general behavior of beaches in the area, but also a great deal of detail about the specific stretch of beach in question.

In 1983, for example, they were called in by a developer whose property at the north end of a barrier island on the South Carolina coast was endangered by the southern migration of Captain Sam's Inlet. RPI relocated the inlet—"which is what nature does, every 40 or 50 years." They relied not on computer modeling but on historical research to determine how the inlet had behaved back as far as 1667, and they undertook a four-year detailed hydrodynamic study of the currents and sand movements. The littoral drift along the South Carolina coast generally runs north to south, moving about 200,000 cubic yards a year—but the studies showed that on the down-drift side of this tidal inlet, the sand actually moved back to the north.

"So if you assumed that your general pattern would hold at the specific site, you'd be wrong," Hayes says. Hayes and his associates were able to show that the inlet normally moved southward about 200 feet annually; they opened a new inlet half a mile north and closed the existing inlet. They predicted that the new inlet would migrate south at the same rate, reaching the original location in 11 years. And that is exactly what it did.

"The cost was relatively small, compared with trying to stabilize the inlet, which would have been very difficult," Hayes says. "The cost was about $250,000, and the lots saved were going for about that price, for half an acre."

RPI has been involved with oil spills since 1975, when it was called in to help with the 53,000-tonne *Metula* spill in the Strait of Magellan, a substantially larger spill than the 37,000 tonnes leaked by the *Exxon Valdez* in 1995. One could make a good case for the oil business as the first truly global industry, pumping oil in Nigeria or Texas, Libya or the North Sea, shipping it to Hong Kong or London or Buenos Aires (or Come-by-Chance, Newfoundland) in tankers officered by Brits and crewed by Asians and owned by Greeks, buying and selling cargoes while the ships are still at sea, colluding and competing as the occasion demands, refining and delivering its product in every country on Earth. The oil business is beyond the reach of any one set of government regulations; indeed, sometimes it behaves as if it were beyond the rule of law altogether.

Most of the world's oil moves by sea, arriving in major ports in supertankers and being transshipped up and down the coast by smaller vessels, some of them little more than rubber bladders hauled by tugboats. Every minute of every day, somewhere on Earth, oil is spilling into the water. Venezuelan crude, Bunker C, jet fuel, diesel, motor oil, it spills into creeks and harbors, leaking from storage tanks, dribbling from cracked transfer pipes, spilling over from filler pipes, splashing into the offshore waters from tankers illegally cleaning their tanks at sea. The Mediterranean rarely has large oil spills, though it carries 35 percent of the world's oil trade, but every year its constant small spills release 17 times as many tons of oil as escaped from the *Exxon Valdez*—the equivalent of a Persian Gulf spill every 26 months or so.

Oil spills are a constant of industrial life, and it is only the big ones —*Amoco Cadiz, Braer, Torrey Canyon*—that make the headlines. (The 2010 BP spill in the Gulf of Mexico represented a whole new order of magnitude.) But the steady occurrence of small spills creates a steady demand for the services of a little company of experts like RPI.

In 1976, RPI's people developed a concept that became known as Environmental Sensitivity Index mapping, classifying minute stretches of coastline in terms of their vulnerability to oil. Level 1 shorelines are solid rock. Level 3 is fine compact sand; Level 4 is coarse sand, into which the oil penetrates more deeply. The most sensitive of all are tidal flats (Level 9) and salt marshes (Level 10)—the very shorelines most affected by the Gulf War spill.

RPI's concept was first tested in 1979, when the company produced ESI maps of the Texas coastline just before the arrival of slicks from the Ixtoc 1 oil well blowout off the coast of Mexico. Since then, it has mapped almost the entire coastline of the United States, and exported the technology to numerous other countries. Originally the maps were produced by hand, but later maps are digital. By 1992 the company was producing a Southeast Alaska ESI Atlas in digital form.

The great benefit of ESI maps is that they allow emergency crews to concentrate their efforts on the areas of greatest potential damage. Never mind the rocks: block the marshes. On Level 1 and 2 shores, Hayes says, "I would never recommend a cleanup. Nature will do it." On Level 3 shores, the oil lies on the surface, and a bulldozer can scrape it up.

"Whenever you recommend beach cleaning, though, you have to be very careful that the recommendation doesn't involve hauling off large volumes of sand, because there will be either a real or perceived problem afterward related to erosion. Sand is a very valuable resource; it costs a lot of money in terms of nourishment and so forth. But the ideal situation is to let nature clean the beach itself."

On low-sensitivity beaches, the surf will break the oil into tiny particles, which are consumed by microorganisms. On gravel and cobble beaches, an oiled berm can be bulldozed into the surf to help this process along. On tidal flats and salt marshes, though, the only strategy worth pursuing is to keep the oil out in the first place.

If oil does get into those low-energy environments, the outlook is grim. Under the asphalt layer in the Persian Gulf, Hayes and his associates found another such layer, the legacy of the *Nowruz* spill of 1983. So what are the prospects that the spicy shores of Araby will recover?

Miles Hayes shook his head.

"The future of the upper intertidal zone is not good at all," he said soberly. "That oil will be there for decades."

8. The Politics of The Beach

... a foolish man ... built his house upon the sand;
And the rain descended, and the flood came, and the
winds blew, and beat upon that house; and it fell;
and great was the fall of it.
　　　—Matthew 7: 26-27

Who owns the beach in the first place? In Roman law, both the sea and its shores were *res communes*, things owned in common by all citizens. In medieval England, the waterways were legally the King's highways, so the shore belonged to the monarch up to the high tide line—but even the Crown's title was limited by an increasingly well-established right of the general public to use the shores and waterways. The common law of England was also the underlying law of the British colonies that became Canada and the United States, except where the U.S. Constitution altered its provisions—but the Constitution was silent on beaches and shores.

Six colonies passed ordinances extending private ownership to the low tide line: Delaware, Maine, Massachusetts, New Hampshire, Pennsylvania and Virginia. Other states went the other way, specifying that public ownership included the "dry sand beach" between the high tide line and the first line of vegetation. Elsewhere, since nobody thought of building permanent structures on the dry sand beach, it effectively became a public space, used by anyone who needed it, and the social patterns that developed from that use came to play a significant role in beach law. Such principles include customary use, the doctrine of public trust and the principle of implied dedication, by which a landowner who knows and permits his property to be used by others is considered to have dedicated the land to public use.

Several U.S. cases based on the public trust doctrine have established not only that the public owns the waterways and tidelands, but also that even the legislature cannot give them away, as the Illinois legislature attempted to do in 1869, when it granted a tract of land under Chicago Harbor to a railway company. No, said the U.S. Supreme Court, the legislature cannot "make a direct and absolute grant of the waters of the state, divesting all citizens of their common right."

What, exactly, is "the high tide line," and where are the boundaries of a piece of "land" that shifts and moves? Here the courts have held that when property gradually erodes, the boundary moves with the slowly retreating shoreline. Strangely enough, in legal language this process is called *accretion*, which is the exact reverse of its plain English meaning. Land which is lost in a sudden catastrophic storm, however, is said to have suffered *avulsion*, and it retains its original boundaries; the owner would normally have the right to reclaim it.

These principles have been hammered out pretty thoroughly in the U.S. courts, but in Canada, says one lawyer, there is surprisingly little case law on these matters. No doubt that is because the issues are urgent in the United States, where a population ten times the size of Canada's is migrating steadily toward the coasts. There is no such migration going on in Canada; even the relentless growth of Vancouver is in the city and the Fraser Valley, not on the shoreline.

The laws derive from politics. The political process—the commitment of public funds and the establishment of public policy—provides the framework in which beach development occurs. Public policy permits and even supports building on the shoreline. Public funds replenish and armor the beach and provide disaster relief when the ocean wrecks the developments. All this is done for the benefit of private property owners. Why? That is one of the big political questions about the beach.

Again, as sea level rises, what do we preserve: the buildings or the beach? That is a second major political question. Populists, environmentalists and democrats will fight to preserve the beach, but they are scattered and unfocused. Waterfront property owners are concentrated on the spot, and usually influential.

"We're always dealing with very small numbers of people who live next to the beach and who are causing the problem, relative to the number of people who want to use the beach," says Orrin Pilkey. "It's a really important principle that the number of people who are causing the problem are minuscule compared to the population. Eighty percent of the population wants to use the beach, but they don't want to live there."

Who has the right to use the beach—the landowners or the general public? That is a third political question. In *The Corps and the Shore*, written with Katharine L. Dixon, Pilkey reviews a proposed 33-mile replenishment project in New Jersey, which has been described as an engineering task comparable in scale to the Panama Canal project. The Army Corps of Engineers thinks it will cost $250 million over 50 years; Pilkey and Dixon argue that its cost will be $6 to $12 *billion*. It's all tax money, but how does it benefit the public? The two authors quote a *New York Times* article pointing out that "Two miles of new beaches in Sea Bright will have access paths spaced 2,500 feet apart with virtually no place to park, no public facilities and no lifeguards. Another half mile is occupied by private beach clubs that were given the right to keep non-members off the new sand. Only 12 public parking spaces exist along the two miles."

The barriers to access were not accidental; the borough council in nearby Monmouth Beach was actively taking steps to *reduce* beach use by the general public. They were responding to a petition from taxpayers concerned that "All kinds of people will be wandering around if we encourage them to stop and park." So much for the eight million New Yorkers who helped pay for the beach enhancements. But the whole debate was overwhelmed in 2012, when Hurricane Sandy rearranged the entire Jersey shore

Again, since the replenishment of a beach has to be done on a holistic, beach-long basis, the decision to undertake such a project must also be a collective decision, a communal decision—in other words, a political decision. Who should have the right to make such decisions, or to veto them? Nourishment projects have sometimes been thwarted by a single landowner's refusal to participate. The Miami project was delayed for years because all such projects undertaken by the U.S. Army Corps of Engineers must include public access—and a few hotel owners were offended that the plebes and proles would thereafter have just as much entitlement to the beach in front of their properties as any of the paying guests. Only when the beach had entirely vanished and the waves were sucking at their seawalls and foundations did they consent.

The requirement of public access sometimes has comic results. In Hull, Massachusetts, Peter Rosen pointed out a four-foot shelf high on the face of a million-dollar revetment. The shelf starts in the air and ends in the air. To reach it one would have to scale the face of the revetment, like a mountain climber. What is it?

Peter Rosen grinned.

"It's a public walkway," he said.

⤳

Underlying the political debates about the beach are two utterly opposed visions of the beach and its relationship to human beings.

One view holds that the beach is a piece of marketable real estate, no different from any other real estate, for sale to the highest bidder.

The market will ensure that it is put to what realtors call its "highest and best use" —*highest* and *best* being measured in money. If the cost of the land is so high that only a high-rise building could carry the mortgage, then the market will force a high-rise to be built. The beach is to be used and enjoyed—like a home in an exclusive subdivision— by those who can afford to pay for it, and they are entitled to expect the government to protect the security of their tenure.

The alternative view sees the beach as *res communes* still, the common property of the whole community and a unique environment in its own right. On this view, anything built on the beach should be regarded as temporary and should be removed by its owners when the beach retreats enough to threaten it. No public money should be spent, either directly or indirectly, to support beach development or to help those who have suffered by building where they should not have built. As one such person said, "If these people were building on the lip of a volcano, nobody would think of giving them disaster relief. Why should it be any different if they build on an eroding beach?"

These issues are especially well-focused on the barrier coast of the United States, where the explosion of population on a retreating coast gives them an urgency they lack in less densely settled regions. The United States, for all its political and ideological quirks, has an admirably robust democracy and a vigorous scientific community. Divisive issues get aired by lobbyists and citizens' groups, publicized by the media, debated in legislatures, jousted over in learned journals, argued in court. The issues are thus most sharply defined and articulated in the United States, and especially on the unstable barrier islands of the east coast. For two generations or more, property owners have largely had their way on the barrier coast. Now the pendulum seems to be swinging back toward *res communes*—and not only in the United States.

WESTHAMPTON, LONG ISLAND, APRIL, 1993

I am looking at a set of expensive houses—elaborately casual architects' designs in glass and weathered wood—standing on stilts twenty feet above the surf. They were built on pilings driven deep into the sand of Pike's Beach; now the sand has gone away, leaving them looking like architect-designed offshore oil rigs, their severed umbilicals of sewer and power swinging beneath them in the wind. Two bicycles are chained together on an utterly inaccessible sundeck, locked against thieves who would need a boat and climbing equipment to reach them.

The waves are breaking beneath the ruined houses and pouring through an inlet half a mile wide where last summer there was a road and a dozen more houses. A U.S. Army amphibious dukw lurches across what has already been named "Pike's Inlet," carrying homeowners, insurance adjusters and officials to the isolated houses still standing on what has now become, unexpectedly, an island.

This is Dune Road after a powerful December nor'easter was followed by a blizzard in March. The two storms inflicted heavy damage all down the coast, from Scituate, Massachusetts, to New Smyrna Beach, Florida. They pounded the barrier beaches of Long Island more heavily than any storm in decades. At Long Beach they unearthed jetties built in the 1920s. The storms cast up human bones along with hull sections from schooners stranded generations before. At Gilgo, they washed away a nearly completed $7.9 million beachfill. They wrecked houses in Kismet and Saltaire.

"Nobody can recall a winter like this," said Gary Joyce, looking out at the new inlet. "You get one big storm and it'll take out two or three houses on Dune Road, and that's it. I'd say these storms did as much damage as the '38 hurricane—and we haven't had a hurricane. These have just been big storms."

Gary Joyce was a magazine editor who had been surfing the beaches of Long Island for 30 years. At 44, he was short and fit, dense and sinewy as leather jerky. He had tried to reach the beach during the height of the December storm.

"You couldn't get over to these beaches. On the second day of the December storm I was at Smith's Point bridge, on the mainland,

and you could see the waves feathering over the dunes a good three quarters of a mile away. You could see a full wave, not just stuff blowing off the top. The storm went through three high tide cycles along with a full moon, and the tides were running seven to ten feet above normal. I'm calling the wave height 25 feet, maybe more. I'm sure the guys in Hawaii are used to waves that size, but this was an extraordinary event for Long Island."

Among the things washed away by the storm, said a report in *Newsday*, was "the middle ground in the decades-long debate over whether, and how, the shoreline should be shielded from the sea ... The debate now centers on two extremes: massive shoreline protection—attempting to halt the forces of nature, as barrier island residents say is necessary—or simply letting nature take its course as it continues the job it began about 12,000 years ago of slowly pushing the barrier beaches closer to the shore."

The problem on Dune Road was caused in large part by earlier attempts to stabilize the beach. After a breakthrough in Pike's Beach in 1962, Suffolk County started to build a field of 21 groins. The engineers wanted to start downdrift, at the west end of the beach, but political pressure caused the project to be started updrift, at the east end, choking off the sand supply at its source. After 16 groins had been built, the job was halted. The two 1993 breaches occurred right at the end of the groin field.

"It didn't take a soothsayer to predict the break would occur at Pike's Beach in a storm of this magnitude," said Bill Daley, chief of New York's Coastal Management Section. This time, however, it appeared that the larger issue might well be settled by the ruinous cost of any major repair job. New York State, said Secretary of State Gail Shaffer, "cannot simply fight Mother Nature in every part of the shoreline." Yes, the state would move to protect threatened roads, water tanks and similar public facilities. It would fill the new gap at Dune Road. But it would not pay to rebuild dunes and beaches all along the barrier coast of Long Island.

The owners of the 180 houses isolated by the new inlets, however, were already suing the county, the state and the federal government for causing excessive erosion of their properties by building the groin field at the wrong end of the beach. They had not been getting the support they needed from the Town of Southampton, so they seceded. In November, 1993, they incorporated the new village of Westhampton Dunes. A month later they had reached a settlement in the lawsuit.

"We started getting public officials on the stand under oath," says Gary Vegliante, the ebullient, funny saloon owner who had become mayor. "That lasted about six days. *Nobody* wanted to testify." Beach experts privately conceded that the homeowners had the governments dead to rights and could well have received as much as $300 million. In the end they settled for a 50-year-long $80 million package, starting with a $35 million program to fill in the inlets and trim the last few groins so the field would pass at least a modest budget of sand along to the famished beach. The Corps would maintain the beach for 50 years.

"I think we got a tremendously sensible solution to a hotly contested and emotional issue," says Vegliante. "The real issue was access. And that's fine, I'm a big beach-access advocate myself. We couldn't look like we're fixing up some rich guy's front yard and blocking off the beach. And we're not rich—we're the poor cousins anyway. There's nobody from Wall Street on this part of the shore. Of the 246 houses here before the storm, probably 50 were really nice, but the huge majority was Middle America—teachers, policemen, firemen, people whose families had been here since the thirties."

Under the settlement, the first 75 feet from the road toward the ocean remained under the exclusive control of the property owner. From there to the front of the dunes, the owner granted a conservation easement which meant that the land had to be undisturbed; the owner could erect one walkover across the dune, but nothing else. ("He still owns it, and he has to pay taxes on it, but he can't use it," Vegliante chuckles.) From the dunes to the water, the beach has been deeded back to the public, with no compensation to the owner. The public can reach the beach by using any of seven walkovers spaced along the village's 2.25-mile length. Bicycle racks are being installed at each walkover. A parking lot at one end of the village provides space for 1,300 cars, and a second lot in the middle of town can accommodate another 200.

"I came into a meeting and said, 'Well, there's good news and bad news,'" Vegliante remembers. "The good news is, the beach is gonna be rebuilt. The bad news is, you aren't gonna own it. Boy, that went over like a fart in church." The deal didn't make the village unduly popular with neighboring towns, either; it diminished the rights of property owners and signaled a very clear resurgence of *res communes.* But it shrewdly accommodated a changing political reality, and thus made the settlement possible.

To Vegliante, the whole experience teaches some dramatic lessons.

"Some people say, 'Let nature take its course,'" he says. "Well, this beach historically had an erosion rate of about a foot a year before they put in the groins. What happened to us was about as natural as a therapeutic abortion."

The episode, he says, sensitized residents to environmental issues. The homeowners are obliged to plant beach grasses, and they have become partners in the maintenance of the beach and the wildlife habitat. In 1996, the village had the highest success rate of piping plover and least tern nesting in the northeastern United States.

"The birds need a beach for that," says Vegliante. "They don't nest in mid-air. They don't copulate on the fly. So now they've got a beach, and you've got 300 families protecting it." The secret is creating the blend of uses, with homeowners, beach-goers and wildlife all living together.

"Let nature take its course. You can't fight Mother Nature," he snorts. "Baloney. Look at Westhampton, right next to us. There hasn't been a washover there since they built the groin field. You can build groins all down the shore. You can stabilize the situation. But you need leadership, and you've got to create that blend.

"And one other thing: don't listen to Orrin Pilkey."

Another clear lesson, one would think, is that if you mess with the shore—as the Corps did with the original groin field—you expose yourself to liability suits. But that exposure is hardly avoidable, says coastal geologist Jay Tanski, of the New York Sea Grant program; modifying the shoreline is almost inevitable. "You could not even have a fishing fleet," he says, "without manipulating the beach."

Because of the lawsuit, Westhampton Dunes was a special case. Other parts of the Long Island shoreline fared less well. After the storms, residents of Saltaire threatened to withhold their taxes: if their wrecked houses and eroded lots had no market value, what was there to tax? Long Beach city manager Edwin Eaton conceded that "we don't belong here on this barrier island, but 90 years ago someone decided to develop it, and now you have 50,000 people living here, and those people aren't going away any time soon." Should additional millions be spent to protect the investment already established on the beach? "My answer is yes."

Gary Joyce didn't agree.

"The beach is just going to keep on moving," he said. "It's got places to go, people to see, things to do. We're the least of its worries. It doesn't belong with houses on it, not anything permanent. Semi-permanent, fine. Take the loss, take the hit—but don't come back and build again. And don't cry when it's all gone, because that's just the nature of the beast. This beach is like a constantly moving organism, only it's a real big organism. It's going out to sea, going into the bay, going that way, shrinking this way. For people to come and build on it and then want the rest of us to subsidize any kind of repair work, I don't think it's fair."

Lee Koppelman, director of the Long Island Regional Planning Board, regards it as not merely unfair but quixotic.

"What people who have homes on the barrier beaches have tried to do is to make this spit of land stable, which is entirely impossible," he said in 1993. By 1997, however, Koppelman was no longer advocating retreat; he was recommending continuous monitoring of the beaches so that preventive measures could be taken in places where the islands were obviously weak. Had he changed his mind?

"I lost," he said bluntly. "When I started arguing about it, there were 2,200 houses on the beaches. Now there are 4,000, and public policy supports that kind of usage, so you have to protect those properties in some way. But there's no question it's ultimately a losing battle, all the same."

⌒

The first state to move decisively to a policy of retreat was South Carolina, after a prolonged battle in 1988 between developers and conservationists. The resulting compromise law prohibited new construction beyond a setback line based on the 40-year erosion rate, limited the size of shorefront buildings and forbade the construction of new seawalls or the replacement of existing ones.

The law gave rise to a pivotal court case launched by an affected landowner named David Lucas. Lucas had been a developer on the Isle of Palms, and though he had sold his interest in the actual development, he had paid $975,000 for two beach lots, intending to build a house for himself and another on speculation.

But the 1988 law made it illegal for Lucas to build on his lots and, Lucas argued, it had thus made the lots valueless. That amounted to a "taking of private property for public use without just compensation," contrary to the Fifth Amendment of the U.S. Constitution. Lucas won in the original trial, lost an appeal to the South Carolina Supreme Court, and finally, in 1992, won in the U.S. Supreme Court, which held that legislation or regulation amounts to unconstitutional taking if it deprives the owner of *all* economically beneficial uses of the land.

The decision seemed to attack the very basis of the South Carolina law. One legal scholar said the decision "elevates investor-backed expectations of speculative profit, no matter how unrealistic those expectations may seem to objective observers, to the sanctity of a constitutional right," but it was consistent with the Supreme Court's current outlook. Under Chief Justice William Rehnquist, the court had been "systematically unresponsive to environmental concerns." Orrin Pilkey was blunter: he called the decision "environmentally irresponsible."

The law was subsequently amended to accommodate the Lucas decision. For anyone who purchased seafront land in South Carolina after 1988, of course, the issue of "taking" does not arise; they knew the property was subject to the law when they bought it. The most contentious issue posed by the law has been the ban on new hard structures, which has been generally supported by the courts. With rare exceptions, the only erosion control now permitted is small sandbags and "scraping."

"Scraping?" Here is geologist Stanley Riggs, describing it:

> I watch as the high spring tide laps around the staircases, swimming pools and foundations of a group of ostentatious oceanfront beach "cottages" that are part of the gated Wild Dunes community on the northeast end of Isle of Palms, S.C.—a barrier island northeast of Charleston. As the tide begins to drop, three trucks, a bulldozer, and backhoe from the Dirt Cheap Trucking Company come to life.
>
> For several days during each bimonthly spring tide, the heavy equipment returns to excavate sand from the ebb-tide delta during low tide and use it in a futile attempt to build sand berms in front of 17 lots—many of which support pretentious million-dollar houses. And every time, the subsequent high tide removes the entire sand berm. Ocean waves again lap around the base of the structures.
>
> This bizarre ritual is repeated during each spring tidal cycle and continues until the moon wanes into the respite period of

the neap tide. The owners buy a little more time in a desperate effort to hold on to their beachfront properties.

Among the threatened properties are the two Lucas lots. Riggs points out that this particular type of barrier island swings back and forth between accretion and erosion; when such islands accrete, their ends swell, and they are then known as "drumstick" islands, a form very common on the Gulf Coast of Florida. The Lucas lots themselves were wholly or partially underwater from 1957 to 1973; the beach then accreted until about 1980, when it began to retreat again. But elaborate "cottages" had been built on the accreted land—the lots are worth $600,000, and the houses more than $1 million—and the owners defended them with rock bulkheads. The shore has continued to retreat, but the law now forbids homeowners to build new seawalls. The homeowners' only legal alternative is the Dirt Cheap Trucking Company.

And so they continue, tide after tide, trucking up sand for the surf to carry away.

∽

Canada has no constitutional provision against taking, but the very issues which were at stake in the *Lucas* decision were featured in one of the few Canadian legal actions involving development on beach property.

The case arose in Lower Kingsburg, Nova Scotia, in 1995. Like many other coastal villages in eastern Canada, Kingsburg hangs somewhere between the nineteenth century and the twenty-first. These are traditional communities with long-established habits, and until recently they used their beaches in traditional ways—as places to build and repair boats, mend nets, dry fish. In the last 40 years, however, the inshore fishery has largely gone away, and so have most of the young people. New people have been moving in, some only for the summer, some year-round: a publisher's representative, a photographer, a university administrator. By and large, the newcomers have melded with the oldtimers; they have come not only for the sea and the meadows and the beaches, but also for the lifestyle, the country humor, the folkways and conversation of the people.

Canada's beaches have not faced the same stresses as the American and European beaches, though that is more a matter of good luck than good management. The Canadian population is concentrated in inland provinces; only one of its eight largest cities is on the sea. In the United States, by contrast, seven of the 16 largest cities are on the coast. The two largest, New York and Los Angeles, have a combined population roughly one-third as large as the entire population of Canada.

But one can easily predict growing pressure on the east coast of Canada. Although the Canadian coastline is more than 152,000 miles long—the longest in the world—most of it does not invite development. The Arctic Sea is no place for beach resorts, and although the west coast is magnificent—deep-cut fjords, snow-dusted mountains, great rain forests—most of it is too wild, precipitous and remote to attract development. The developable coastline is chiefly in the four underpopulated, economically depressed eastern provinces: New Brunswick, Nova Scotia, Prince Edward Island, Newfoundland.

Canada's Atlantic shoreline is stunning—rocky forelands enclosing pocket beaches, long stretches of beige sand, clean cold ocean surf, a view that stretches to Ireland. In summer, the shallow enclosed water on New Brunswick's Gulf of St. Lawrence shoreline heats up quickly; it becomes the warmest saltwater north of Florida. (The province's Bay of Fundy shoreline has some of the coldest.) The Gulf shore has miles and miles of uninhabited sandy beaches, chains of barrier islands, unspoiled salt marshes and salmon-fishing rivers. It remains undeveloped because most Canadians live far away, and most other people in the world think that "a Canadian summer" is an oxymoron. But land is cheap, communities are hungry for jobs and development, and New Brunswick is only a long day's drive from Boston.

The Atlantic provinces have made some efforts to protect their beaches; Nova Scotia has a Beaches Protection and Preservation Act, under which it has protected 95 beaches. Hirtle's Beach, next to Kingsburg, had been designated a protected beach, and Kingsburg Beach was also supposed to be protected. Indeed, the government believed it had been designated. But somehow it slipped through the net, and when a developer presented himself at the Lunenburg County building inspector's office looking for a permit to build a house in the Kingsburg dunes, the surprised inspector found that he had no legitimate excuse to refuse.

That first building permit "opened the floodgates," says John Duckworth, a spokesman for the quickly formed Committee to Protect Kingsburg Beach. "Once one person got a permit, that established a market and market values for all the previously worthless property in the dunes and wetlands." It was a substantial value, in Nova Scotian terms: lots in the dunes were suddenly worth $60,000, in a province where raw land often sells for less than $1,000 per acre. Appalled, the committee petitioned the provincial government to designate Kingsburg Beach at once. The government did, but by the time it had acted, five foundations had been poured in the dunes, and two of them had houses on them.

Meanwhile, some of those who owned other lots in the dunes sued the government, which—by freezing further development—had rendered their land worthless once again, depriving them of a lush windfall. Essentially, this was the *Lucas* issue: landowners suing the government for regulating away the economic value of their land. The plaintiffs claimed they were entitled to notice that their waterfrontage was being considered for designation, and to be heard before the final decision was made.

Mr. Justice David MacAdam found that the government had the right to take action to "leave [the beaches] unimpaired for the benefit and enjoyment of future generations," and that it had done exactly that at Kingsburg. Though "the designation of the plaintiffs' lands as beaches under the Act was unlawful," he said, the fact that the province had made a procedural error "must not jeopardize the public interest in the beaches of Nova Scotia as set out in the Act. That public interest is for the benefit, education and enjoyment of present and future Nova Scotians."

Mr. Justice MacAdam found in favor of the plaintiffs—but he did not overturn the government's action. Instead, he ordered the government to give the plaintiffs a hearing that satisfied the requirement of procedural fairness. The government held hearings, and eventually ruled that those who had received building permits before the beach was designated could proceed with construction—but no further construction would be allowed. The decision rewarded fast-footed developers and punished the less-aggressive owners of neighboring lots, but the government hoped it would prevent what might have been a prolonged series of further actions, appeals, suits and counter-suits. It did not: the decision did indeed lead some of the landowners to sue the province for compensation for the loss of value in their land. But when the dust settled, the decision stood.

The better solution would have been to expropriate the entire dune, pay fair compensation to all owners, and remove the foundations and houses. But such a precedent might require the government to pay compensation every time it designated a beach. And the province's hands are not clean; the provincial government does a fair amount of beach armoring, protecting roads and highways and building causeways across wetlands and inlets.

John Duckworth cites Hirtle's Beach, right next to Kingsburg, as an example of good beach management. The province recently teamed with Lunenburg County to buy the half of the beach it did not already own, and placed the beach's management in the hands of a broadly based and conservation-oriented Management Committee struck by the local Board of Trade.

For Duckworth, one image from the battle for Kingsburg Beach glows in memory: the image of a woman named Meredith Mackay—

who now sits on the Hirtle's Beach Management Committee—standing up at a public meeting, her voice choked with emotion, telling the community that of all the things her father had done in his life, one act had made her more proud to be his daughter than any other.

Her father had owned half of Hirtle's Beach. And he had given it to the people of Nova Scotia.

∽

Pro-development forces have an edge in such battles because the structural weight of law and regulation is based on a long and deeply entrenched tradition of reshaping the shoreline as though it were any other piece of land. Katharine Dixon, Orrin Pilkey's collaborator, has noted more than 50 programs of the U.S. federal government which encouraged or supported development on the shore. Some of these are general development subsidies, which are available to citizens everywhere; beach dwellers use the normal housing assistance programs as well as roads, sewage and other infrastructure programs. But they also benefit from disaster relief measures, tax deductions for casualty losses, tax-funded coastal works by the Corps of Engineers, and various other subsidies.

If one wanted to discourage people from building homes in hazardous places, one could start by restricting the subsidies. Instead, the U.S. government has created special subsidies which have the effect of *helping* people to own homes on the beaches and river floodplains.

The most striking instance is the National Flood Insurance Program, a prime example of a good idea gone awry. Flood insurance was virtually impossible to obtain from private insurers, who have a marked aversion to losing money. Enacted in 1968, the government program was designed to help state and local governments discourage building in locations exposed to flooding.

To obtain federal flood insurance, homeowners had to be located in participating communities, which in turn had to implement specific zoning and construction regulations. In addition to the carrot of insurance, the program had a stick: homeowners within participating communities who did not purchase flood insurance would be ineligible for other federal financial assistance, including disaster relief and home-mortgage insurance.

"It was a well-meaning program," says Peter Rosen. "People already in the flood zone would have protection, and no other insurance would be offered for new structures. But whenever there was an insurance claim people would rebuild a little bit better, a little bit nicer; perhaps summer homes would be winterized, and so forth. So what started out in the forties and fifties and sixties as cottages on the beach are now very nice year-round homes, largely paid for by flood-insurance claims.

"And while flood-insurance regulations prevented people from building in the flood zone, it didn't prevent them from building *above* the flood zone—so houses elevated over the 100-year-flood level were eligible for subsidized insurance. Once again flood insurance was subsidizing development on the coast, which is the exact opposite of what the program was designed to do."

The number of U.S. households located in flood hazard areas grew by 40 percent in 30 years. By 1996, the United States had an estimated 276,000 households living within reach of storm surges, and another 2.4 million in floodplains nearby. The National Flood Insurance program had 2.5 million policies in force, 72 percent of them on the marine coasts. From 1978 to 1987, the program paid out $657 million more in claims than it collected in premiums. It had $500 million on hand, but a single catastrophic hurricane season could generate up to $4 billion in claims, and the total potential liability of the program was a staggering $300 billion. All U.S. taxpayers were carrying that risk, but the benefits were flowing to only a few of them.

"The original goal of the NFIP has been ignored and perverted," charged the Coastal Alliance, the National Wildlife Federation and Friends of the Earth. "In effect, the NFIP has become a financial safety net for shoreline developers. Why should the taxpayer take on the insurance risk for risky beachfront developments that private insurers will not?"

A good question, and a highly political one.

$\backsim$

For conservationists, one clear lesson is that the time to act is always *now*. As time passes, populations grow, prices rise, environmentally important areas are cleared and paved. It will never be any easier than it is now. And your children will thank you for your foresight, as Oregonians—and tourists—are grateful to two forceful and determined public servants named Oswald West and Sam Boardman.

Oregon's shoreline is young, bold, dramatic. Through most of its length it rises abruptly from the sea, deeply indented, with steep rocky cliffs, dark forested capes and stream-fed beaches tucked among its rocky coves. Its northern sections are nourished by the cascade of sediments carried from the vast watershed of the Columbia River. Its southern sections are dominated by miles of wandering dunes created by the rapid erosion of the sandstone bedrock. The sandstone crumbles; the water carries it seaward; the winds blow it back. The dunes adjust themselves to the seasonal wind changes and creep inland three or four feet a year.

The whole coast is speckled with state parks; they pass almost as regularly as milestones. They are not big parks, only a few square miles between the highway and the sea. One of the northernmost is Oswald West State Park, which includes about five miles of shoreline incorporating pocket beaches, mountains, a 900-foot cape and many acres of towering rain forest.

Oswald West was governor of Oregon from 1911 to 1915. Theodore Roosevelt said he was "a man more intelligently alive to the beauty of nature ... and more keenly appreciative of how much this natural beauty should mean to civilized mankind, than almost any other man I have ever met holding high political position." As governor, West induced the legislature to claim all the state's beaches as public highways, and to end sales of land between the lines of high and low tide, thus preserving the state's magnificent beaches for all the citizens.

At the other end of the coast is Boardman State Park—11 miles of shoreline with arched rocks and sea caves, deep canyons and monstrous offshore rocks, curling sand beaches and abandoned mine workings. The road you drive was built only in 1962; before its construction the area was almost inaccessible.

Boardman State Park honors the memory of Oregon's other great prophet of shoreline conservation, Samuel H. Boardman. Born in Massachusetts, Boardman homesteaded on the Columbia River at what is now the town of Boardman. He became interested in beautification of the spreading road system and set up volunteer groups that planted thousands of trees along the highways. In 1919 he joined the highways department, and in 1929 he became the first superintendent of state parks, a job he held for 21 years.

When Boardman started, Oregon had 6,444 acres of state park; when he retired in 1950, at 75, that had risen to 57,195, arguably the finest state park system in existence. Boardman was a great salesman, and he had persuaded the owners of nearly 20,000 acres to donate their land to the park system. In the 1940s, for example, he was assembling land for a park, and he noticed that a borax company had once mined a mineral called pricetite along the coast. Borax Consolidated, of London, still owned about two miles of coastline. Boardman persuaded them to give it to the state, retaining only the mineral rights. That strip of land is now part of Boardman State Park.

In building a parks system, Boardman once said, you must "build when your sinews are young. Build before time makes your recreational heritage prohibitive through cost. Husband that which you have; build unto that which you would preserve."

The Oregon coast affords many great spectacles, including some of the highest and roughest surf most of us will ever see, spouting high into air as it smashes against the solid rock of the cliffs. Near Heceta Head is the only known year-round rookery of Steller sea lions; you can visit them in their home by taking an elevator down through the rocky cliff to the sea-cave where they live. You can look to seaward at the isolated spire of the old lighthouse on Tillamook Rock, where the sea has been known to heave rocks the weight of a man's body clear over the light, 139 feet above sea level. The lighthouse was abandoned in 1957; today it is the Eternity at Sea Columbarium, and if you like you can arrange to have your ashes deposited there after your death. You can explore 40 miles of dunes—not only the living dunes by the shore, but also the old vegetated dunes, 300 feet high. At Cape Kiwanda you can see dories shoved into the surf, heading out for a day's fishing. Near Brookings you can visit forests of myrtle, redwood and azalea.

If plumes of surf, azalea forests and wandering dunes move you to reverence, you might want to direct some of your prayers toward the repose of Oswald West and Sam Boardman.

And if you want to see how not to do it, just keep driving south from Boardman State Park. In half an hour you'll be in California. In a day you'll be in Encinitas, where houses have been sliding down the eroding cliffs into the sea for more than 100 years.

It's a terrible place for houses. It might have made a fine state park.

☙

Slowly, belatedly, we are growing more sensitive to Gaia's well-being— and in the process we are creating a market for environmentally sensitive development. If we are going to live on barrier islands, for instance, we do not have to live right in the dunes in order to enjoy the beach.

When Alan Bisbort, co-author of the guidebook *Life Is A Beach*, was asked to recommend one beach on the whole U.S. east coast, he replied, "Kiawah Island."

Good choice. Fat and stunning Kiawah, 10,000 acres in area, lies 21 miles from Charleston, South Carolina. Ten miles long and a mile and a half wide, Kiawah is relatively stable; it lies along a low-energy coastline, and it is actually two islands in one, a modern retreating island that has merged with a much older barrier from an earlier geological epoch.

In 1974, when OPEC was riding high and Arab money was splashing into investments all over the Western world, the Kuwait Investment Company bought this former plantation. From the start, Kiawah was intended to be an environmental and architectural jewel. The Kuwaitis began with a $1.3 million environmental study—wildlife, plants, archaeology, geology—which took 16 months to complete. The geologist on the team was Miles Hayes, who did a careful review of the island's shape, both now and in the past. He recommended very conservative setback lines and he specified them for every precinct of the shore.

The foredunes were left untouched. The mature maritime forest—myrtles, palmettos, magnolias, live oaks—was left largely untouched. So were the salt marshes, the lazy rivers, any area of special environmental value. Houses were grouped not just along the beach, but throughout the island, beside golf courses and tidal creeks, among the trees, behind the dunes, beside ponds and parks. Biking trails provide everyone with access to the exquisitely clean, wide beaches. Most of the island is not developed at all. One suspects that such planning makes good business sense: the whole island becomes desirable, not just the strip along the beach.

Bisbort loves Kiawah's beaches but dismisses the development as "a compound of rich people who play golf." Well, yes—rich, but not, like, *rich*. In 1993, when I was there, lots were running from under $70,000 to more than $700,000, houses from just less than $100,000 to something more than $1 million. You could have sold a decent house in any major city and replaced it with one in Kiawah without suffering a grave financial hernia. And if developers are to leave a good deal of land in its natural state, the price has to go up on the parcels they select for development.

Still, this is far from modest housing. Kiawah's people certainly do play golf: the island has four courses, designed by the likes of Gary Player and Jack Nicklaus. Kiawah's glossy promotional kits, with their magnificent photographs, parchment pages and tumescent prose, discreetly reveal that this is a "security development." It may offer "low-country roasted oysters and Southern barbecue accompanied by bluegrass music and glorious riverfront sunsets," not to mention "ten miles of flawless Atlantic beach ... sweeping vistas of green and golden marsh grass ... a centuries-old maritime forest, draped with Spanish moss"—but it also has gates and guards to keep the world at bay, and a second set of gates and guards to keep the more exclusive districts safe from the rest of the island's residents. It all evokes a world where such mundane realities as loan payments, rebel teenagers and tooth decay might be considered just a little bit ... vulgar.

Too tame for Alan Bisbort, clearly. And in truth, places like Kiawah are not designed for those who revel in human diversity and who love funky old organically matured communities. Still, Kiawah has deservedly won several awards for environmental sensitivity, ecological planning and land conservation. If one is going to create a new residential district on a barrier island, it is hard to imagine how to do it much better than Kiawah's developers have done.

Sanibel and Captiva islands, on the other hand, did grow organically—at least for a while. These linked islands lie on the Gulf of Mexico, 15 miles southwest of Fort Myers, Florida. Like many islands in the Bahamas, Sanibel has an open, well-defined beach on its seaward side, and an tangle of mangrove swamps and wetlands on its inner face. Between the swamps and the beach, the island is heavily wooded. The wetlands are home to roseate spoonbills, anhingas, alligators and many other species. The swampy side of the island is the Ding Darling National Wildlife Refuge, named for the Pulitzer Prize-winning editorial cartoonist, who was also an ardent conservationist.

In fact 40 percent of the area of Sanibel and Captiva islands is given over to wildlife reserves.

Shells are the great attraction of Sanibel's beach. Miami's beach is made up of broken shell fragments; Sanibel's is constantly replenished with new, complete shells washing in from the shallow waters of the Gulf of Mexico. Sanibel's early settlers waded ashore through drifts of shells two and three feet deep; the beaches are largely made up of broken shells; the waves washing on the shore chime and jingle. Their forms and colors are exquisite: infinitely tiny coral-colored clamshells, scallop shells in all sizes, sea pen shells which look like huge mussels— blue-black outside, iridescent inside. Cockleshells, sea-olives and conchs. Sand dollars, whelks, periwinkles, and many more.

The beach is wide and flat, and the broken shells crunch under your feet when you walk. Just a few yards offshore, the brown pelicans soar and swoop and plunge into the water. Kids caper in the warm gentle surf. Couples walk hand in hand through the gentle swash and backwash, their faces invisible, their shapes black in silhouette against the red sun sliding down toward Mexico.

The islands were once home to the Caloosa people, and were visited by Ponce de Leon in 1521. For a certain period, says an engagingly forthright Chamber of Commerce booklet, it was the hideout of a gang of "second-rate pirates." A group of homesteaders arrived in 1888, but hurricanes wrecked their plantations in 1921 and 1926, and many gave up in despair. A few remained, and some discerning individuals discovered the islands—the writers Anne Morrow Lindbergh, Fletcher Knebel, Edna St. Vincent Millay and Rachel Carson among them—but the area remained a backwater even after a causeway to the mainland was built in 1963.

In the early 1970s, however, development was working its way steadily down the west coast of Florida. It reached Lee County in 1973-74, and Sanibel found itself being carved up into subdivisions and splattered with motels. Residents were horrified. Lee County planners were projecting as many as 35,000 housing units, and a population not far south of 100,000. The Chamber of Commerce publication says bluntly that the county "refused to do anything to preserve the quality of life through zoning or other controls."

Very well, said Sanibel, we secede. In November, 1974, the residents voted to become a town and immediately clapped a moratorium on all new building until consultants could develop a land-use plan. Business interests were furious. One developer went to court to have the new town declared illegal, while the local Bank of the Islands was blocked from providing a $250,000 operating loan to keep the new town afloat until it could collect taxes. The mayor asked the citizens to put up the money, and three days later he had it.

The master plan was adopted in 1976. It called for a maximum of 7,800 homes, to be concentrated in "developable zones." Homes in "hazard zones" faced strict guidelines, including a setback line ranging from 100 to 250 feet beyond which no building whatever could take place. Two years later, the town—having been unsuccessfully sued by various investors under the *taking* provision of the Fifth Amendment—in turn sued a condominium development for building its recreational complex too close to the beach. The developers settled out of court and moved the facilities.

Today the town has a population of 5,500. Its hotels and resorts have an enviable 90 percent occupancy rate, and the place comes across as a genuine community—highly self-aware, conscious of the fragility of its environment, and yet unpredictable, expressive, full of life. In addition to the usual pleasures of swimming, fishing and shelling, it has theaters and restaurants, libraries and Little League teams, museums and marinas, festivals of classical music and jazz. Its old clapboard community center hosts bingo games, movies, art exhibits, card games, square dances, auctions and political rallies.

Sanibel, in short, has many diverse attractions to complement its unique and unfortified beach. It has diversity among its people. It is a lusty little democracy. And it has no gates.

As a better understanding of the shoreline percolates through the population, laws and regulations are slowly changing. Three states, Maine and the Carolinas, now prohibit seawalls and other hard structures outright, and 13 states now have erosion-rate setbacks, including the Great Lakes states of Michigan and Ohio. The laws of Maine also set a height limit of 35 feet on buildings near the shore, and require that they be "readily removable." If a beachfront building is more than 50 percent damaged by a storm, it may not be rebuilt, and the wreckage must be removed at the owner's expense. New construction must be shown to be safe for 100 years, assuming a sea level rise of three feet per century. In some instances, the state requires a demolition plan to be filed with the building plans before it will issue a permit for shoreside construction.

Maine enforces these regulations vigorously. It has denied all applications for high-rises at Old Orchard Beach, for example, since they would fall within the 100-year setback line, and has ordered the removal of residences and commercial buildings erected in defiance of the law. Florida, by contrast, in 1995 passed legislation that left decisions about beach armoring to local communities—a disastrous step, since shoreline engineering on one part of the coastline will have impacts on other places. Coastal processes do not take place within tidy and arbitrary municipal boundaries.

If we are going to live on the shore, then the basic political questions have to do with balancing the competing players who have an interest in the shoreline—not only the human players, but also the plants, the animals and the beach itself. Nowhere do more of those interests coincide than at Sebastian Inlet.

Sebastian Inlet lies on—indeed, constitutes—the boundary between Brevard and Indian River counties on the east coast of Florida, about 40 miles south of Cape Canaveral. It connects the Atlantic Ocean to the Indian River, which is part of the Intracoastal Waterway. The Indian River is a protected waterway and an estuary of national significance; the National Estuary Program is doing studies in it. The inlet is in the middle of the Archie Carr Turtle Refuge, established because the area has the largest population of nesting sea turtles in the northern hemisphere. It is just north of the Pelican Island National Wildlife Refuge, the oldest such refuge in the United States.

Sebastian Inlet is right at the boundary of the tropics and marks the northernmost range for some forms of coral and for several species of tropical fish. It is a nesting area for the least tern and the beach mouse, both endangered species. The highly endangered Atlantic Right Whale gives birth to its young—only a dozen or so a year—off its coast.

The inlet boasts superb fishing off its north jetty, and the jetty has created some of the best surfing conditions on the east coast. On the bank of the inlet is the most visited state park in Florida. The inlet is a promising site for aquaculture. Huge blubbery manatees, another endangered species, plow through its waters. Indian River Lagoon supports considerable shellfish harvesting. Commercial fishermen and recreational boaters constantly pass through the inlet; although the two adjoining counties are the least-populated counties on the coast, they nevertheless contain an estimated 44,000 licensed boats; the local boating industry represents $1 billion in economic activity and supports 17,000 jobs.

If there is a spot on the shore anywhere in the world with more complex competing uses, I cannot imagine where it would be.

The body charged with mediating among all these interests is the Sebastian Inlet Tax District Commission, incorporated in 1918 by the Florida legislature as an independent entity responsible for opening and maintaining a navigable waterway between the ocean and the river. To do that, the district was authorized to levy taxes on properties in the adjacent portions of the two counties. Local residents didn't object; they had long agitated for another inlet through the 100-mile stretch of barrier island between Cape Canaveral and Fort Pierce. At various times, beginning as early as 1888, they had tried to dig one by hand, but the inlet always filled and closed. The tax district's job was to get the damn thing open and keep it open.

That took 50 years, and in hindsight it involved a fair amount of environmental mayhem. Storms closed the inlet for long periods during the 1920s and 1930s, and kept it shut during most of World War II. The basic problem was a rocky reef down the spine of the island. In 1948, the U.S. Navy used some of its war-surplus explosives to dynamite the reef, and the Corps of Engineers built a 250-foot jetty on the north side of the newly reshaped inlet. The jetty has since been extended to 1,000 feet, and a 170,000 cubic yard sand trap has been blasted into the inlet's floor. The tides draw more than 100,000 cubic yards of sand into the inlet annually; it falls into the sand trap, and from time to time it is pumped out and sent on its way to nourish the down-drift beaches of Indian River County.

After 1948 the inlet was a fact of life. It stayed open, but by the early 1980s the commission itself was giving off an odor like citrus slowly rotting in the tropical sun. State auditors were appalled at its lack of proper operating and management systems, its missing records, its dubious bidding and contracting practices, and the questionable—indeed, actionable—travel accounts of three commissioners. State legislators muttered about abolishing the commission altogether.

Enter Carol Ann Senne, a young wife and mother who also happened to be a professional engineer, a graduate of Harvard and MIT with a mind as sharp as an auditor's pencil. Elected to the Commission in 1985, Senne was soon joined by Charles W. Sembler II, a 21-year-old commercial fisherman whose grandfather had chaired the Commission in the 1930s and whose great-grandfather had tried to get the inlet opened as a private venture. The third member of the new team was an educator and former salvage diver named David Howell. The three instituted a set of reforms which ultimately won national recognition.

The born-again commission retained new lawyers and accountants, hired its first full-time administrator, Raymond LeRoux, and engaged an innovative young staff engineer, Kathy Fitzpatrick. It entered into partnerships with the parks system and with all the other levels of government. It went looking for a consulting geologist and found Dr. Randall Parkinson, a coastal geologist at nearby Florida Tech. That led to a wide-ranging relationship with the university.

The commission established an advisory board of leaders from local user groups. It hired a lobbyist in the state capital and commissioned Robert Dean's lab at the University of Florida to build a sophisticated model of the inlet to use in planning and experimentation. It started talking frankly and frequently with the media, an initiative eased by the fact that LeRoux had been editor of a local newspaper before his appointment as the inlet's administrator.

Early on, the rejuvenated commission—at its own expense—developed a comprehensive five-year plan for the inlet. The plan cost $110,000, but staffers speak of it in the reverent tones normally reserved for scripture.

"We sat down with the Department of Natural Resources of the State of Florida and brainstormed," Carol Ann Senne remembered. "We said, If you could manage an inlet, what would you do? What would you look at, besides just the sand? Some of the most wonderful things about Sebastian Inlet are the natural resources. What about the fishery? What about the sea turtles? What about the mangrove shoreline? There's so much down there that's important. How do they all interact? How is the management of the inlet going to affect them?

"You address each one of these issues independently, looking for the optimal management approach, and then you look at them as an integrated system. That's where you get into your decision making process and all your tradeoffs. You come up with a five-year plan, and every year you must update that plan so it's always a five-year plan.

"The wonderful thing about it is, you always know where you're going and you know what you need to monitor ahead of time so that you can make good decisions about when to dredge, where to place the sand and how to take care of your other resources. But you're always weighing and balancing."

As Senne likes to say, you can't manage without data, so the plan turned the commission into a research organization.

"We do a lot of research," says LeRoux. "Every coastal area is unique and different, so it becomes as much art as science. A lot of the strong feelings and attitudes of people are based largely on ignorance and bias, and our search for knowledge has really toned down a lot of the extreme positions in the local community.

"We've invested a quarter of a million dollars a year in coastal zone research and plan to continue doing so. And we've been able to do that while *lowering* taxes for eight years in a row at the same time."

The commission uses infrared aerial photography to monitor the state of the eelgrass. It counts and watches the hatching of turtle eggs. It monitors fish and bird populations. It runs economic analyses of its own effects. Kathy Fitzpatrick does time-lapse photography of the inlet every day. The Commission is planning side-scan sonar mapping of the offlying reef. Randy Parkinson drills cores to determine the effect of a proposed new channel from the inlet to the Intracoastal Waterway.

Carol Ann Senne says she saw an opportunity to establish Sebastian Inlet as a state-of-the-art operation in coastal zone management. Five years after her election, she and her colleagues had done it.

"In 1989," says Ray LeRoux, "we won the Award of Distinction from the Florida Shore and Beach Association, a 90-year-old organization that represents all of the influences that love beaches and coastlines. That was for the best-managed beach program in local government. Two years later we won the State of Florida Award of Distinction for our work with endangered sea turtles—so that was for environment rather than management. We think those two are not mutually exclusive, that good management is good environmental programming. And then in 1992 we won the first-ever award in America for Excellence in Local Government from the National Oceanic and Atmospheric Administration. There really are only three government awards to win, and in three years we won them all."

To LeRoux, it is only logical that the clientele and management of a place like Sebastian Inlet should take the lead in reshaping our attitudes to the shoreline.

"We have to survive with nature, in harmony," he says. "We have to operate in such a way that we're a friend and ally with other species on the planet. And you know, the people who use the water and know the water appreciate it and love it the best."

∽

I have nothing but admiration for people who work with enlightened devotion toward a more intelligent and respectful relationship between human beings and the beach. At the same time I feel a twinge of melancholy. Thoreau's beach was a wild, rank place, with no flattery in it. Sebastian Inlet is not a wild, rank place; it is trained and manipulated, scrutinized and directed, known and measured. A hurricane could turn it wild again, but only briefly. Sanibel Island survives only because it is defended by statutes and bylaws. Kiawah is regulated down to the last cedar shake.

Regulation is the evil twin of conservation, and even the best-intentioned regulations can have quixotic and unfair effects. Nobody loves regulations. Yet fundamentally I do not complain about them: I see no alternative. Left to their own devices, driven by hedonism and greed, market forces turn shorelines into nightmares at once sterile and dangerous. The market gave us Coney Island and Blackpool. Regulation gave us Sanibel and the Oregon coast. Politics gives us the choice.

I am—humbly, I hope—grateful to live among beaches that are still wild and rank, pitiless and elegant. I love the way they shift and move, sleeping for decades and then suddenly breaking apart, changing shape, engulfing forests and exposing shipwrecks, always intent on their intricate dance at the boundary of the sea and the land. They are great teachers of philosophy, demonstrating the poignancy of the human delusion that permanence and stability are possible, that change can be prevented by acts of the will. Look, they whisper, everything changes. Only the processes are permanent.

I talk about beaches as though the damn things were alive.

It is probably fruitful and healthy to think of them that way.

But maybe they really are alive.

The Celtic Mass for the Sea

Certain moments on the shore have a meditative, almost mystical quality: the vastness of the sea; the sky with its ceaselessly evolving patterns of clouds; the curve and curl of sand and wave; the busy scurrying sanderlings, conscious only of their need for food; the calling cards of the clam vents spurting underfoot. Life, in short, and the world, going on as it must have gone on before the arrival of human beings and as it will go on, no doubt, after our departure.

Fragrant maiden of the sea
Thou art full of graces,
Be thine own hand on my rudder's helm
And be mine a good purpose
Towards each creature in creation.

Jennyfer Brickenden located that ancient text and wove it into Scott Macmillan's magnificent *Celtic Mass for the Sea*—a sacred work for our time, rooted in the ancient Celtic reverence for the mysterious sea as preserver, destroyer and giver of life. An ambitious work for string orchestra, Celtic ensemble and massed choirs, the *Celtic Mass* includes incantations and charm poems chanted by mothers as they laid their babies on the beach, surrounding the infants with shells to keep them safe from evil spirits while the mothers went about their work. The *Mass* also includes a prayer, which should be uttered along every shoreline where fishermen live and where fish still remain:

> *That it may please Thee to give and preserve to our use the kindly fruits of the earth and restore and continue to us the blessings of the sea. Let not our faults or our frailty bring disaster upon us.*

Where was that prayer and that sensibility when the draggers were scraping the bottom and towing their baglike nets through the spawning masses of codfish on the Grand Banks? Where is that prayer when herring, intact but for their roe, are pouring like a silver waterfall from the dumptrucks into the municipal landfill? *Let not our faults or our frailty bring disaster upon us.* But they do, they do—and how can we pray for exemption from the consequences of our actions?

> *Tiny plant life keeps us living*
> *Sea weeds till we reach our landing,*
> *Food and drink and tiny plant life*
> *Tiny plant life on swelling oceans.*

The most terrible line in the whole *Celtic Mass*—prophetic, contemporary, uncompromising—is said to come from St. Columba in the fourth century: *He who tramples on the world tramples on himself.*

But the *Mass* also includes this dreamy, lyrical verse:

> *Now lay thine ear against this golden sand,*
> *And thou shalt hear the music of the sea*
> *Those hollow tunes it plays against the land—*
> *I have lain hours, and fancied in its tone*
> *I have heard the languages of ages gone ...*

Lay one's ear against the sand—and hear the languages of ages gone? The reference, says Jennyfer Brickenden, is to "sonorous sands," sands that emit a musical tone when you walk on them, sands that almost seem to speak. Sonorous sands? Is this—like kelpies and fairies—a poetic effusion from the Celtic past?

Come and park the car beside the fisheries museum at Basin Head, on the east coast of Prince Edward Island. Walk over the old cast-iron bridge, which arches across the tiny estuary, with kids cannon-balling off the rope hanging beneath it. Go down the beach past the families with their picnics, the gangly teenage couples, the toddlers with their sand pails, watched by hawk-eyed young mothers. This beach, too, seems endless. It runs out in the heat into obscurity, where it meets the sea and the sky in a white, seamless horizon.

And now listen as you walk. *Squeak. Skrawwk. Squeak. Skrawwk.*

The sound is coming from your feet. Walk toward the dunes, then toward the surf. The sound is weak in the dunes, and the wet sand of the swash zone is silent. The sound is strongest just above the high tide line, where a hint of moisture remains.

Kick the sand, and the sound becomes high, sharp, urgent: *Chip!* Draw your toe slowly through it, and the sand responds with a long, low hum that sounds like the voice of the beach. Draw your foot back and forth over the surface or sweep your hand across it, and you can create an almost continuous sound, like a fiddler making his bow glide back and forth across a string.

Now lay thine ear against this golden sand, and thou shalt hear the music of the sea ...

These are singing sands, which are also found at Manchester, Massachusetts; at Cannon Beach, Oregon; at Kanai, Hawaii; at Eigg in the Hebrides and Bornholm in the Baltic—not to mention Chimney Corner, Cape Breton, just across Northumberland Strait, and the Magdalen Islands, fifty miles north. Until recently, the secret of such a beach seemed to be the character of the sand: pure quartz, with round, regular grains that show up clearly under magnification. Most sand is much less uniform, derived from a variety of sources and made up of a variety of materials. But quartz sand is the hardest of all, and therefore the oldest; when softer materials have been ground to nothing, quartz endures.

But can only quartz sands produce a sound? And how do they do it, anyway? Three scientists at Laurentian University in Sudbury, Ontario, published an article in *Nature* suggesting that the sound comes from a silica gel-like surface layer on the sand grains. The layer occurs naturally not only on some quartz sands, but also on calcareous sands in Hawaii, which derive from shells. To test their hypothesis, the experimenters tried to produce the sound from commercially available silica gel. It sang, too.

Soon we may know how the miracle works, but it will be no less a miracle for that.

⁓

Scott Macmillan is a professional musician who works in almost every musical metier, from gospel and traditional Celtic music to jazz and classical forms. He is a brilliant guitarist, a composer and arranger and general man-about-music; he conducts a series of concerts for Symphony Nova Scotia, writes music for film and TV and has released a superb jazz and Celtic album, *Guitar Souls,* with his longtime friend, the master guitarist David MacIsaac.He and Jennyfer have produced an intimate, collaborative series of albums called *Scott Macmillan Presents The Minnie Sessions.* The title is a play on words: the music—with the simplest of arrangements and a handful of musicians—is recorded in Scott and Jennyfer's summer home in Cape Breton, which was previously owned by a healer named Minnie Adams.

I had the privilege of working with Scott on a project while he was writing the *Celtic Mass,* and I vividly recall sitting in the attic workroom of his little house in the hydrostone district of Halifax while he played snatches of the *Mass* from his computer, describing excitedly how the piece would work, how the sections would be linked and who he hoped would play at the premiere. It was clearly going to be an exciting and powerful work, rooted in a culture that was at its zenith three millennia before Christ—and yet with a concern about the way we treat nature that was as fresh as it was when the words were set down sixteen centuries before.

And I was fortunate enough to be at the premiere, too, when two massed choirs, a brilliant Celtic ensemble and Symphony Nova Scotia presented the new work to a packed house, while the CBC broadcast it live across the country. More than a year later it was recorded in a studio. By then the *Mass* had begun to make its way in the world and had been presented several more times elsewhere in Canada and in the United States.

The Celtic Mass for the Sea was eventually released on the Marquis label and subsequently through EMI Canada. It has since sold many thousands of copies and become the classical music equivalent of a gold record, permanently enriching our musical heritage.

On the hillside I recline
Ever yearning for the lost,
Ever looking to the west,
Where the sun sets in the sea.

9. The Living Beach

What are heavy? Sea-sand and sorrow.
What are brief? Today and tomorrow.
What are frail? Spring blossoms and youth.
What are deep? The ocean and truth.
　　　—Christina Rossetti

"The living beach" is a metaphor shared by dozens of scientists, and many of them admit that they have something approaching reverence for beaches, a feeling evoked by no other geological phenomenon. Like plants and animals, beaches are systems, not mere assemblages of inert material. They are active, unpredictable, willful; they almost seem capable of strategic thinking. Only the rivers have a similar grip on our emotions. If a beach does so many of the things a living creature would do—change, move, adapt, starve, accept nourishment, defend itself and all the rest of it—then can it truly be said to be alive?

"I expected to discover somewhere in the scientific literature a comprehensive definition of life as a physical process," writes James Lovelock, author of *Gaia*, "but I was surprised to find how little had been written about the nature of life itself. Data galore had been accumulated on almost every conceivable aspect of living species ... but in the whole vast encyclopaedia of facts the crux of the matter, life itself, was almost totally ignored."

What does it mean to say that a thing is alive? Even physicians can only infer the presence of life from its activities, the aptly named vital signs. All the same, we know—or think we know—a living thing when we see it. We have, says Lovelock, "a very rapid highly efficient life-recognition programme in our inherited set of instincts."

Well, so it seems to us—but you and I would not agree with Aristotle about what was living and what was not. Aristotle thought that a stone fell to the ground because it was seeking the earth, its natural home. If a stone can seek something—anything—it is at some level sentient and alive. Isaac Newton, the founder of modern science, took hermetic philosophy seriously, and hermeticism rests in part on the idea that all matter can transform itself, in which case all matter must be living.

Perhaps our life-recognition program is not an inherent biological ability conferred on us by creative evolution; perhaps it is a cultural construct, reflecting a widespread but purely social consensus about which things are living and which are not.

But life, the thing itself, remains a profound mystery. There lies a human being, breathing very slowly on a hospital bed. That person is alive and every part of the body is alive—the cells, the organs, the systems that govern breath and circulation and digestion.

And then the breathing stops. The heart falls still. In that instant, nothing physical seems to have changed: all the cells and systems are intact. But life has left the body, and nothing we can do will put it back.

But what was it that left the body?

So far as I can determine, we really have no idea.

The science that descended from Newton treated the world and all its parts as a huge machine; indeed, Newton's worldview was first known as "the mechanical philosophy." Since Newton, science has been relentlessly reductionist, slicing the world into ever smaller pieces and studying those pieces more or less in isolation. The technique has been wildly successful; the whole of our technological civilization rests on it. A century ago, the scientific picture seemed almost complete. True, there were a few anomalies, small clouds on the horizon. But these were merely bits and pieces of unfinished business.

Enter the physicists of the twentieth century—Einstein, Bohr, Pauli, Heisenberg and others. They sail off to the anomalies on the horizon and discover they have sailed right out of Newton's universe. At the most minute subatomic level, they discover, particles do not seem to be matter at all; they are forms of energy dancing with other forms of energy. And reality is not out there, separate from us. We are in reality. We affect reality. In some sense, we create reality.

Reality now appears to be about energy, information, organization. Take two joined particles and separate them electrically. Off they go in opposite directions, each traveling at the speed of light. Now put an obstacle in front of one particle, deflecting it upward. *The other particle instantly deflects downward.* Somehow, information has been conveyed at *twice the speed of light.* The central mystery of quantum mechanics, says Henry Stapp of the Lawrence Radiation Lab, is, "How does information get around so fast?" There is a school of thought that holds that subatomic particles are conscious and are consciously making decisions.

This is a profoundly shocking notion. But, as Gary Zukav puts it in *The Dancing Wu Li Masters: An Overview of the New Physics,* "the philosophical implication of quantum mechanics is that all of the things in our universe (including us) that appear to exist independently are actually parts of one all-encompassing organic pattern, and that no parts of that pattern are ever really separate from it or from each other."

One specific implication of the new physics, says Zukav, is that "the distinction between organic and inorganic is a conceptual prejudice." *Everything* is part of a single, living whole.

Including those particles.

And including the beach.

The vision of reality we glimpse in the new physics is fascinating and stimulating, but it is also abstract and emotionally unsatisfying. Our life-recognition system may be a cultural construct, but it is still the only system we have. And even if *organic* and *inorganic* prove to be fundamentally meaningless concepts, they *seem* meaningful to us. Plants and animal do die, whatever that means, and death is one of the most important facts in human life.

Turn to the field of computer science known as artificial life —not artificial intelligence, but artificial *life.* A computer scientist named Chris Langton contends that artificial life—a field he largely invented— is the inverse of conventional biology, just as much as the new physics is an inversion of conventional reductionist physics. Conventional biology proceeds by *analysis,* dividing and dissecting the natural world into species, organs, cells and so on. Artificial life, by contrast, attempts to understand life by *synthesis,* trying to create entities on the computer that are programmed to obey simple rules, and then putting those entities together in groups to see whether their interaction will generate more complex, lifelike behavior.

Langton belongs to a group of scientists from a wide range of disciplines—economics, physics, chemistry, mathematics, biology, neuroscience, archaeology—that came together at the Santa Fe Institute, established in the late 1980s precisely to bring the group together. Their credentials were celestial. A number of them were Nobel Prize winners. They had a few crucial things in common: for instance, a nagging suspicion that reductionism might not be the only route to truth, and an interest in physicist Ilya Prigogine's basic concern: Why does the universe display order and structure?

How are organisms organized, for instance? Or, for that matter, stars or food webs or markets or societies? Is evolution really just a matter of chance encounters and sporadic mutations, or is there some deep organizing principle at work in nature? Could that principle, whatever it is, account for the pattern by which long periods of relative stability—the era of the dinosaurs, say, or the Cold War—conclude in cascades of tumultuous change?

The new hypothesis being explored at Santa Fe suggests that if you take a large group of independent agents capable of interaction—atoms, aardvarks, corporations, whatever—and you set them all down together, they spontaneously organize themselves. Order emerges. Hence they became known as *emergent systems.* Take a pot of soup or water. Heat it slowly, and the lazy movement within it seems to be formless and random. But then, just before the soup boils, hexagonal patterns appear on the surface: convection cells with hot fluid rising in the center and colder liquid dropping down the edges. Order. Pattern. An emergent system.

Chris Langton's particular riff on this fundamental idea was that you might be able to create a group of agents on a computer and that they might organize themselves in this way. And maybe that would tell you about the way order arises in nature, and about the system of organization that drives organisms, and that we call *life.*

Langton convened the first workshop on artificial life in September 1987. One presentation at that workshop seems to capture something essential about the whole concept. Craig Reynolds of the Symbolics Corporation in Los Angeles had been trying to understand how and why groups of animals formed themselves into flocks or schools and moved as though they were a single being. He created a bunch of birdlike critters on his computer—he called them *boids* —and he put them into an environment full of poles, walls and other barriers. He gave them three simple instructions: Try to match your velocity with your neighbor's. Try to move toward the center of your group of boids. Try to maintain a minimum distance from other objects, including other boids.

Following only these three individual, local rules, the boids organized themselves into a flock. They flowed between and around obstacles just as a school of fish does. On one occasion, a boid hit a pole, and after a momentary disorientation flew off to join the flock.

Nothing in the rules said anything about flocking together. The three simple rules had yielded complex, organized behavior.

Order. Pattern. Emergence.

An arresting thought ultimately flows from this work on emergence and complex adaptive systems in general. Maybe—just maybe—certain molecules, jostling around in the primordial soup of basic matter 4,500 million years ago, came together in some similarly emergent fashion to create the earliest forms of life. And maybe that's how evolution works: agents interacting at every level to form ever more complex adaptive systems, which themselves become parts of larger systems in a branching pattern of organic order spreading endlessly across the planet. Langton speculates that evolution hasn't stopped; it's just moved on to "the social-cultural plane." Nations, markets, the beginnings of a global society.

"Suppose that these models about the origin of life are correct," says Stuart Kauffman, another of the Santa Fe scientists. "Then life is the natural expression of complex matter. And that means we're at home in the universe. We're to be expected. How welcoming that is!"

∽

At some point Santa Fe, going up, meets James Lovelock on his way down, like businessmen from the ground floor and the penthouse taking elevators to a meeting halfway up the office tower. Santa Fe starts with molecules and atoms and finds them organizing themselves upward into life, into ever more complex systems; Lovelock finds the whole Earth to be living and traces its physiology downward into life forms that perform its internal functions, like respiratory or circulatory systems.

Lovelock's Gaia hypothesis proposes that the Earth is in fact alive: a single, self-regulating system maintained by and for life. To say that the Earth is living does not necessarily mean it is any more conscious or intelligent than a potato, of course, but a further extension of the idea suggests that the planet is evolving a mind. Gaia's mind would be human thought. You and I may be among Gaia's brain cells.

Lovelock formulated the Gaia hypothesis when he was asked by the U.S. National Aeronautics and Space Administration to devise a test for the presence of life on Mars. He attacked the problem by turning the situation around. If he were a Martian scientist, how would he know there was life on Earth? Looking at the Earth through an imaginary telescope on Mars, he told David Cayley of CBC Radio's *Ideas*, he found "an atmosphere that was wildly anomalous, a strange, wonderful and beautiful anomaly that sort of shouted a song of life right across the solar system, right into the galaxy."

Lovelock focused on the atmosphere, which may be considered the circulatory system of the planet. There he noted the simultaneous presence of oxygen and methane in the air. The two gases normally react and destroy one another. But our atmosphere *always* has oxygen as 21 percent of its volume and methane at one and a half parts per million. The two gases are always reacting and destroying one another, but the amount of each in the atmosphere is always the same. The only explanation is that something is producing methane and oxygen at exactly the same rate they are being used up—and the only something that can do that is life.

Such anomalies led Lovelock and his colleagues to say, "Maybe we're looking at it the wrong way round. The atmosphere isn't an environment for life, it's something that life has made as an environment for itself. It's something it has chosen and deliberately keeps going because it likes it that way. And that, of course, was the Gaia hypothesis."

Science is fundamentally about stories, says Doyne Farmer, another Santa Fe scientist. It does for us what mythology did for the ancients: it gives a credible explanation of what the world is like and how it came to be that way. It lets us contemplate, in a useful and coherent way, our understanding of who we are and how we relate to the world in which we find ourselves.

Stories and ideas hang around in our consciousnesses like seeds, waiting for the right moment to bud and leaf and grow. Gaia is not a new idea; also known as Ge, Gaia was the ancient Greek personification of the Earth as a goddess, and the prefix *geo* (as in *geology* and *geography*) derives from her name. Lovelock was not the first scientist to postulate the Gaia hypothesis; he writes that "the first *scientific* expression of a belief that the Earth was alive came from James Hutton in 1785 in a lecture before the Royal Society of Edinburgh. He thought also that the proper study of the Earth was through physiology and compared Harvey's discovery of the circulation of the blood with the cycling of the elements. Hutton was the father of Geology. I wonder where and when things went wrong."

∽

We were not ready to hear the Gaia story in 1785. We seem to be ready now. The Gaia hypothesis strikes many of us, scientists and nonscientists alike, as intuitively right. The new story in science is a story of unity, order, relatedness. More and more, the Earth does look like a seamless fabric of interdependence, movement and renewal.

And so perhaps it becomes less important to determine whether the beach is truly alive. It is an interesting question in theory, but it may not matter very much in practice. The distinction between *living* and *nonliving* may even be irrelevant. Ultimately the beach deserves exactly the same care and stewardship as the rest of Gaia.

But what does stewardship mean? If stewardship became a major objective for us, what would we do differently?

Geologist Stanley Riggs suggests that we might begin by giving legal rights to beaches and other natural objects. He proposes that beaches should have legal standing in the courts; they should become jural persons, with rights the courts would be obliged to consider. The idea is disorienting at first, but then so is the present situation. If I sue my neighbor over ownership of some dune land, is there not something absurd about the fact that the law considers my interests and my neighbor's, but not those of the dunes? Surely Gaia is also a party to this dispute.

The courts already consider the legitimate interests of persons who are unable to speak for themselves—infants and the mentally incompetent, for instance. Other entities that are, literally, legal fictions are "persons" in the courts, including corporations, trusts, estates and nations. In many jurisdictions, animals have at least minimal rights, such as the right not to be treated cruelly. Even ships are sometimes treated as jural persons.

If a ship or an estate, why not a beach, a mountain, a stream?

"Throughout legal history, each successive extension of rights to some new entity has been a bit unthinkable," writes Christopher Stone, a law professor at the University of Southern California, in *Should Trees Have Standing? Towards Legal Rights for Natural Objects*. It was Stone's provocative essay that prompted Riggs to propose rights for beaches. "We are inclined to suppose the rightlessness of rightless 'things' to be a decree of Nature," says Stone, and "not a legal convention acting in support of some status quo."

This is the critical consideration in Stone's argument; the dividing line between property, with which we have no ethical relationship, and things-with-rights, with which we do. There is no *natural* boundary between them; the border reflects a social consensus, usually unvoiced. We are usually not aware of the consensus any more than a fish is aware that it lives in water.

Things without rights, says Stone, are mere property. One can do what one wants with property—neglect it, alter it, give it away, destroy it. A property owner's rights confer privileges but no obligations. If something has rights, however, we may *not* do anything we like to it;

we have an obligation to treat it according to a set of rules adumbrated and often enforced by a third party.

The history of Western law shows a steady migration of items of property into the category of things-with-rights. In Roman law, a man had absolute power over his children, even to the point of denying his paternity or putting them to death. In 1858, a U.S. court could say explicitly that "a slave is not a person, but a thing." Blacks, Natives, Jews, Chinese, women (especially married women), animals—all of these have at various times been considered property and have been denied the most basic of rights. In the industrialized West, all of them have a substantial basket of rights today, though not always a full basket of identical rights.

We may hear an echo of Santa Fe here. As order and organization spread, as evolution moves into the social and cultural plane, our range of ethical relationships broadens. More and more of our property relationships are transformed into ethical relationships.

Stone argues that natural objects should have at least three basic rights: the right to institute legal action at their own behest; the right to have injuries to them taken into account in determining legal relief; and the right to benefit from that relief. Since trees and beaches cannot exercise those rights themselves, individuals or groups should be able to apply to the court for legal guardianship and for the right to litigate on behalf of the natural object.

Is it necessary, though, to extend rights to natural objects in order to have their interests protected by the courts? Perhaps not, says Stone, but legal terms like *rights* have meaning in informal speech, and those meanings provide the context of legal discourse. Furthermore, "judges who could unabashedly refer to the 'legal rights of the environment' would be encouraged to develop a viable body of law—in part simply through the availability and force of the expression." The new set of rights could prompt the courts to perform "the very task that is called for: of summoning up from the human spirit the kindest and most generous and worthy ideas that abound there, giving them shape and reality and legitimacy."

Stone's whole essay expresses the growing consciousness of our need for an ethical relationship with nature and a plea that we start to think in less homocentric terms. We are not protecting natural objects for future generations; we are protecting them *for themselves.* The environment does not exist for humanity; it may be that humanity exists for the environment.

It is a powerful argument, and an alluring one. It represents something practical we could do tomorrow, a concrete step toward genuine stewardship of the natural world.

~

At one point Stone also suggests that there is a case for having representation in legislatures to speak for the environment. This, too, seems odd at first thought. At second thought, the present situation seems even odder.

Leave aside the question of national boundaries for the moment and look at the map of North America. What natural or logical explanation can there be for Saskatchewan or Wyoming, or for many of their internal divisions? Four straight lines ruled on the prairie, and presto: a state, a province, a township, a farm. John Wesley Powell, explorer of the Colorado River and later head of the U.S. Geologic Survey, thought that state boundaries in the arid west—where the most important factor for settlement was the availability of water—should have followed major watersheds. The state of Upper Platte River. The state of Yellowstone. The state (or states) of Columbia. In Canada, where the national map echoes the east-west trend of the drainage basins, such a scheme might have given us the provinces of North and South Saskatchewan, Churchill, Athabasca, Red, Peace. And, by extension, provinces of Upper and Lower St. Lawrence, Atlantic Coast and Pacific Coast, Rocky Mountains, Canadian Shield.

Perhaps it is not too late. All over the world, large nations are straining to hold together, and many are breaking up. Futurist John Naisbitt predicts 1,000 member countries in the United Nations by the middle of the next century—microcountries, many of them. Andorra, which in 1993 became the 184th United Nations member, has a population of 47,000. Countries that remain united will need a reason to stay together.

Divided by language, culture and a vast geography, Canada has wrestled with problems of national unity for generations. What would happen if it became a federation of bioregions? William Thorsell, former editor of the *Globe and Mail*, suggested that the country needs what the French call *un projet de societe*, an objective that unites a society in a common purpose. He proposed that Canadians undertake to be "the finest trustees in the world of our sovereign natural environment."

Thorsell is quite serious about redrawing the map of Canada in terms of its distinctive ecosystems, an act that would in itself transform our politics. He would invent new instruments and structures that would place the environment at the core of our lives together.

"We would have to invent a co-operative national instrument by which to study, debate and act out our responsibilities," he writes. Evidently he would leave the provinces more or less as they are, since he calls for "some kind of internal treaty or covenant ... to bind our legislatures to participate in and act upon our decisions."

Thorsell is not very specific about his "new instruments," but they might begin with Canada's appointed Senate, always a source of controversy. We might have the senators elected from ecosystems, with a specific charge to represent the environment as well as the people. We might adopt a constitution that included a bill of rights for the environment. We might institute green tax reform—a package of increased taxes on pollution, fossil fuel use, nonrenewable resource use and the like, combined with reduced taxes on incomes and investment. When we begin to think about making sweeping political changes in the interest of the environment, the possibilities seem endless.

The opportunity, Thorsell writes, "requires debate, consensus and collective action at some collective cost. It permits of individual action. It is not essentially selfish and self-referential. It contributes to the rest of the world's well-being. It allows for a spiritual and ethical dimension. It creates a constructive example for others. It raises our eyes from the present to the future in a broader cause." And, he notes, "because Canada constitutes a large part of the Earth, it will matter to the Earth itself."

The *Globe and Mail* is not a mushy tree-hugging fringe publication; it purports to be Canada's national newspaper, and its sympathies generally lie with the Cossacks of Canadian capitalism. That such an electrifying proposal should emanate from such a source suggests that Thorsell is right: this is an idea with the power to bridge many of the gaps that divide us—French, English, Aboriginal, immigrant, native-born, male, female, old, young, left, right. Canadians should be debating it excitedly. It could transform our politics and our country, and even our individual lives.

∽

Is the beach truly alive? At the outset, perhaps the question seemed important because a genuinely living beach would demand that we develop toward an ethical relationship with it. For me, however, it has become difficult to see how we can have anything but an ethical relationship with it, or how it can be disconnected ethically from everything else on this living and beautiful planet. The instruments of thought and language allow us to think about the beach as though it were separate from the sea and the land and the air. But within the realm of Gaia, nothing is truly separate from anything else.

For me, the beach emerges as an eternal process with a perpetually mutable form, an ever shifting boundary, an image at once of change and stability. It is a paradox, a union of opposites. It reveals that stability is an illusion—and that change is also an illusion. It thus brings us face to face with perhaps the greatest theme in literature, science and philosophy: the nature of time and human dismay at our own meager allotment of it. The span of a human lifetime is the flare of a match against endless darkness; but it is all the time we have.

What are we looking for when we gaze into the surf?

I think we are looking for God—for reassurance, that is, that we are somehow connected with a unity too fundamental to name. Alan Watts, the spiritual commentator, called it the great self; theologian Paul Tillich called it the "Ultimate Ground of Being"; David Bohm, an eminent physicist, calls it "That Which Is." We hunger to understand what Watts considered to be the great secret: the knowledge that the world is a single Self, and that we can no more separate ourselves from the great Self than the wave can separate itself from the trough, or the sand from the beach. Language makes distinctions, but the Self remains One.

Nowhere in our normal experience is the great unity of things—even of stability and change—more available to our apprehension than it is at the beach. Ultimately, looking at the tumbling waves and the restless sands, we are looking into the nature of reality: ceaseless variety within an eternal process.

We may even perceive that each of us, too, is a process, a part of the great Process, and that both reverence and joy should flavor our own brief dance upon the sands.

Further Reading

Abbott, R. Tucker. *Kingdom of the Seashell.* (1972) Melbourne, FL: American Malacologists, 1993.

Amos, William A. and Amos, Stephen H. *Atlantic and Gulf Coasts* (The Audubon Society Nature Guides) New York: Alfred A. Knopf, 1985.

Bascom, Willard. *The Crest of the Wave: Adventures in Oceanography.* New York: Harper and Row, 1988.

Bascom, Willard. *Waves and Beaches.* New York: Doubleday, 1980.

Bird, Eric C. F. *Beach Management.* New York: John Wiley, 1996.

Carson, Rachel. *Under the Sea Wind.* New York: Oxford University Press, 1941.

Carter, Robert. *Sail Far Away: Reflections on Life Afloat.* New York: Norton, 1978.

Gosner, Kenneth L. *A Field Guide to the Atlantic Seashore.* (The Peterson Field Guide Series) Boston: Houghton Mifflin, 1978.

Johnson, Douglas W. *Shore Processes and Shoreline Development.* New York: John Wiley, 1919.

Kaufman, Wallace, and Pilkey, Orrin. *The Beaches are Moving: The Drowning of America's Shoreline.* Durham, NC: Duke University Press, 1983.

King, Cuchlaine A.M. *Beaches and Coasts.* London: Edward Arnold, 1959.

Leatherman, Stephen P. *Barrier Island Handbook.* College Park, MD: University of Maryland Laboratory for Coastal Research, 1988.

Lovelock, J.E. *Gaia: A New Look at Life on Earth.* New York: Oxford University Press, 1979, repr. 1987.

Manley, Sean, and Manley, Robert. *Beaches: Their Lives Legends and Love.* Philadelphia: Clinton, 1968.

Paine, Stefani Hewlett. *Beachwalker: Sea Life of the West Coast.* Vancouver: Douglas and McIntyre, 1992.

Pilkey, Orrin, and Dixon, Katharine L. *The Corps and the Shore.* Washington, DC: Island Press, 1996.

Reisner, Marc. *Cadillac Desert: The American West and its Disappearing Water.* (1986) Vancouver: Douglas and McIntyre, revised ed., 1993.

Roodman, David Malin. *Getting the Signals Right: Tax Reform to Protect the Environment and the Economy.* Worldwatch Paper 134. Washington, DC: Worldwatch Institute, 1997.

Waldrop, M. Mitchell. *Complexity: The Emerging Science at the Edge of Order and Chaos.* New York: Simon and Shuster, 1992.

Zukav, Gary. *The Dancing Wu Li Masters: An Overview of the New Physics.* New York: William Morrow, 1979.

Index

A

Abbott, R. Tucker, 146-7
accretion, 187, 195, 222, 233
Alaska, 43-4, 53, 219
algae, 106, 108-9, 118, 126-127, 130, 138, 179
American Conchologist, The, 143-6
anatomy of the beach, 23
Apulae, 81
Aristotle, 141, 259
artificial life, 261-2
Arnold, Matthew, 58
Asia, 81, 136, 176-7
avulsion, 222

B

backshore
    defined and described, 23, 105
    as biological environment, 105-115
barrier beach/island defined, 87
    formation of, 88
    Kiawah Island, SC, 241
    Long Island, NY, 225-233
    movement of, 87-98
Bascom, Willard, 42, 50-7, 192
beach armoring, 184-215
    Corps of Engineers, U.S. Army, 199-208
    dewatering, 204-5
    dolosse, 199
    groins and jetties, 194-7,
    miscellaneous methods, 211
    replenishment, 204-10
    scraping, 232-3
    seawalls,
beachcombing, 148-50
beachface *see* foreshore
Bedford Institute of Oceanography (Canada), 19
berm, 23-4, 67, 206, 207, 219, 232
Bird, Eric, 172
birds of the shore, 131-8
Bisbort, Alan, 241-3
Blackpool, UK, 163-4, 251
Boardman, Samuel H., 239-41
Bohm, David, 271
Bombard, Alain, 161-2
Brickenden, Jennyfer, 253-5
Brighton, UK, 162-3
British Columbia, 21, 67
Browning, Robert, 140
Byron, George Gordon, Lord, 24, 166

C

California, 52-4, 57, 59-60, 67-8, 87, 121, 167-8, 171, 173, 203, 241, 266
Cameron, Lulu Terrio-, 34, 36, 92, 109
Campbell, Sir Malcolm, 169
Cape Canaveral, FL, 169, 247-8
Cape May, FL, 87, 203
Carroll, Lewis, 104
Carson, Rachel, 65, 244
Carter, Robert and Cynthia, 80-1
Cato, Wayland, 100-3
Celtic Mass for the Sea, (Macmillan), 253-7
Clarke, Arthur C, 45, 55
climate change, 86, 177
coastal geology, origins of, 69-70
    cobble, 22, 26, 70-2, 81, 152, 179, 219
    conchology and conchologists, 140-7
    Coney Island, 163-4, 174, 251
    conservation, 239-52
        in Oregon, 239-41
Cook, Capt. James, 73-4, 142-3, 167

Corne, St. Luc de la, 155
Corps of Engineers, U.S. Army
    beach armoring, 199-207, 237
    in California, 68
    in Cape Hatteras, NC, 186
    in Florida, 249
    in Long Island, NY, 228, 230
    in Nantasket, MA, 71
    in New Jersey, NY, 223
    in Oregon, 196-7
    Lim Vallianos, 174
crustaceans, 65, 107-8, 115, 123-7, 131,135, 138
Cuming, Hugh, 143
Cummings, Albert, 76-7

D

Daley, Bill, 227
Dan, Donald, 144, 147
Danish Geotechnical Center, 205
Darwin, Charles, 55, 150, 180
Davis, Robert F., 36
Dean, Robert, 192-6, 208, 214, 249
Defoe, Daniel, 148
development projects, 237-8, 241-52
    subsidies, for, 237-8
dewatering, 204-5
Dixon, Katharine L., 223, 237
Doland, Robert, 36
dolosse, 199, 206
Doucet, Charlie, 16, 32, 69, 79, 138, 186
Draper, Lawrence, 39
drumlins, 70-4, 87, 92
Duckworth, John, 235-6
dukw, 52, 57, 226
dulse, 118, 182
dune/dunes
    and island migration, 87-94
    as geological evidence, 69-70
    formation of, 110-11
    life forms of, 110-12
    movement of, 92-6
    on West Coast, 60-1

E

Eaton, Edwin, 230
Einstein, Albert, 260
Eliot, T.S., 49
emergent systems, 262
Everson, Gene, 140-7
Exxon Valdez, 216, 218

F

Fitzpatrick, Kathy, 249-50
Florida
    Cape Canaveral, 169-20, 247-8
    Daytona Beach, 169
    Florida Keys, 37, 65, 113, 177
    Hutchinson Island, 172-3, 205
    Indian River, 105, 247-8
    restoration, 206, 208-9, 232-3
    sand, 65, 196-7
    Sanibel-Captiva, 243-50
    Sebastian Inlet, 246-52
    shells, 140-1, 143-5
Flynn, Brian, 207, 209
Forbes, Don, 62
foredunes, defined, 105
foreshore (beachface), 66-7
    as biological environment, 115-25
    defined, 23
    oil spills, 217-8
Frost, Robert, 184
Fundy, Bay of, 20, 47, 62, 118, 135, 234

G

Gaia: A New Look at Life on Earth
    (Lovelock) 20, 258
Gaia hypothesis, 83, 116, 241, 258, 263
Gastropods, 121
Genesis, Book of, 24
Geological Survey of Canada, 19, 62, 72
Georgia, 64, 89
Gibbons, Euell, 149-50
glacier, glaciers, 59, 61-4, 72, 79, 81-3
global warming, 63, 83-6, 97
Globe and Mail, 269-70

Godfrey, Paul, 84, 94

Goldberg, Richard, 145-6

Gosse, Sir Edmund, 181

Gosse, Philip, 180-1

groins and jetties, 174, 185-7, 193-7, 203-4

Guzman, Rafael, 214-5

Guzzwell, John, 40-1

H

Haugdahl, Sig, 169

Hayes, Miles O. 216-20, 242

Hirohito, Emperor, 141

Holland, 84, 195, 212-3

Holmes, Oliver Wendel, 51

hurricanes, 175-8, 244

Hutton, James, 180, 265

I

Indian Ocean disaster, 45

inlet,

in barrier island, defined, 87

Pike's Inlet, NC, 226-8

Sebastian Inlet, FL, 246-52

Isle Madame, NS, 22, 36, 48, 62, 70-1, 152

J

Japan, 39, 43-5, 118, 124, 128, 141, 143, 165-6, 192, 195

jetties and groins, 174, 185-7, 193-7, 203-4

Johnson, Douglas, 57, 69, 94

Joyce, Gary, 226, 230

K

Kahanamoku, Duke, 167

Kauffman, Stuart, 263

Kaufman, Wallace, 32-3, 39, 83, 177, 187

Kiawah Island, SC, 241-3, 251

Koppelman, Lee, 230

L

lagoon, 68, 89-91

defined, 23, 87

ecosystem, 104-9, 112-3

Langton, Chris, 261-3

law and legal issues, 226-36, 246

at Westhampton Dunes, NY 226-31

Lucas, David, and South Carolina law, 231-3

at Lower Kingsburg, NS, 233-7

legal rights for beaches, 266-8

legislative representation for, 268-70

LeRoux, Raymond, 249-51

lifeboats, 77, 160-1

Linnaeus, Carolus, 142

littoral, 66-7, 90, 195, 217

Long Island, NY 61-2, 64, 67, 70, 91, 157, 174, 225-31

Lovelock, James, 20, 258-9, 263-5

Lucas, David (and U.S. court case), 231-5

Ludington, Dick, 113, 172-3, 207

M

MacAdam, David, 235-6

MacDonald, John D., 178

MacMillan, Scott, 253-6

Magdalen Islands, QC, 37, 75-6, 155, 199, 255

Maine, 108, 137, 221, 246

malacology, 140, 145

maritime forests, 87, 93, 104, 111, 242-3

McPhee, John 192

Merrifield, Eric, 199

Miami, 67, 88, 172, 175, 195, 207-9, 224, 244

Mieremet, Ben, 85-6, 176

Mississippi River, 65, 201-2

mollusks, 120-3, 130-1, 140-7

N

Nantasket, MA, 68-71, 94

National Flood Insurance Program (U.S.), 237-8

National Hurricane Centre (U.S.), 175, 178

National Institute of Oceanography (UK), 39

New Brunswick, 35, 129, 153, 168, 234

New Jersey, 65, 119, 158, 163, 191 203, 223

Newfoundland

Cape St. Mary's, 133-4

capelin, 153
Grand Banks, 68
nor'easter, 37
terrain, 63, 234
wrecking, 157-8
Newton, Isaac, 259-60
nor'easters, 36-8
North Carolina
Cedar Island, 99-103
lagoon, 23
nor'easter, 37
Outer Banks, 89, 91, 154, 157, 168
Shackleford Banks, 93
Nova Scotia
beach use, 152
common tern, 136-8
geology, 19, 64, 68, 70, 84
Lower Kingsburg, 234-7
shoreline, 74
Symphony Nova Scotia, 256-7

O

oceanography, oceanographers, 50-7
Odyssey (Homer) 155, 159
oil spills, 216-20
Oregon, 60, 155, 196, 239-40, 251, 255
overwash, 26, 89-90, 92, 98
overwash channels, defined, 26
overwash fans, 90, 92
ownership and legal status, 221-2 oysters, 108-9

P

Pamlico Sound, 23, 89, 101
Parkinson, Randall, 64, 249-50
Persian Gulf, 218-20
Pilkey, Orrin
armored beaches, 184-90, 193-4, 197, 206-8, 211-5, 233
barrier beach islands, 87-9, 97-8
Corps of Engineers, 200-2
erosion, 96
shore development, 232-3, 237-8
storms, 175-8
plankton, 56, 107-9, 112, 115-8, 125, 162
Point Roberts, WA, 28-30

political issues, 221-5
Pondville Beach, NS. 22-4, 49, 61
Powell, John Wesley, 268
Prince Edward Island, 33, 92, 119, 178, 234, 255

R

Reisner, Marc, 201-3
res communes, 221, 225, 229
resonance, 47-8
retreat, as alternative to armoring, 213-4, 231-3
Riggs, Stanley, 232-3, 265-6
Romans, 141, 165, 187-8, 191, 211, 221, 267
Roosevelt, Teddy, 239
Rosen, Peter, 69, 73, 94, 189-90, 224, 238
Rosenberg, Gary, 142, 146
Rossetti, Christina, 258
Rumpf, Georg Eberhard (Rumphius), 142

S

Sable Island, 48, 157-60, 178
salt marsh, 22-4, 62, 72, 106-9, 219, 234, 242
salvage, 157-8
sand see sediment
sandbar, 19, 26-7, 66-7, 196
sand castles, 75-7
sand waves, 195
Sanibel-Captiva Island, FL, 65, 141, 243-5, 251
Santa Fe Institute, 261-5, 267
Scheu, Lynn,143
sea level
eustatic and relative, 82-4
and global temperatures, 82-7
shoreline response to, 87-98
stand of, defined, 79
sea mount, 41-2
seawall, 36, 83, 86, 97-8, 169, 174, 185, 187-93, 197, 203-4, 207, 210, 212, 224, 231, 233, 246
Orrin Pilkey on, 184-6
Peter Rosen on, 189-90
Robert Dean on, 192-6
seaweed, see algae
Sebastian Inlet, FL, 246-51
sediment

cobble, 22, 26, 70-2, 80, 152, 179, 219
  defined, 59
  sources of, 59, 61-6, 71
  movement of, 66-8, 73-4
  "singing" sands, 255-6
  sortation of, 71
  suitability for replenishment, 205-7
seiche, 48
Senne, Carol Ann, 248-50
Shaffer, Gail, 227
Shaw, John, 72, 74
shell-collecting, *see* conchology
Shelley, Percy Bysshe, 166
shipwrecks and lifesaving, 155-61
shoreface, 23, 26-7, 105, 126, 190, 206
  defined, 23
  as biological environment, 126-31
Should Trees Have Standing?(Stone), 266
Simpson, Robert H., 174
Slocum, Joshua, 55, 158
Smeeton, Miles and Beryl, 40-1
sonorous or singing sands, 255-6
sortation, 71-2
South Africa, 45, 125, 136, 167, 199
South Carolina, 185-6, 217, 231-2, 242
Stapp, Henry, 260
Stevenson, Robert Louis, 32, 147-8, 197
Stevenson, Thomas, 197-8
Stone, Christopher, 266-8
storm surge, 37, 98, 177-8, 211, 238
surfing, 167-8, 247
swash, 23, 25, 49, 66-7, 98, 123, 206, 255
swell, 38-9, 48
swimming, 161-7

T
"taking," U.S. Constitutional provision against, 231-3, 244-5
Tanski, Jay, 230
Taylor, Robert, 19-23, 25-27, 36-7, 59, 62, 72, 74
Tennyson, Alfred, Lord 79, 151
tetrapod, 192, 199
Thames Barrier, 212

The Beaches Are Moving, (Kaufman and Pilkey), 32, 83, 187
The Dancing Wu Li Masters, (Zukav), 260
Thoreau, Henry David, 24, 149, 159-60, 251
Thorsell, William, 269-70
tidal deltas, 90, 196
Tillich, Paul, 271
tombolo, tombolos, 70-3, 76
tsunami, 43-5, 53, 168

U
U.S. Army Corps of Engineers,
  see Corps of Engineers, U.S. Army

V
Vallianos, Lim 174, 200, 203-4, 209
Vegliante, Gary, 228-30
Vietnam, 54, 140, 176-7

W
Washington, State of, 28, 53, 60, 85, 164, 171, 176, 200
Watts, Alan, 271
wave/waves
  constructive and destructive, 25
  force of, 198-9
  formation of, 33-36
  in open ocean, 35, 38-42
  internal, 42-3
  measurement of, 34-6
  resonance of, 48-9
  rogue waves, 40-1
  sand waves, 195
  seiche, 48
  storm surges, 37
  subsurface, internal, 42-3
  surfing, 167-8
  swell, 39
  tides as waves, 45-8
  tsunamis, 43-5
  wave trains, 40
wave tank, 38
Waves and Beaches, (Bascom) 42, 54-6
Weber, Ernst and Wilhelm, 38

West, Oswald, 239-41
Westhampton Dunes, NY, 91,226-231
Whitman, Walt, 32
Wright, Wilbur and Orville, 168

Z

Zukav, Gary, 260